PENGUIN BOOKS

STOP-TIME

Frank Conroy was born in New York City
in 1936. He attended schools in New York
and Florida and was graduated from Haverford College in 1958. He now lives on
Nantucket Island, where he writes, reads,
plays the piano, and fishes for striped bass.
His most recent novel is *Body & Soul*.

STOP-TIME

Frank Conroy

PENGUIN BOOKS

To Danny and Will

PENGUIN BOOKS
Published by the Penguin Group
Penguin Group (USA) Inc., 375 Hudson Street, New York, New York 10014, U.S.A.
Penguin Books Ltd, 80 Strand, London WC2R 0RL, England
Penguin Books Australia Ltd, 250 Camberwell Road, Camberwell, Victoria 3124, Australia
Penguin Books Canada Ltd, 10 Alcorn Avenue, Toronto, Ontario, Canada M4V 3B2
Penguin Books India (P) Ltd, 11 Community Centre, Panchsheel Park, New Delhi – 110 017, India
Penguin Books (N.Z.) Ltd, Cnr Rosedale and Airborne Roads, Albany, Auckland, New Zealand
Penguin Books (South Africa) (Pty) Ltd, 24 Sturdee Avenue,
Rosebank, Johannesburg 2196, South Africa

Penguin Books Ltd, Registered Offices: 80 Strand, London WC2R 0RL, England

**First published in the United States of America
by The Viking Press 1967
Viking Compass Edition published 1972
Reprinted 1973 (twice), 1974, 1975
Published in Penguin Books 1977**

40 39 38 37 36 35 34 33 32

**Copyright © Frank Conroy, 1965, 1966, 1967
All rights reserved**

Library of Congress Cataloging in Publication Data
Conroy, Frank, 1936–
Stop-time.
First published in 1967.
1. Conroy, Frank, 1936–   —Biography.
2. Authors, American—20th century—Biography.
I. Title.
[CT275.C7643A3   1976]   973 [B]   76-53807
ISBN 0 14 00.4446 9

Printed in the United States of America
Set in Linotype Times Roman

Grateful acknowledgment is made to Alfred A. Knopf, Inc., for permission to quote lines from "Less and Less Human, O Savage Spirit" *(The Collected Poems of Wallace Stevens).*

Portions of this book appeared originally, in somewhat different form, in *The New Yorker, The Paris Review, Partisan Review,* and *The Urban Review.*

It is the human that is the alien,
The human that has no cousin in the moon.

It is the human that demands his speech
From beasts or from the incommunicable mass.

If there must be a god in the house, let him be one
That will not hear us when we speak: a coolness,

A vermilioned nothingness, any stick of the mass
Of which we are too distantly a part.

—WALLACE STEVENS

Contents

Prologue

WHEN we were in England I worked well. Four or five hundred words every afternoon. We lived in a small house in the countryside about twenty miles south of London. It was quiet, and because we were strangers, there were no visitors. My wife had been in bed for five months with hepatitis but stayed remarkably cheerful and spent most of her time reading. Life was good, conditions were perfect for my work.

But I would go to London once or twice a week in a wild, escalating passion of frustration, blinded by some mysterious mixture of guilt, moroseness, and desire. I wasn't after women, but something invisible, something I never found. I'd get drunk at the Establishment Club and play the piano with the house rhythm section (ecstatic if it went well, sick with disappointment and shame if not, nothing in between), all of this leading up to—in fact nothing more than an elaborate ritualized introduction to—the drive home at three A.M. in my Jaguar. The drive home was the point of it all.

Fifty to sixty miles an hour through the empty streets of South London. No lights. Slamming in the gears, accelerating on every turn, winding up the big engine, my brain finally clean and white, washed out by the danger and the roar of the wind, I barreled into the countryside. Now the headlights came on, and the speed opened up to ninety and a hundred. Once even to a hundred and fifteen on the narrow, moonlit English road.

In the few villages along the way I pulled every trick I could think of to make up for the slower speeds, driving in the wrong lane, cutting corners on the wrong side of the pylon, mounting the sidewalks, running red lights—anything at all to keep the speed, to maintain the speed and streak through the dark world.

1

Savages

MY FATHER stopped living with us when I was three or four. Most of his adult life was spent as a patient in various expensive rest homes for dipsomaniacs and victims of nervous collapse. He was neither, although he drank too much, but rather the kind of neurotic who finds it difficult to live for any length of time in the outside world. The brain tumor discovered and removed toward the end of his life could have caused his illness, but I suspect this easy out. To most people he seemed normal, especially when he was inside.

I try to think of him as sane, yet it must be admitted he did some odd things. Forced to attend a rest-home dance for its therapeutic value, he combed his hair with urine and otherwise played it out like the Southern gentleman he was. He had a tendency to take off his trousers and throw them out the window. (I harbor some secret admiration for this.) At a moment's notice he could blow a thousand dollars at Abercrombie and Fitch and disappear into the Northwest to become an outdoorsman. He spent an anxious few weeks convinced that I was fated to become a homosexual. I was six months old. And I remember visiting him at one of the rest homes when I was eight. We walked across a sloping lawn and he told me a story, which even then I recognized as a lie, about a man who sat down on the open blade of a penknife embedded in a park bench. (Why, for God's sake would he tell a story like that to his eight-year-old son?)

At one point in his life he was analyzed or took therapy with A. A. Brill, the famous disciple of Freud, with no apparent effect. For ten or fifteen years he worked as a magazine editor, and built up a good business as a literary agent. He died of cancer in his forties.

I visited him near the end. Half his face was paralyzed

from the brain-tumor operation and jaundice had stained
him a deep yellow. We were alone, as usual, in the hospital
room. The bed was high to my child's eye. With great effort
he asked me if I believed in universal military training. Too
young even to know what it was, I took a gamble and said
yes. He seemed satisfied. (Even now I have no idea if
that was the answer he wanted. I think of it as some kind
of test. Did I pass?) He showed me some books he had
gotten to teach himself to draw. A few weeks later he died.
He was six feet tall and at the end he weighed eighty-five
pounds.

Against the advice of his psychiatrists my mother divorced him, a long, tedious process culminating a year before his death. One can hardly blame her. At his worst he
had taken her on a Caribbean cruise and amused himself
by humiliating her at the captain's table. Danish, middle-
class, and not nearly as bright, she was unable to defend
herself. Late one night, on deck, his fun and games went
too far. My mother thought he was trying to push her over
the rail and screamed. (This might be the time to mention
her trained mezzo-soprano voice and lifelong interest in
opera.) My father was taken off the ship in a strait jacket,
to yet another (Spanish-speaking) branch of the ubiqui-
tous rest home he was never to escape.

I was twelve when my father died. From the ages of nine
to eleven I was sent to an experimental boarding school in
Pennsylvania called Freemont. I wasn't home more than a
few days during these years. In the summer Freemont became a camp and I stayed through.

The headmaster was a big, florid man named Teddy who
drank too much. It was no secret, and even the youngest
of us were expected to sympathize with his illness and like
him for it—an extension of the attitude that forbade the
use of last names to make everyone more human. All of us
knew, in the mysterious way children pick things up, that
Teddy had almost no control over the institution he'd
created, and that when decisions were unavoidable his wife
took over. This weakness at the top might have been the
key to the wildness of the place.

Life at Freemont was a perpetual semihysterical holiday.
We knew there were almost no limits in any direction. A
situation of endless, dreamlike fun, but one that imposed

a certain strain on us all. Classes were a farce, you didn't have to go if you didn't want to, and there were no tests. Freedom was the key word. The atmosphere was heavy with the perfume of the nineteen-thirties—spurious agrarianism, group singing of proletarian chants from all countries, sexual freedom (I was necking at the age of nine), sentimentalism, naïveté. But above all, filtering down through the whole school, the excitement of the *new thing,* of the experiment—that peculiar floating sensation of not knowing what's going to happen next.

One warm spring night we staged a revolution. All the Junior boys, thirty or forty of us, spontaneously decided not to go to bed. We ran loose on the grounds most of the night, stalked by the entire faculty. Even old Ted was out, stumbling and crashing through the woods, warding off the nuts thrown from the trees. A few legitimate captures were made by the younger men on the staff, but there was no doubt most of us could have held out indefinitely. I, for one, was confident to the point of bravado, coming out in the open three or four times just for the fun of being chased. Can there be anything as sweet for a child as victory over authority? On that warm night I touched heights I will never reach again—baiting a thirty-year-old man, getting him to chase me over my own ground in the darkness, hearing his hard breath behind me (ah, the *wordlessness* of the chase, no words, just action), and finally leaping clean, leaping effortlessly over the brook at exactly the right place, knowing he was too heavy, too stupid as an animal, too old, and too tired to do what I had done. Oh God, my heart burst with joy when I heard him fall, flat out, in the water. Lights flashed in my brain. The chase was over and I had won. I was untouchable. I raced across the meadow, too happy to stop running.

Hours later, hidden in a bower, I heard the beginning of the end. A capture was made right below me. Every captured boy was to join forces with the staff and hunt the boys still out. My reaction was outrage. Dirty pool! But outrage dulled by recognition—"Of course. What else did you expect? They're clever and devious. Old people, with cold, ignorant hearts." The staff's technique didn't actually work as planned, but it spread confusion and broke the lovely symmetry of us against them. The revolution was no longer simple and ran out of gas. To this day I'm proud that I was the last boy in, hours after the others. (I paid a price though—some inexplicable loss to my soul as I crept around all that time in the dark, looking for another holdout.)

We went through a fire period for a couple of weeks one winter. At two or three in the morning we'd congregate in the huge windowless coat-room and set up hundreds of birthday candles on the floor. They gave a marvelous eerie light as we sat around telling horror stories. Fire-writing became the rage—paint your initials on the wall in airplane glue and touch a flame to it. At our most dramatic we staged elaborate take-offs on religious services, complete with capes and pseudo-Latin. We were eventually discovered by our bug-eyed counselor—a homosexual, I recognize in retrospect, who had enough problems caring for thirty-five boys at the brink of puberty. As far as I know he never touched anyone.

Teddy announced a punishment that made the hair rise on the backs of our necks. After pointing out the inadequacies of the fire-escape system he decreed that each of us would be forced to immerse his left hand in a pot of boiling water for ten seconds, the sentence to be carried out two days hence. Frightened, morbidly excited, we thought about nothing else, inevitably drawn to the image of the boiling water with unhealthy fascination. We discussed the announcement almost lovingly till all hours of the night, recognizing a certain beauty in the phrasing, the formal specification of the "left hand," the precision of "immersed for ten seconds"—it had a medieval flavor that thrilled us.

But Teddy, or his wife (it was done in her kitchen), lost his nerve after the screams and tears of the first few boys. The flame was turned off under the pot and by the time my turn came it didn't hurt at all.

The only successful bit of discipline I remember was their system to get us to stop smoking. We smoked corn silk as well as cigarettes. (The preparation of corn silk was an important ritual. Hand-gathered in the field from only the best ears, it was dried in the sun, rubbed, aged, and rolled into pipe-sized pellets. We decimated Freemont's corn crop, ineptly tended in the first place, by leaving ten stripped ears rotting on the ground for every one eventually harvested. No one seemed to mind. Harvest day, in which we all participated, was a fraudulent pastoral dance of symbolic rather than economic significance.) With rare decisiveness Teddy got organized about the smoking. The parents of the only non-scholarship student in the school, a neat, well-to-do Chinese couple, removed him without warning after a visit. The faculty believed it was the sight of students lounging around the public rooms with cigarettes hanging expertly from their rosy lips, while we maintained it was the toilet-paper war. The parents had walked through the front door when things were reaching a crescendo—endless white rolls streaming down the immense curved stairway, cylindrical bombs hurtling down the stairwell from the third-floor balcony to run out anticlimactically a few feet from the floor, dangling like exhausted white tongues. The withdrawal of the only paying student was a catastrophe, and the smoking would have to stop.

Like a witch doctor, some suburban equivalent of the rainmaker, Mr. Kleinberg arrived in his mysterious black panel truck. Members of the staff were Teddy, George, or Harry, but this outsider remained Mister Kleinberg, a form of respect to which it turned out he was entitled. We greeted him with bland amusement, secure in the knowledge that no one could do anything with us. A cheerful realist with a big smile and a pat on the shoulder for every boy in reach, he was to surprise us all.

The procedure was simple. He packed us into a small, unventilated garage, unloaded more cigarettes than the average man will see in a lifetime, passed out boxes of kitchen matches, and announced that any of us still smoking after ten packs and five cigars was excluded from the new, heavily enforced ban on smoking. None of us could resist the challenge.

He sat behind his vast mound with a clipboard, checking off names as we took our first, fresh packs. Adjusting his glasses eagerly and beaming with friendliness, he distributed his fantastic treasure. The neat white cartons were ripped open, every brand was ours for the asking—Old Gold, Pall Mall (my brand), Chesterfields, Wings, Camels, Spud, Caporals, Lucky Strike (*Loose Sweaters Mean Floppy Tits*), Kools, Benson & Hedges. He urged us to try them all. "Feel free to experiment, boys, it may be your last chance," he said, exploding with benevolent laughter.

I remember sitting on the floor with my back against the wall. Bruce, my best friend, was next to me.

"We're supposed to get sick," he said.

"I know."

We lighted up a pair of fat cigars and surveyed the scene. Forty boys puffed away in every corner of the room, some of them lined up for supplies, keeping Mr. Kleinberg busy with his paperwork. The noise was deafening. Gales of nervous laughter as someone did an imitation of John Garfield, public speeches as so-and-so declared his intention to pass out rather than admit defeat, or his neighbor yelled that he'd finished his fourth pack and was still by God going strong. One had to scream through the smoke to be heard. It wasn't long before the first boys stumbled out, sick and shamefaced, to retch on the grass. There was no way to leave quietly. Every opening of the door sent great shafts of sunlight across the smoky room, the signal for a derisive roar—boos, hoots, whistles, razzberries—from those sticking it out. I felt satisfaction as an enemy of mine left early, when the crowd was at its ugliest.

The rest of us followed eventually, of course, some taking longer than others, but all poisoned. Mr. Kleinberg won and smoking ended at Freemont. With dazed admiration we watched him drive away the next day in his black truck, smiling and waving, a panetela clamped between his teeth.

A rainy day. All of us together in the big dorm except a fat boy named Ligget. I can't remember how it started, or if any one person started it. A lot of talk against Ligget, building quickly to the point where talk was not enough. When someone claimed to have heard him use the expression "nigger-lipping" (wetting the end of a cigarette), we decided to act. Ligget was intolerable. A boy was sent to find him.

I didn't know Ligget. He had no friends even though he'd been at school longer than the rest of us. There was some vagueness about his origins, probably his parents were dead and relatives cared for him. We knew he was in the habit of running away. I remember waking up one night to see three men, including a policeman, carrying him back to his bed. He fought with hysterical strength, although silently, as if he were afraid to wake the rest of us. All three had to hold him down for the hypodermic.

On this rainy day he didn't fight. He must have known what was up the moment he walked through the door, but he didn't try to run. The two boys assigned to hold his arms were unnecessary. Throughout the entire trial he stood quite still, only his eyes, deep in the pudgy face, swiveling from side to side as he followed the speakers. He didn't say anything.

The prosecutor announced that first of all the trial must be fair. He asked for a volunteer to conduct Ligget's defense. When it became clear no one wanted the job a boy named Herbie was elected by acclamation. It seemed the perfect choice: Herbie was colorless and dim, steady if not inspired.

"I call Sammy as a witness," said the prosecutor. There was a murmur of approval. Sammy was something of a hero to us, as much for his experiences in reform school as for his fabulous condition. (An undescended testicle, which we knew nothing about. To us he had only one ball.) "The prisoner is charged with saying 'nigger-lip.' Did you hear him say it?"

"Yes. He said it a couple of days ago. We were standing over there in front of the window." Sammy pointed to the end of the room. "He said it about Mark Schofield." (Schofield was a popular athletic star, a Senior, and therefore not in the room.)

"You heard him?"

"Yes. I got mad and told him not to talk like that. I walked away. I didn't want to hear him."

"Okay. Now it's your turn, Herbie."

Herbie asked only one question. "Are you sure he said it? Maybe he said something else and you didn't hear him right."

"He said it, all right." Sammy looked over at Ligget. "He said it."

"Okay," said the prosecutor, "I call Earl." Our only Negro stepped forward, a slim, good-looking youth, already vain. (A sin so precocious we couldn't even recognize it.) He enjoyed the limelight, having grown used to it in the large, nervous, and visit-prone family that had spoiled him so terribly. He got a package every week, and owned a bicycle with gears, unheard of before his arrival.

"What do you know about this?" asked the prosecutor.

"What do you mean?"

"Did you ever hear him say what he said?"

"If he ever said that around me I'd kill him."

"Have you noticed anything else?"

"What?"

"I mean, well, does he avoid you or anything?"

Herbie suddenly yelled, "But he avoids everybody!" This was more than we had expected from old Herbie. He was shouted down immediately.

"I don't pay him no mind," said Earl, lapsing uncharacteristically into the idiom of his people.

The trial must have lasted two hours. Witness after witness came forward to take a stand against race prejudice. There was an interruption when one of the youngest boys, having watched silently, suddenly burst into tears.

"Look, Peabody's crying."

"What's wrong, Peabody?" someone asked gently.

Confused, overwhelmed by his emotions, Peabody could only stammer. "I'm sorry, I'm sorry, I don't know what's the matter. . . . It's so horrible, how could he . . ."

"What's horrible?"

"Him saying that. How could he say that? I don't understand," the boy said, tears falling from his eyes.

"It's all right, Peabody, don't worry."

"I'm sorry, I'm sorry."

Most of the testimony was on a high moral plane. Children are swept away by morality. Only rarely did it sink to the level of life. From the boy who slept next to Ligget: "He smells."

We didn't laugh. We weren't stupid boys, nor insensitive, and we recognized the seriousness of such a statement.

"His bed smells, and his clothes, and everything he has. He's a smelly, fat slob and I won't sleep next to him. I'm going to move my bed."

Sensing impatience in the room, the prosecutor called the prisoner himself. "Do you have anything to say?"

Ligget stood stock still, his hidden eyes gleaming. He was pale.

"This is your last chance, you better take it. We'll all listen, we'll listen to your side of it." The crowd voiced its agreement, moved by an instant of homage to fair play, and false sympathy. "Okay then, don't say you didn't have a chance."

"Wait a second," said Herbie. "I want to ask him something. Did you say 'nigger-lip' to Sammy?"

It appeared for a moment that Ligget was about to speak, but he gave up the effort. Shaking his head slowly, he denied the charge.

The prosecutor stepped forward. "All those who find him guilty say aye." A roar from forty boys. "All those who find him innocent say nay." Silence. (In a certain sense the trial was a parody of Freemont's "town meetings" in which rather important questions of curriculum and school policy were debated before the students and put to a vote.)

The punishment seemed to suggest itself. We lined up for one punch apiece.

Although Ligget's beating is part of my life (past, present, and future coexist in the unconscious, says Freud), and although I've worried about it off and on for years, all I can say about it is that brutality happens easily. I learned almost nothing from beating up Ligget.

There was a tremendous, heart-swelling excitement as I waited. The line moved slowly, people were taking their time. You got only one punch and you didn't want to waste it. A ritual of getting set, measuring the distance, perhaps adjusting the angle of his jaw with an index finger —all this had to be done before you let go. A few boys had fluffed already, only graying him. If you missed completely you got another chance.

It wasn't hurting Ligget that was important. but rather the unbelievable opportunity to throw a clean, powerful punch completely unhindered, and with none of the sloppiness of an actual fight. Ligget was simply a punching bag, albeit the best possible kind of punching bag, one in human form, with sensory equipment to measure the strength of your blows.

It was my turn. Ligget looked at me blankly. I picked a spot on his chin, drew back my arm, and threw as hard a punch as I could muster. Instant disappointment. I hadn't missed, there was a kind of snapping sound as my fist landed, and his head jerked back, but the whole complex of movements was too fast, somehow missing the exaggerated movie-punch finality I had anticipated. Ligget looked at the boy behind me and I stepped away. I think someone clapped me on the back.

"Good shot."

Little Peabody, tear-stained but sober, swung an awkward blow that almost missed, grazing Ligget's mouth and bringing a little blood. He moved away and the last few boys took their turns.

Ligget was still on his feet. His face was swollen and his small eyes were glazed, but he stood unaided. He had kept his hands deep in his pockets to prevent the reflex of defense. He drew them out and for a moment there was silence, as if everyone expected him to speak.

Perhaps it was because we felt cheated. Each boy's dreams-of-glory punch had been a shade off center, or not quite hard enough, or thrown at the wrong angle, missing perfection by a maddeningly narrow margin. The urge to try again was strong. Unconsciously we knew we'd never have another chance. This wild freedom was ours once only. And perhaps among the older boys there were some who harbored the dream of throwing one final, superman punch, the knock-out blow to end all knock-out blows. Spontaneously, the line formed again.

After three or four blows Ligget collapsed. He sank to the floor, his eyes open and a dark stain spreading in his crotch. Someone told him to get up but it became clear he couldn't understand. Eventually a boy was sent to get the nurse. He was taken to the hospital in an ambulance.

X rays revealed that Ligget's jaw was broken in four places. We learned this the day after the beating, all of us repentant, sincerely unable to understand how it had happened. When he was well enough we went to visit him in the hospital. He was friendly, and accepted our apologies. One could tell he was trying, but his voice was thin and stiff, without a person behind it, like a bad actor reading lines. He wouldn't see us alone, there had to be an adult sitting by him.

No disciplinary action was taken against us. There was talk for a while that Sammy was going to be expelled, but it came to nothing. Ligget never returned.

It is two o'clock in the morning. I lie in bed watching the back of my wife's neck. She sleeps, she is part of the night. The baby wakes at seven, her sleep is for both of them. Sleep is everywhere. I am like a bather at the edge of a pool.

My faith in the firmness of time slips away gradually. I begin to believe that chronological time is an illusion and that some other principle organizes existence. My memories flash like clips of film from unrelated movies. I wonder, suddenly, if I am alive. I know I'm not dead, but am I alive? I look into the memories for reassurance, searching for signs of life. I find someone moving. Is it me? My chest tightens.

I get so uncomfortable floating around like this that I almost gratefully accept the delusion that I've lived another life, remote from me now, and completely forgotten about it. Somewhere in the nooks and crannies of memory there are clues. As I chase them down a kind of understanding comes. I remember waking up in the infirmary at Freemont. I had been sick, unconscious for at least a day. Remembering it I rediscover the exact, spatial center of my life, the one still point. The incident stands like an open window looking out to another existence.

Waking in a white room filled with sunshine. The breeze pushes a curtain gently and I can hear the voices of children outside, far away. There's no one in the room. I don't know where I am or how long I've been there. It seems to be afternoon but it could be morning. I don't know who I am, but it doesn't bother me. The white walls, the sunlight, the voices all exist in absolute purity.

2
Space
and a Dead
Mule

I'D BEEN waiting at the main road since early morning, watching cars. The day was clear and sunny and from my seat on top of a stone gate pillar I could see about a mile. Much of the time the road was empty.

I kept a running calculation on the mathematical probability of the next car being the one I was waiting for. Each time one passed I would glance at my watch and recalculate the odds. A schoolmate sat on the other pillar arguing that my figures were wrong, that the chances were equal for every car. I got angry and eventually he left. When the big long-distance trucks passed I would wave, and almost always the drivers waved back.

I'm sure that leaving Freemont was an emotional experience—saying goodbye to my friends, tying my duffel bag on top of the car, driving down the gravel road for the last time. Possibly I cried. But I can't really remember. My last image is from on top of the stone pillar, recognizing the car and watching it come toward me. In a sense it's as if it never reached me, as if approaching me, it drove into invisibility. Perhaps children remember only waiting for things. The moment events begin to occur they lose themselves in movement, like hypnotized dancers. Another example occurs to me. The arrival home of my father late one night. I ran down the hall, opened the door, and looked up at him. My last memory is that something was wrong. The outlines of his body spread a corona of power. He emanated force. I've been told that on that night he got rough and chased me all over the apartment. When my mother came home I was hiding under the bed, but my memory ceases at the opening of the door. The image is vivid and detailed to the point of remembering the weave of his suit—gray-blue herringbone—and the smell of his breath. Bourbon, but after that, nothing.

On that same night occurred the only preterna[tural phe]nomenon in my experience. I knew my father was [c]several hours before his arrival, and said so to my sist[er. I] hadn't seen him in years and seldom thought about him— the knowledge simply arrived in my brain out of nowhere. I might have caught a glimpse of him on the street without realizing it, but since he came direct from a rest home three hundred miles away on unauthorized leave, I have to discard the idea. My mother left her job that night, the only time she ever did, because of an uneasy feeling that something was wrong at home. For which I'm grateful. Father was zeroing in on me when she arrived.

Driving to Florida in a musty-smelling 1936 Ford with brand new woven-straw seat covers. The radio, cigarette lighter, heater, right windshield wiper, horn, and speedometer were broken. Top speed was fifty miles an hour.

I was in the back with Alison, my older sister. We liked each other without having much in common. Besides the differences of sex and age we were separated by opposing philosophies. Next to me, she would start singing:

"We're on our way, and we ain't comin' back,
We're on our way, and we ain't comin' back,
We're on our way, great God, we're on our way . . ."

To avoid the chaos of family life Alison looked to the larger world outside, as if what was going on at home didn't matter. "Out there" was where she'd discover who she was. This gave her an aura of independence and strength, useful enough in dealing with the family—all of us, cut off from the outside world, too easily believed in her connectedness. But as she was fifteen and knew little of what was happening "out there," her independence was no more than a courageous bluff. But it was all she had. In her loneliness she saw the world only vaguely—thus her tendency to color life with ready-made tints. She would take the song of escaping slaves and equate it with her own experience, falsifying both.

My philosophy, at age eleven, was skepticism. Like most children I was antisentimental and quick to hear false notes. I waited, more than anything else, waited for something momentous to happen. Keeping a firm grip on

nse importance. My vision had to be
"it" happened I would know. The mo-
ld clear away the trivia and throw my
erspective. As soon as it happened I
what was going on, and until then it was
spectacularly unsuccessful philosophy
happened.)

other, rather tall for a woman, with an
abundance of blond hair and wide, cleanly cut features.
She radiated the robust freshness of a farm girl—her fore-
bears were, in fact, Danish country people—missing ideal
Scandinavian beauty only because her face lacked sugges-
tiveness. Studying it you noticed that things were a little too
big. She was handsome rather than beautiful, but for all
that men's heads never failed to turn.

Next to her, in the driver's seat, was Jean, a man of almost impossible Gallic good looks. The ne'er-do-well son of
a collapsed aristocratic New Orleans family, he had been
around for years, seeing my mother while my father was
away. He was six feet tall, slim, and sported a black mustache. The bones of his face and head were extraordinarily
delicate and well proportioned, just slightly smaller than
life size, accentuating their fineness. A perfect Greek head,
but without the Greek effeminacy. His features were
French and masculine. Dark, almost black eyes, a thin
humorous mouth. He smoked cigarettes through an F.D.R.
holder but affected the mannerisms of the proletariat. I
rather liked him, which was lucky. From this trip on, for
the next eight years, he was my stepfather.

We didn't have much money. Stopping only for gas and
food, we drove straight down the east coast. Our destina-
tion was a town called Fort Lauderdale.

During the Florida real-estate boom of the late nineteen-
twenties vast tracts of land in the interior were bought up
by speculators. Heavy machinery came out from the cities
on the coast—Caterpillar tractors, graders, steam shovels,
heavy trucks, earthmovers. Selected islands in the woods
were cleared. Scrub pines were bulldozed into the sand,
palmettos poisoned with kerosene, road beds laid, sidewalks
poured, fire hydrants installed, building lots measured off,
streets named—all the preparations for the conversion of

wasteland into suburbia. Then came the crash of twenty-nine. There was no more money to continue development. Inflated land values collapsed, in some cases from thousands of dollars an acre to a dollar or less in the space of a few months. Inaccessible without city transportation, without city water, sewage, or electricity, without stores or gas stations, without, in most instances, a single soul living on the premises, the speculators' subdivisions weren't even worth cannibalizing. Like neat surgical scars on the surface of the earth they were left, empty, under the hot Florida sun.

Ten miles back of Fort Lauderdale, well hidden in the woods, was one of these islands. Untouched for twenty years, it had fallen into the hands of a socialist from Wisconsin named Doc, a bovine fellow dedicated to giving the workers homes of their own. For no money down and a few dollars a month anyone prepared to build with his own hands could get a plot of land. It was to be a workers' community, or more precisely, a white workers' community.

The land had come full circle, from the big money boys of the twenties to the smalltimers of the forties. In every respect Doc's plan was the antithesis of the older plan—instead of the middle class, the lower class, instead of speculators, homeowners, instead of money, labor—as if he had a religious obligation to take ground tainted by the capitalist fantasies of the boom and wash it clean with the down-to-earth realities of socialism. Lying in his trailer at night did Doc dream his dream? The rediscovery of an older, better America. Cabin raisings. Town meetings. Simplicity. Was he to be the father of these children? Probably. With pathetic optimism he had named the project "Chula Vista," beautiful view, and the name if not the project marked Doc as a social visionary. The view in all directions was exactly the same. Flat, sandy land, underbrush, and stunted pine trees. Dismal, to say the least. We bought two lots.

Building the house brought out the best in Jean. He threw himself into the planning with uncharacteristic fervor, making hundreds of crude drawings and designs, struggling with figures and lists. Profoundly anti-traditional, his answer to the problem of building a house was not to see how other men had done it, but to start completely from scratch and work it out on his own. His theory that the intelligent layman could do a job better than someone who'd been trained (trained = brainwashed) was to be applied in the construction of his own home. Unlike the rest of us, he was more interested in the act of building the house than in the house itself. Minor innovations in design struck him as major conceptual breakthroughs, small technical victories ballooned into great philosophical verities. Every nail and stick of wood became endowed with his persona, and as a result he worked hard. Harder no doubt, than he ever had before.

Reclaiming the land came first. Small trees and underbrush had to be cleared. The young pines fell easily under a sharp ax or machete, but the palmettos were more difficult. Showing only a knee-high fringe of palm above ground, these plants were in fact immense subterranean growths of appalling toughness. Their fat, hairy roots joined together deep in the sand, so that when you'd worked your way down to the bottom of one plant you sometimes had to work your way back up along another. And if they didn't go down they ran horizontally, interweaving—ten or fifteen feet of root as thick as a man's waist. I became a specialist in extracting them, a job I enjoyed because it was tough. No one else had the patience. It took days to clear even the small plot where the house would stand.

In the terrific heat we drank case after case of Nehi orange soda kept cool under fifty pounds of ice in the trunk of the Ford. Even Jean, a food faddist, forgot his principles and guzzled it down with relish. Our bodies glistening with sweat, we took salt pills twice a day and ate sandwiches of white bread and lunch meat. A preparation called 6-12 kept the mosquitoes under control, but clouds of gnats swirled continuously around everyone's head. Sometimes at night we'd work by Coleman lanterns, and flying roaches, drawn by the brightness, would smash against the hot glass with a metallic snap.

It was an exciting scene at night. Great stacks of lumber looming at the edge of darkness, hammers and axes throwing sparks into the air. In the sharp-edged light, faces changed mysteriously, and each figure spilled a huge shadow over the underbrush.

Notwithstanding Jean's self-representation as an original thinker, he had the foresight to design an extremely simple building, perhaps unconsciously recognizing that the minor innovations he held in such high regard would lose their significance to the world at large if the house collapsed. He was led, inevitably, to one of nature's strongest and simplest forms, the cube.

We built the floor first, a twenty-five-by-twenty-five-foot platform set on concrete blocks in the sand. I remember some nervous discussions about *anchoring* the house. It was finally decided that *gravity* would *anchor* the house and no more was thought about it. Problems in construction were solved as they arose. Jean and my mother sounding like philosophers at work on first principles: "If this holds up that, then what holds up this?" "Why, that, of course!" etc. After the floor came the framework of the walls and roof, then the lathing, roofing, windows, and finally two coats of paint outside. The interior was never finished.

The house was actually one large room. The kitchen was hidden by a curtain and Alison and I slept in a double-decker bed behind a partition. There was a pump in the yard and a privy in back.

I don't remember everything about meeting Tobey. One day we faced each other in the middle of the white coral road, hesitating to speak, staring. We were the only boys for miles around. I remember wondering how he could walk on the hot, sharp coral without shoes.

"Don't your feet hurt?"

He shakes his head.

"Do you live around here?"

"Back there. Around the corner."

"Hey, that's great. I live in the new house by the woods."

"I saw you working on it," he says.

"We ought to get some wire and a couple of dry-cell batteries and string it up between our houses. We could learn Morse code and send messages."

He looks up from the road. "You think we could?"

"Sure."

"Have you got a bike?"

"Yes." I had just gotten it.

"Let's go swimming. I know a rock pit back in the woods. It's got an island in the middle."

"Okay. I'll have to get my bathing suit."

"Hell, you don't need a suit. There's nobody around."

"How far is it?"

"A couple of miles. It's a great place," he says.

All that summer we were together. My days started with
Tobey calling from the road. "Fra-yunk . . . hey, Fra-
yunk . . ." I'd swallow some milk, grab a piece of bread,
and rush out, the screen door slamming behind me. There
he'd be, straddling his bike, bare feet in the white dust, a
brown arm waving, beckoning me out into the blinding
glare.

We spent most of our time in the woods. The first project
was a tree-house built precariously high in a tall pine.
The climb was difficult for anyone who didn't know the
secret hand-holds we'd constructed at the hardest parts.
Lazing around in the sun we'd tell stories and pick the
black pine tar off our hands and feet. Far below us the
earth dozed. Occasionally we'd glance back to Chula Vista
—when a car started, or a man on a roof flashed his
hammer. (Down would come the arm in dead silence,
then, too late, the sharp snap of the blow.) Above, the fat
white clouds drifted in the blue. Great sedate clouds,
rich and peaceful. We lay on our backs watching them, getting dizzy as they slipped along behind the branches, as if
our tree was falling.

On the ground we laid out track and field games. Hour
after hour our bodies fell like bundles into the softened
sand. Tobey once high-jumped his own height. We kept a
record in a nickel notebook, carefully noting down our per-
formances and progress.

We had caches of canned food and comic books at
different places in the woods. We rarely used them; it was
the idea that pleased us.

Best of all was the rock quarry. Down the long white
coral road on our bikes, mile after mile into the deserted
woods. Leaving the bikes against a tree we walked across
the sand. The air buzzed with sun and sleepy insects. If
we saw a king snake, all six feet wrapped black and shiny
in the shade of a palmetto, we'd break off a pine branch
and kill it, smashing the small head till the blood ran.
Rabbits were rare; if we saw one we'd throw a stick.

Once we found a dead mule, bones picked almost clean, ants streaming through the eyes. The stench was too much for us and after poking the corpse we ran away, gasping for breath. We talked about that mule for weeks. What was its fascination? Death dramatized, something of unbelievable importance being revealed right in front of us. But something else too. We rambled over a tremendous amount of space every day, over vast areas of silent, empty woods (a pine woods on sandy ground is more like a'desert than anything else), rambled over miles of wasteland trying to find the center of it, the heart, the place to *know* it. We sensed the forces around us but they were too thinly spread, too finely drawn over all the miles of woods for us to grasp them. The forces eluded us. We would run into a clearing knowing that just a moment ago, in that instant before we had arrived, something of importance had happened there. But when we found the dead mule we knew we were close, suddenly very close. Those forces spread like air over the woods had converged here, on this animal the moment he died, and were not yet altogether gone.

We could see the abandoned quarry behind the trees, the tall white island in the center seeming to move as we ran. Two black hawks lifted from the pinnacle, swerving away over the water and up into the blue air, their wings beating slowly, synchronized in movement like a double image in a dream. Impossibly still, the water lay against the shining coral shore like brown glass. We ran to the edge, shouting to break the silence.

"Yodela-ay! Yodelay-io!"

"Ali-ali-ali-ali-ali-*in*-free!"

Or just "Yay!"

We did a lot of shouting—phrases from childhood games, dirty words, satisfying noises of all kinds. We were afraid, but only a little afraid, of the silence around us. Usually there was enough breeze in the tops of the pines to make a faint rustling noise behind the day, but I remember times, hot, airless days, sitting in the woods alone in perfect silence, paralysis creeping over my limbs, my ears deaf without sound to hear, my eyes frozen without movement to watch. We shouted in joy and fear, sending our voices ahead to animate the bleakness, supremely conscious of ourselves as pinpoints of life in a world of dead things, impurities that sand, coral, water, and dead mules were only tolerating.

It was easy to undress. We wore only blue jeans. I remember a mild shock at the absence of anything but air against my skin. Running to the edge of the bank we threw ourselves into the water, instantly setting the whole broad surface alive with movement and dappled light. Our legs kicked up thin sheets of water that sparkled in the sun and the slapping of our cupped hands echoed away into the woods. The water was always warm.

Neither one of us knew how to swim properly. We'd simply crash through, with a tremendous amount of wasted movement, toward the island, our progress slow but steady. We never raced, knowing, I suppose, that as bad as we were it was pointless. Halfway across we'd tread water.

"It's great nobody ever comes here," I'd say, spluttering.

"I bet nobody even knows about it except us."

"If any kids from Dania find it we can put up signs saying the water is poisoned."

"Hey, maybe it is!"

We'd laugh.

"You know that big old turtle we saw on the bank?"

"Yes?"

"I bet he could take your peter off in one bite."

"Jesus Christ!" I'd yell, only half joking, my legs propelling me up in the air. "Jesus Christ!"

At the highest point of the man-made island a bed of soft green moss had grown over the coral. We'd lie with our chins in our hands looking out over the miles of pine woods, the sun hot against our backsides.

"We ought to build a shack out here."

"Have to carry all the wood."

"We could build a raft and float the stuff over."

"Hmm . . ."

Often we'd fall asleep, tired from the long ride and the swim, a drowsy, dreamless half-sleep in the sun. When one awoke the colors of the world had deepened, as if the whole scene had just been created.

Riding back we'd keep an eye out for cars parked in the woods. Two or three times we spotted one, and hidden in the tops of nearby trees had watched the gentle rocking motion of the chassis on its greased springs, silent and comically sinister. We were too scared to get close enough to see anything, except a heart-freezing glimpse of a woman's arm being raised, or the sudden flash of sunlight on a bald pate. We knew what we were watching, but somehow we could never quite believe it. From the safety of the trees we'd whistle and screech till the car drove away. Scrambling down we'd race over to find the prophylactic, holding it up on the end of a long stick, grimacing with disgust. Neither of us knew exactly what it was, accepting it nevertheless as proof that the unbelievable act had taken place. We hid our ignorance from each other, making oblique wisecracks to cover it up.

Jean. At about this time our fates, his and mine, began to affect one another. And fate is the appropriate word. He dropped from nowhere to become my father. I emerged from behind my mother's skirts looking, to his eyes, something like a son. We had in common that we were male inhabitants of the U.S.A., and my mother, and nothing more. Life had placed us together. We faced each other like two strangers trapped in an elevator.

Jean was one of three brothers. His father, a professor of chemistry, died young and left the family almost nothing except the house they lived in. The mother was charming but somewhat scatter-brained. The boys, particularly Jean, were too much for her and ran wild. All three—Dan the youngest and most self-effacing, Victor the most earnest, and Jean the wildest—led difficult lives as if they shared a common psychic wound. The most obvious characteristic of each man mushroomed uncontrollably, rushing to fill a vacuum, and each man grew lopsided and awkward with the weight of it. Victor's puritanical earnestness led him to alcoholism, Dan's self-effacement to loneliness and misanthropy, and Jean's wildness to the private dreamworld of the mentally unbalanced.

Jean left school early and began a long series of jobs, never staying long in one position. He went to sea, was a longshoreman, floor-walker, counterman, male model, carpenter, migrant laborer, waiter, dancing teacher, and on and on. He'd been married twice before he met my mother, very briefly to a New Orleans debutante and then to a young girl who eventually lost her mind, leaving his bed for a padded cell. The third marriage must have seemed his last chance at a normal life. Whether or not a normal life is something to be prized, and whether or not he ever truly wanted it, it turned out he was too fond of his old ways to risk a change.

He brought us to Florida, and undoubtedly somewhere in his mind was the halfhearted desire to emulate Victor, the steadiest brother, who lived a fair imitation of the typical American middle-class life as a small-time real-estate broker in Fort Lauderdale. Unfortunately Victor's alcoholism was progressive, and soon after our arrival the first ominous fissures began to appear in his tidy world. Before long he collapsed entirely.

Asleep on the couch in Victor's living room, drifting between the half-light of dreams and the reality of morning sun. A noise opens my eyes. Still asleep I see a tall figure pass the foot of the couch, a dark uncle, a fast-moving Victor figure crossing to the desk. I watch his back as he sits writing. Uneasiness creeps forward from the back of my head, waking me with a silent danger signal. Don't move! Don't make a sound! I watch his solid figure. In the early morning silence small sounds are magnified—the scratch of his pen, a bird outside, the creaking chair. Don't move! It's coming! The pen stops and his shoulders stiffen. My eyes widen slowly. Now! His arms jerk straight up into the air as if pulled on strings from above. The pen flies from his fingers and crashes against the ceiling. The chair clatters to the floor as his body lunges upward and his feet leave the ground. His hair seems to stand out from his head as though electrified. In space his mouth opens and his back arches, every muscle stretched to rock hardness. Stiff-legged he drops two inches, a petrified man. From somewhere inside his rigid form a scream materializes, a long sound that winds lazily up the scale, higher and higher till his voice breaks. The scream turns into something I'd never heard before. Emitting a steady, unwavering blast of noise his body falls backward, stiff as a board. When he hits the floor the house shakes. His eyes are rolled back in his head making him look oddly Japanese.

I wish I could say I went to his aid. In fact I left the scene immediately, rising from the couch, hurdling the armrest, through the door and away in one continuous fluid streak of speed, arms and legs pumping like the shafts of an engine. Victor's wife and son passed me in the hall going in the opposite direction. Amazed, I saw tears in Lucky's eyes. He must have started to cry the very instant his father screamed, as if he'd been waiting for it. They barely looked at me.

I was too scared to do anything but run. Perhaps my father's dramatic visits home had given me a low tolerance for insane behavior. At the moment of breakdown Victor seemed less like someone I had talked and laughed with than the Wild Man of Borneo. He was possessed, and God alone knew what he'd do to me if he had the chance. I'd been too scared even to look at him, afraid somehow that his image on my retina was dangerous.

Rushing from the house in my underwear, I streaked around a palm tree and ran full tilt into the back of a parked car. It was the primitive symbolism of the comic strips come to life. My head hit the trunk with a tremendous CLONG while stars and colored lights swirled in profusion. For one silly instant, listening to the huge sound reverberating down my entire life span, it seemed I *was* a comic strip character, a cartoon somehow living out the plot and reading it simultaneously. Spread-eagled over the deck of the car, sinking back into a sleep from which no more than sixty seconds ago I had awakened, sinking as well from the trunk to the ground, slipping slowly off the hot metal, limp as a dishrag, it came to me that the world was insane. Not just people. The world.

So Victor was no help to Jean. If anything the example of his brother confirmed Jean's distrust of ordinary workaday life. He was damned if *he'd* get caught like so many others. Occasionally when money ran out he'd take a week's work as a carpenter, but most of the time he puttered around the house or went to the beach. There was always a project in the future he could think about as he lay in the sun.

Jean made a terrible mistake. Not only did he live off his wife (who worked far more often than himself), but worse, far worse, he lived off what were, symbolically at least, his children. Every month two checks arrived at our Chula Vista mailbox, two one-hundred-dollar checks from an old lawyer in Jacksonville, drawn against a trust belonging to my sister and me. The money was for our support. For eight years—in Florida, New York, and Connecticut—our support checks were Jean's largest source of income. Without them he would have to have gone to work. Only a small fraction was spent on Alison and me. Jean and my mother spent many thousands of dollars before we were old enough to realize what was going on. (At seventeen years of age, when I had left home and gone to Europe, I unsuspectingly accepted forty dollars a month, on which I lived, while my mother skimmed off sixty for herself and Jean.) Had Jean been less proud he might have lived this way without hurting himself, but as it was, anger built up with every year. Some anger came out, but most of it went inside himself. He built a maze inside to keep the anger moving, to keep it bouncing in his head, its destructive energy trapped in a cycle of movement. He became a sort of emotional pinball machine.

But that comes later. In Florida Jean was relatively cheerful. He enjoyed telling stories, particularly dialect stories, and always made my mother laugh. He swam a mile a day, read Erskine Caldwell and James M. Cain in paperback, ate well, slept well, and was content. When I started to become a problem he felt uninvolved and left discipline to my mother. He was probably right. I doubt that he could have helped me.

It began slowly: balking at my chores (helping with the dishes, watering the sandy lawn with its nonviable baby palm trees, sweeping the floor, all the countless empty jobs adults give children), never coming home on time, sulking. Gradually I slipped into the state of *being in trouble*, a pedal point of tension that was to grow steadily until I understood little else about myself, until the fact of being alive became synonymous with the fact of being in trouble.

The first year in Florida was my last good year until I became a man. The woods, Tobey, bikes, running, nakedness, freedom—these were the important things. It was the end of childhood.

At night we'd ride our bikes down a long, flat, empty road through the woods to the drive-in movie at the edge of town. Kids were allowed in free. We'd sit on a long bench just under the screen, or lie on the sandy ground and stare up at the immense figures moving against the sky. Going home, the movie would stay with us for a while. We'd act out the best scenes, shouting the lines. Nervous, filled with passion, we stood up on the bikes for more speed and pedaled deeper and deeper into the woods. Halfway home the movie was gone. We'd ride easily through the balmy air, gliding, listening to the faint hiss of the tires on the asphalt. We'd sing Hoagy Carmichael ("Ol' buttermilk SKY!") or swerve the bikes stylishly in long arcs back and forth. The road was always empty. There were no houses, no lights—only the stars.

3

Going North

JEAN had a plan: to build a house next to ours and rent it out. All he needed was money. For that we'd go back North where wages were higher.

Tobey came to see me off. I remember him standing in front of the house as we pulled out of the driveway. He waved once and then stood quietly. I'd told him I was coming back the following summer, that I'd come back even if it meant running away. I watched him walk over to get his bike from against the tall pine in the yard, watched him spin the pedal with his foot and lift his head. I waved through the back window and then we turned a corner and he was gone.

A curious thing happened in the car. Nobody spoke. For miles and miles we rode in silence. It couldn't have been sadness. They were leaving nothing behind, not a single friend, no lovers, no enemies. They could pick up and leave for New York as easily as going to the beach. Jean and my mother always lived that way. They were rarely asked anywhere, made no friends, and lived, except for an occasional boarder in the house, in total isolation from the rest of humanity.

Alison was glad to go back North. For her it was the end of a period of loneliness and disturbing proximity to the rest of the family. She was older than me, and living without privacy, almost in the same room with Mother and Jean, was extremely difficult. I was certainly no help to her. My favorite trick, when I saw her making for the outhouse, was to sneak up behind her, push a sapling through a crack in the wall, and tickle her bare behind. She never failed to scream. In fact, on the first occasion she burst through the door of the privy and out into the sunlight screaming her heart out—blue jeans around her ankles, white tail in the air, fast-shuffling toward the safety of the house like an hysterical majorette. The few tentative friends she'd made at school lived miles away, and in any case couldn't, she felt, be asked home. Living in Florida she had neither a real family nor a supporting outside world. She was glad to go North, and as it turned out, she never came back.

For my mother the decision to return to New York was undoubtedly a relief. All year she'd been secretly holding back money from her pay checks in an attempt to keep one or two hundred on hand for emergencies, and all year Jean, with an uncanny sixth sense, had known just when he could go over the budget. Instead of acting as a safeguard her emergency fund encouraged Jean's already dangerous financial irresponsibility. He began to believe he couldn't be broke with his wife around. In eight years with my mother he never held a steady job. It may be significant that once he was alone, without emergency funds, or support checks for his children, faced in fact with the appalling prospect of being broke with nowhere to turn, he settled down to driving a taxicab and has worked hard ever since.

Jean went North with some apprehensiveness, but he knew he needed money to finance the building of the house, and he was willing to work if it meant easy street later on. He liked Florida because it was warm. The warmth meant something to him and he was uneasy leaving it. (When he split up with my mother he went straight to Florida. I've seen the same reaction in other people. A friend from college, in terrible shape after leaving school, breaking up with his girl, and leading a lonely life in New York suddenly announced he was going to Florida "because it's warm.")

I didn't want to leave Fort Lauderdale. Tobey had become my best friend. There was nothing waiting for me in New York.

Our first stop was Jacksonville, Florida, my father's birthplace. Alison and I were to see Minnie, our grandmother, who lived there with a hired companion. Minnie was old and rich, and a little crazy.

Through the quiet suburban streets of Jacksonville. Early morning, and the sun is still cool. The car moves forward smoothly under the trees. My mother turns to check our appearance. For the first time in a year or more I am wearing a tie.

"Maybe she'll take us out to lunch," Alison says, remembering a day in New York when Minnie took us to the Waldorf-Astoria. She smooths the skirt of her dress, pleased at looking nice. "Someplace downtown."

"Here we are," Jean says, pulling up to the curb. "Too late to turn back." Easy for him to laugh, I think. He doesn't have to go in.

We get out slowly. Mother leans down and says to Jean through the open window, "I'll be back in a second." Our footsteps seem unnaturally loud on the pavement. I look down at my feet. The polished shoes seem unfamiliar, as if they didn't belong to me. I make a point of stepping on the cracks in the sidewalk.

"Remember not to talk about Jean," my mother says. "All right. Here we are." She rings the bell.

The door is opened by Miss Smith, a pleasant-looking woman of fifty-five or sixty. She wears a dress with large green flowers in the design and around her neck a string of pink pearls, rosy against the dry skin. The moment she sees us she smiles. "Well, just look who's here!"—as if she hadn't been expecting us—"Isn't this nice!"

My mother steps back from the door. "I won't come in just yet. I'll say hello when I come back for the children."

"That's fine," says Miss Smith, nodding her head, still smiling. "That'll be just fine." Her voice has a kind of sing-song rhythm, vaguely reassuring, as if nothing could surprise her. "All right, children." She leads us into the hall, closing the door behind us. The house is cool and dark, with a peculiar musty, sweet odor hanging in the air. At the end of the hall she gently puts her hand on my shoulder, stopping me, and goes into a room. "Minnie!" We hear her voice raise slightly in pitch. "Isn't this nice? Frank and Alison are here to see you."

My grandmother's response is electrifying. Her voice ascends in a strange shrill noise, a cross between a shriek and a coo, a cracked, warbling, shaky cry, meant, I finally realize as Miss Smith returns still smiling, to indicate pleasure. Again the gentle hand on my shoulder, this time urging me forward into the sitting room.

Minnie sits by the window in an old-fashioned wooden wheelchair. Puffy, snow-white hair explodes radially from her face in a halo of brightness and her sharp blue eyes move back and forth between us. "The children. The children . . ." she murmurs. As we approach she lifts her skinny hands from the armrests and holds them fluttering in the air like two weak birds.

To my complete amazement Alison goes right up to the old lady and kisses her on the cheek. Minnie is suddenly calm, her eyes look straight at me, almost as if Alison weren't there. Miss Smith gives me a surreptitious nudge and I go forward. Under the slippery black sleeve my grandmother's arm is impossibly thin, not much thicker than a walking stick and just as hard. Her cheek is cool against my mouth, not unpleasant, but a strong odor rises from her body—lavender, urine, a sweet decay. Dry fingers light as feathers touch my cheek. "Well, well, well . . ." her cracked bird-voice says in my ear. I step away, glancing at Miss Smith. We all sit down and Miss Smith begins to chat, filling the silence.

Hours later. The room is getting warm and an old electric fan has been turned on. Standing on a table in the corner, it sweeps slowly back and forth, a huge black insect turning its head. At Minnie's insistence Alison and Miss Smith have gone downtown to get Alison a new dress. I sit on a kitchen chair facing my grandmother, who has dozed off. A horn sounds from the street and her eyes open.

"Do you know where your father is?" she asks.

"In the hospital."

"Do you know why?"

"He's sick."

"Yes, of course," she says sharply, "but what's wrong with him?"

After a moment I say, honestly, "I don't know."

For some reason this seems to please her. "Will you go and see him?"

"Yes."

"When was the last time you saw him?"

I try to think. "I can't remember. I'm sorry."

Her long ropey hands tremble in her lap. She says nothing for several moments, and then out of nowhere suddenly asks, "Do you love me?"

My face flushes with heat. "Yes. Of course."

She leans forward from the wheelchair, a fierce bird, her eyes on mine. "Do you really love me?"

"Of course I love you, Grandmother." The unfamiliar
word seems overformal but I don't know what else to call
her.

With an ambiguous sigh she leans back, her eyes finally
releasing me. "I *am* your grandmother," she says unnecessarily. "Miss Smith always wants me to send you money.
She always says, 'Don't you think it'd be nice to send something to Frank and Alison?' "

"Thank you for the check on my birthday."

"Birthdays and Christmas, Christmas and birthdays. You
don't have to thank me. Do you keep it or give it to your
mother?"

"Oh, we keep it. She cashes it for us."

"You need a new suit. Get one in New York and have
her send me the bill."

"Yes. Thank you very much. Thank you."

She slams her hand against the armrest. "Shut up."

I watch the black head of the electric fan moving back
and forth, back and forth.

"Why should I give you money? You're her children,
not mine." Soon she falls asleep again.

Alison and Miss Smith return. Minnie remains in the sitting room while we eat sandwiches in the kitchen. Alison
talks animatedly to Miss Smith. Sipping at my Coke I am
envious of my sister. She can jolly up Minnie, too, in a way
that seems completely genuine. Is it? I look up at Alison's
flushed, smiling face. Does Minnie mean anything to her,
an old woman we've seen three or four times in our lives?
Am I missing something that Alison is getting? She's older
than me, of course. Suddenly I know that Alison is only
acting. She plays it out as if we were ordinary grandchildren
visiting an ordinary grandmother, as if we were the sort of
people Alison had read about in the magazines. I look at
Miss Smith, at her kind face, her lips moving in encourage-
ment as Alison talks. My mind halts. I'm too young to know
what I'm watching. Two women, one old, one young, keeping up appearances.

Our '36 Ford was a remarkable car. Driven nonstop from
Jacksonville to New York, it never complained, never faltered. Its small V-8 engine drank very little gas, its temperature and oil pressure remained reassuringly constant, and
in every respect it seemed dependable if not indestructible.

Jean had bought it second hand for two hundred dollars. At three o'clock in the morning, humming along through the flat swamplands of the Carolinas in the moonlight, he and I watched the odometer move from 99,999.9 to 00,000.0.

"That engine hasn't been opened once in a hundred thousand miles," Jean said. "Of course it's just luck. I got this and someone else got a lemon."

"What does it mean, really, when a car is a lemon?"

"Every once and a while on the assembly line a car gets put together the wrong way. Everything goes wrong—little things at first and then bigger and bigger things. If you ever buy one sell it right away before it gets expensive."

"Did you ever buy one?"

"No."

The idea fascinated me. Watching the empty road ahead of us I turned the concept of lemon over and over in my mind. It seemed the perfect word—a bright yellow car mysteriously endowed among all its brothers with an individual fate. Automobile number 142241, ostensibly the same as all the others, but actually a composite of manufacturing errors, a collection of mistakes. It made a great deal of sense to me. Instead of spreading the mistakes equally over all the cars produced, certain cars, known as lemons, were packed efficiently with everything that could possibly go wrong with an automobile. In this way one knew that the other cars were okay.

"How often do they turn up?" I asked.

"Oh, I don't know. Every couple or three thousand."

"They ought to do something about it. They shouldn't sell them."

"They don't care. Now you take the Tucker. There was a really modern automobile. He cared about making a good car and look what they did to him."

"It's too bad we'll never be able to get one."

"They squeezed him right out." Jean's voice rose suddenly and in the back seat Mother and Alison stirred in their sleep. "He was too good. They squeezed him out."

"Victor says Tucker was a thief. An embezzler."

"Victor! What does Victor know? I've seen the car. The embezzlement charge was a conspiracy of the big automobile manufacturers. It's the same old story. They couldn't meet the competition so they framed him."

"Can they get away with that?"

"Get away with it?" Jean laughed hoarsely, his choked cry even more explosive than usual. "They can get away with anything they damn please! They run the whole show. Don't you know that yet?"

"Hush up. We're trying to sleep," Mother said from the back.

"For someone who's supposed to be so smart," Jean said softly, turning to me with a faint smile, "you don't use the old bean very much." This was a familiar phrase of Jean's, a favorite accusation against me, and always, like some final incantation at a religious rite, a signal that the dialogue was over, a reminder that Jean, as leader, was privy to secrets beyond my ken. It was an appeal to my faith, delivered gently, with an almost apologetic smile whenever he sensed hesitancy in my response to him. I always took it as a compliment.

I did hesitate, though, at his explanations—not so much because I didn't believe him as because the way in which he delivered explanations left very little room for response. Jean's intellectual touchstone was clarity. All problems were reduced to a simple proposition—race prejudice was exclusively an economic problem, dentists refused to tell people not to eat sugar because in doing so they would put themselves out of business, religion was nothing more than superstition, if you ate the right foods you would never get sick, there was no such thing as heredity, everything started from zero when the sperm cell met the egg cell, no one could learn to play the piano except by practicing eight hours a day—and so forth and so on. His style almost never varied. First a slow and elaborate introduction to the subject at large, and finally, at the right moment, a sudden reduction to the essential. It was simple and remarkably successful—after the bewildering opening verbiage many people grasped the cleverly introduced reduction with the tenacity of bulldogs. (Jean once had a bulldog.) He would turn eagerly, his eyes sparkling and his head thrown forward in a parody of anticipation to see the effect of his logic. It was always a difficult moment. Jean wanted more than a sign of recognition, a sign that you had understood; he wanted you to *become him,* to discard immediately all ideas of your own and totally accept the closed frame of reference in which he saw whatever problem it was you were discussing.

Jean's technique and tremendous verbal energy impressed me, but I could never surrender completely. I sensed he was too tricky to be altogether right. (Yet even now, knowing what I know, I am vaguely ashamed of my hedging.) But in those days Jean was good-humored about the resistances he found in his fellow men. He was accustomed to them after all. Half his life had been spent wandering like some profane messiah telling people not to eat white bread and they had gone right on doing it. He had a certain good-natured stoicism in those days.

Jean was a sucker for any diner with a truck in front of it—we were even fooled once by a huge cardboard cut-out of a semi cleverly half hidden in the shadows. "Trucks Welcome. Trucks Stop Here! Truckers! Eats Bunks Showers . . ." In all of them the juke boxes played one tune, "Red Silk Stockings and Green Perfume," a long, twangy hillbilly dirge. I remember a place in Virginia where the waitress had a glass eye.

"Howdy," Jean said. He always used this curious word with working people, saying it slowly and tentatively as if to reassure them that despite his aristocratic profile he was just plain folks. Howdy. A cross between cowboy talk and mountain talk, it was as exotic to Jean as it was to me.

"What'll it be?" she said, peering through her one movable eye.

"What kind of pie've you got?"

"Apple cherry blueberry rhubarb pecan and banna cream."

"Coffee and apple pie."

"Who's this, your relief?" she asked, nodding at me. Mother and Alison were asleep in the car.

"That's right," said Jean.

"What's your pleasure, honey?"

"Cherry pie and a glass of milk."

We watched her walk to the end of the counter. Her white uniform was spotless.

We ate silently, slightly stunned at being out of the car. The pie was bad, sweet and gelatinous inside and soggy outside. Jean ordered more coffee to stay awake. A truck driver dropped some coins in the juke box.

"There it is again," I said.

"Look at the build on that guy." Jean was watching the truck driver, an immense fellow with shoulders twice as wide as his own. "I wouldn't mix with him," he said unnecessarily. A slight man, Jean had never, as far as I knew, mixed with anybody. But as a boxing fan he knew the language and enjoyed salting his speech with an occasional fight reference. It took me years to discover the surprising fact that Jean was somewhat self-conscious about his body. He thought he was too thin, and despite his height had the touchiness of a small man. He saw all forms of beauty dimly, but most particularly his own. The delicacy and grace of form that had been the delight of so many women went unrecognized by the owner. If he'd had the discipline he would have ruined himself by working out with bar bells.

The waitress returned. "There's a shower and stuff in the back if you want."

Jean looked up. "No. I guess the coffee will keep me awake. Thanks."

Outside, we walked through the hot black air toward the car. Gravel crackled under our feet. "Good-looking woman," Jean said.

"The waitress? But she only had one eye!"

Half to himself, his voice fading as we went around opposite sides of the car, he said, "If the rest of her is real it doesn't make too much difference about the eye."

Jean started the motor and worked the tall, floor-mounted gear shift. We rolled onto the highway and the diner fell behind us, bars of light drifting slowly around the interior of the car, waning, angling into nothing. In the darkness we heard the wind, the humming of the engine, the steady creaking and rumbling of the old chassis as we gathered speed, rushing back into a trance. Alison leaned forward and asked sleepily, "Where are we?"

"Nowhere," I said. "Virginia. Go back to sleep."

"I feel like I've been on this trip all my life," she said, sinking back under her blanket.

4
White Days and Red Nights

JEAN and my mother had weekend jobs as wardens at the Southbury Training School, a Connecticut state institution for the feeble-minded. Every Friday afternoon we drove out deep in the hills to an old cabin they had bought for a few hundred dollars on the installment plan.

The first dirt road was always plowed for the milk truck, but never the second, and in the snow you could see the tracks of wagon wheels and two narrow trails where the horses had walked. A mile down the road was the Greens' farm. Every morning they hauled milk to the pick-up station, a full silent load up to the hill, and then back, the empty returns from the previous day clanging raucously behind the horses as if in melancholic celebration. No one else ever used the road. If it was passable we drove to the cabin, if not, we walked, single file, in the horses' tracks, our arms full of food.

Every Friday the cheap padlock was opened, every Friday I stepped inside. A room so dim my blood turned gray, so cold I knew no human heart had ever beaten there— every line, every article of furniture, every scrap of paper on the floor, every burned-out match in a saucer filling me with desolation, depopulating me. A single room, twelve feet by eighteen. A double bed, a bureau, a round table to eat on, and against the wall a counter with a kerosene cooker. In the exact center of the room, a potbellied coal stove. All these objects had been watched by me in a state of advanced terror, watched so many long nights that even in the daytime they seemed to be whispering bad messages.

My mother would make a quick meal out of cans. Corned-beef hash or chili. Conversation was usually sparse. "I have a good cottage tonight."

"I can't remember where I am. We'd better stop at the administration building."

Outside, the lead-gray afternoon slipped almost imperceptibly into twilight. Very gradually the earth moved toward night and as I sat eating I noted every darkening shadow. Jean sipped his coffee and lighted a Pall Mall. My mother arranged the kerosene lamp so she could see to do the dishes.

"Frank, get me some water."

Through the door and into the twilight, the bucket against my thigh. There was a path beaten through the snow, a dark line curving through the drifts to the well. The low sky was empty, uniformly leaden. Stands of trees spread pools of darkness, as if night came up from their sunken roots. At the well I tied a rope to the handle of the bucket and dropped it into the darkness upside down, holding the line. The trick was not to hit the sides. I heard a muffled splash. Leaning over the deep hole, with the faintest hint of warmer air rising against my face, I hauled the bucket hand over hand until it rose suddenly into view, the dim sky shimmering within like some luminous oil. Back to the house with the water. Absolute silence except for the sounds of my own movement, absolute stillness except for a wavering line of smoke from the stovepipe.

While Mother did the dishes Jean and I sat at the table. He sipped at his second cup of coffee. I fished a dime out of my pocket. "Could you get me a couple of Baby Ruth bars?"

Jean sucked his teeth and reached for a wooden pick. "The stuff is poison. It rots your teeth."

"Oh Jean, I know. It won't take you a second. There's a stand in the administration building."

"You're so finicky about food and you go and eat that stuff. Can you imagine the crap in those mass-produced candy bars? Dead roaches and mouse shit and somebody's nose-pickings."

"Jean, for heaven's sake!" My mother laughed.

"Well, he won't touch a piece of perfectly good meat and then he'll eat that junk."

"It'll only take you a second." I pushed the dime across the table.

"I know the trouble with you. You're too lazy to chew your food. You wash everything down with milk." He glanced at the coin, his eyes flicking away. "All right. If you want to kill yourself. Keep the dime." He finished his coffee and cigarette slowly, savoring the mixed flavors and the moment of rest. Since he'd stopped using the holder his smoking style had changed. He'd take a quick drag, blow out about a third of the smoke immediately, inhale the rest, and let it come out as he talked. I often made it a point to sit in such a way that a strong light source behind him showed up the smoke. It was amazing how long it came out, a fine, almost invisible blue stream, phrase after phrase, changing direction smoothly as he clipped off the words. For some reason I admired this phenomenon tremendously. I could sit watching for hours.

Jean pushed back his chair and stood up, stretching his arms and yawning exaggeratedly. Even this he did gracefully. Like a cat, he was incapable of making an awkward move. Looking out the window he sucked his teeth noisily. "Well," he said slowly, "the lions and tigers seem to be under control tonight."

I felt my face flush and quickly turned away. It was a complicated moment. My fear of staying alone in the house had been totally ignored for weeks. For Jean to mention it at all was somehow promising, and I was grateful despite the unfairness of his phrasing. He knew of course that it wasn't lions and tigers I was afraid of—by using that image he was attempting to simplify my fear into the realm of childishness (which he could then ignore in good conscience) as well as to shame me out of it. Jean was telling me, with a smile, that my behavior was irrational and therefore he could do nothing to help me, something I would never have expected in any case. I knew perfectly well that no one could help me. The only possible solution would have been for me to stay in the city on weekends with Alison, but that battle had been lost. Jean and Mother wanted me with them. Not because they felt they had to look after me but because I was useful. I drew the water. I tended the fire so the house would be warm in the morning when they returned.

"We'd better go," Mother said, lifting the last dripping dish from the plastic basin. "Frank, you dry the dishes and put them away."

I watched their preparations with a sense of remoteness. It was as if they were already gone. Mother dried her

hands carefully and put on her heavy coat. Jean bent over
the row of paperback books and pulled out an Erskine
Caldwell. "I won't be able to read tonight but I'll take it
anyway."

"All right?" Mother asked. They stood for a last moment,
waiting, making sure they hadn't forgotten anything, sensing in each other the precise moment to leave. Then they
were through the door and away. I followed a few moments later, stepping in their footprints to the road. I
watched them walk into the darkness underneath the trees.
My mother turned at the top of a rise and called back to me
over the snow. "Don't forget to set the alarm!" She hurried
to catch up with Jean. As they moved down the hill it was
as if they sank deeper and deeper into the snow. Dimly I
could make out the top halves of their bodies, then only
their shoulders, their heads, and they were gone.

I went back to the house. After an initial surge of panic
my mind turned itself off. Thinking was dangerous. By not
thinking I attained a kind of inner invisibility. I knew that
fear attracted evil, that the uncontrolled sound of my own
mind would in some way delineate me to the forces threatening me, as the thrashing of a fish in shallow water draws
the gull. I tried to keep still, but every now and then the
fear escalated up into consciousness and my mind would
stir, readjusting itself like the body of a man trying to
sleep in an uncomfortable position. In those moments I felt
most vulnerable, my eyes widening and my ears straining
to catch the sound of approaching danger.

I dried the dishes slowly and put them away, attempting
to do the whole job without making a sound. Occasionally a
floorboard creaked under my weight, sending a long, lin-
gering charge up my spine, a white thrill at once delicious
and ominous. I approached the stove nervously. The coal
rattled and the cast-iron grate invariably banged loudly
despite my precautions. I had to do it quickly, holding my
breath, or I wouldn't do it at all. Once finished I checked
the window latches. There was nothing to be done about
the door; it couldn't be locked from the inside and mother
refused to lock it from the outside because of the danger
of my getting trapped in a fire.

By the yellow light of the kerosene lamp I sat on the
edge of the bed and removed my shoes, placing them carefully on the floor. The Big Ben alarm clock ticked off the

seconds on a shelf above my head, and every now and then a puff of coal gas popped in the stove as the fuel shifted. I got under the covers fully clothed and surveyed the stillness of the room, trying to slow my breathing. For an hour or more I lay motionless in a self-induced trance, my eyes open but seldom moving, my ears listening to the sounds of the house and the faint, inexplicable, continuous noises from outside. (In this state my ears seemed rather far away. I was burrowed somewhere deep in my skull, my ears advance outposts sending back reports to headquarters.) As I remember it the trance must have been close to the real thing. It was an attempt to reach an equipoise of fear, a state in which the incoming fear signals balanced with some internal process of dissimulation. At best it worked only temporarily, since fear held a slight edge. But for an hour or two I avoided what I hated most, the great noisy swings up and down. The panic and the hilarity.

At the first flashing thought of the Southbury Training School I sat up and took a book from the shelf. Escaped inmates were rare, and supposedly harmless, but I knew that a runaway had ripped the teats from one of the Greens' cows with a penknife, and that another had strangled four cats in a barnyard. I read quickly, skimming the pages for action and dialogue while most of my mind stood on guard. Book after book came down from the shelf, piling up on the bed beside me as I waited for sleep. I knew that if I left the lamp on I would stay awake most of the night, so when the pages began to go out of focus I set the alarm clock, cupped my hand over the mouth of the lamp chimney and blew myself into darkness.

Being sleepy and being scared do not cancel each other out. After hours of waiting the mind insists and slips under itself into unconsciousness. The sleeping body remains tense, the limbs bent as if poised for flight, adrenalin oozing steadily into the blood. Every few minutes the mind awakens, listens, and goes back to sleep. Fantastic dreams attempt to absorb the terror, explaining away the inexplicable with lunatic logic, twisting thought to a mad, private vision so that sleep can go on for another few seconds.

I wake up in the dark, a giant hand squeezing my heart. All around me a tremendous noise is splitting the air, exploding like a continuous chain of fireworks. The alarm clock! My God, the clock! Ringing all this time, calling, calling, bringing everything evil. I reach out and shut it off. The vibrations die out under my fingers and I listen to the silence, wondering if anything has approached under the cover of the ringing bell. (Remember a children's game called Giant Steps?)

I sit up cautiously. My body freezes. Rising before me over the foot of the bed is a bright, glowing, cherry-red circle in the darkness, a floating globe pulsating with energy, wavering in the air like the incandescent heart of some dissected monster, dripping sparks and blood. I throw myself backward against the wall behind the bed. Books tumble around me from the shelves, an ashtray falls and smashes on the floor. My hands go out, palms extended, towards the floating apparition, my voice whispering "Please . . ." Impossibly a voice answers, a big voice from all around me. "FRANK! FRANK!" My knees give out and I fall off the bed to the floor. I can feel the pieces of broken ashtray under my hands.

From the corner of my eye I see the red circle. I keep quite still, and the circle doesn't move. If I turn my head I seem to sense a corresponding movement, but I can't be sure. In the blackness there is nothing to relate to. Step by step I begin to understand. My body grows calmer and it's as if a series of veils were being whisked away from my eyes. I see clearly that the circle is only the red-hot bottom of the stove—a glowing bowl, its surface rippling with color changes from draughts of cool air. The last veil lifts and reveals an image of magic beauty, a sudden miracle in the night. I fall asleep watching it, my shoulder against the bed.

Hours later the cold wakes me and I climb up under the covers. When dawn comes my limbs relax. I can tell when dawn has come even though I'm asleep.

I woke up when the wagon went by, creaking like a ship, passing close, just on the other side of the wall by my head. Chip would be driving, I knew, with Toad in back watching the cans. They never spoke as they went by. Sometimes Chip would murmur to the horses, "Haw, gee-aw." The traces rang quietly and the tall iron-rimmed wheels splintered rocks under the snow.

It was hard to get out of bed. The air was cold. Water froze in the bucket and the windows were coated with ice. The light was gray, exactly the same quality as the twilight of the night before, devoid of meaning. I cleaned out the stove, laid paper, a few sticks of kindling and some coal, splashed kerosene over everything, and struck a match. With a great whoosh the stove filled with flames. My teeth chattering, I rushed back under the covers. I fell asleep waiting to get warm.

When Jean and my mother came through the door I woke up. They seemed tremendously alive, bustling with energy, their voices strangely loud.

"It's freezing in here. What happened to the fire?" I sat up in bed. The fire had gone out, or more likely had never caught after the kerosene had burned.

"You forgot to set the alarm," my mother said.

"No I didn't."

She knelt and relit the fire. Jean stood in the open doorway, knocking snow off his galoshes. He closed the door and sat on the edge of the bed, bending over to open the buckles. "My God, it's cold. We should have stayed in Florida."

"I vote for that," I said.

"Just get your ass out of that bed." He rubbed his stocking feet and twisted up his face. "How about some coffee?"

"Just a second," my mother said, still fussing with the stove.

Jean stood up and undid his belt. "Okay. Let's go." He waited till I was out of bed, took off his trousers, and climbed in. The heavy black and red flannel shirt he wore in cold weather was left on, buttoned tight over his narrow chest. He ran a finger over his mustache and waited for his cup of coffee.

Mother made it for him while I fixed myself a bowl of cornflakes.

"It's not very much to ask to keep the stove going," my mother said. "I never ask you to do anything."

I ate my cornflakes. The stove was beginning to give off a little heat and I pulled my chair closer, arranging it so my back was to the bed. I heard Mother undressing, and then the creak of the rusty springs as she got in beside Jean. From that moment on I was supposed to keep quiet so they could sleep.

There was no place else to go. Outside the land was hidden under two and a half feet of snow. The wind was sharp and bitter (I found out later that locals considered it the worst winter in forty years) and in any case I didn't have the proper clothes. Even indoors, sitting in the chair with the stove going, I kept a blanket wrapped around me Indian style. The time dragged slowly. There was nothing to do. I tried to save the few books for nighttime, when my need of them was greater. I drew things with a pencil—objects in the room, my hand, imaginary scenes—but I was no good and quickly lost interest. Usually I simply sat in the chair for six or seven hours. Jean snored softly, but after the first hour or so I stopped hearing it.

Midway through the morning I remembered the candy bars. Certain Jean had forgotten them, I looked anyway, getting up from the chair carefully, tiptoeing to his clothes and searching through the pockets. Nothing. I watched him in bed, his face gray with sleep, his open mouth twitching at the top of each gentle snore. My mother turned to the wall. Jean closed his mouth and rolled over. The room was absolutely silent. I went back to the chair.

They awoke in the early afternoon and stayed in bed. Although the small stove was working it was still the warmest place. Freed from the necessity of keeping quiet, I walked around the room aimlessly, getting a drink of water, rubbing the haze off the windows to look outside. My mother raised her voice and I realized she was talking to me.

"Take some money from my purse and go down to the Greens' and get a dozen eggs."

The trip to the Greens' would take an hour each way. Outside the temperature was five or ten degrees below zero and it was windy. I didn't want to go. My heart sank because I knew I had to.

Children are in the curious position of having to do what people tell them, whether they want to or not. A child knows that he must do what he's told. It matters little whether a command is just or unjust since the child has no confidence in his ability to distinguish the difference. Justice for children is not the same as justice for adults. In effect all commands are morally neutral to a child. Yet because almost every child is consistently bullied by older people he quickly learns that if in some higher frame of reference all commands are equally just, they are not equally easy to carry out. Some fill him with joy, others, so obviously unfair that he must paralyze himself to keep from recognizing their quality, strike him instantly deaf, blind, and dumb. Faced with an order they sense is unfair children simply stall. They wait for more information, for some elaboration that will take away the seeming unfairness. It's a stupid way of defending oneself, but children are stupid compared to adults, who know how to get what they want.

"Couldn't we wait until they come up with the wagon?"

"No. The walk will do you good. You can't sit around all day, it's unhealthy."

"Oh Mother, it'll take hours."

Suddenly Jean sat up, his voice trembling with anger. "Look, this time just go. No arguments this time."

I looked at him in amazement. He'd never even raised his voice to me before. It was against the unwritten rules —my mother was the disciplinarian. I could see he was angry and I had no idea why. Even my mother was surprised. "Take it easy," she said to him softy. "He's going."

Jean's anger should have tipped me off, but it didn't. Wearing his galoshes and his overcoat I went to the Greens' without realizing why they had sent me.

It was no secret that I wanted to go along to the training school at night, to sleep on an extra bed somewhere. For months Mother put me off, but when she realized I would never get accustomed to staying alone she gave in. She was tired of dealing with me, tired of my complaints and my silences. (Alternative unconscious motivations for her change of heart: one, she felt guilty about me; two, she decided to show me something that was worth being afraid of—namely, the worst men's cottage, to which Jean was assigned the night I tagged along.)

We drove slowly down the steep, twisting road to Southbury, our headlight beams traversing back and forth across the snow. Jean leaned over the wheel, craning his neck to watch for the cutoff through the black truncated trees. "It's along here somewhere."

"We have to pass that boarded-up farmhouse," my mother said.

"Here it is." He applied the brakes slowly and the tires pulled against the sanded road. We were entering the grounds through the back, saving a mile. The car bumped along through the woods for a few hundred yards and then emerged at the top of a hill.

The Southbury Training School spread below us like a toy village in a Christmas display. Small dormitories disguised to look like suburban homes were spread evenly over a square mile of stripped and graded hillside. Halfway down, the two administrative buildings rose into the air, their white cupolas lighted by floodlights. Weaving across the hillside in every direction were the lines and curves of a network of private roads, described in the darkness by chains of street lights winking on slender poles.

Jean edged the Ford over the lip of the hill and the bumpy dirt road changed immediately to a smooth, carefully plowed asphalt ribbon. We rolled along silently, watching the powdered snow drift across the surface of the road under the headlights.

"There it is," my mother said as we approached one of the dormitories. "Number Twelve."

Jean pulled up in the driveway. There was a brass knocker on the front door, and a mailbox, and a green metal tube on a stand with *"Danbury Times"* written in elaborate lettering. I caught some movement out of the corner of my eyes. The blinds were raised in one of the ground-floor windows and a girl stood combing her hair with long, even strokes. She saw the lights of the car and smiled. Half her teeth were gone. I looked away quickly.

My mother rang the bell and stood close to the door to be out of the wind. Almost immediately it swung open, spilling a long bar of yellow light across the snow. She lifted her hand in a signal that could just as easily have meant we should wait a moment as to wave goodbye, and was gone.

We drove slowly across the hill toward the boys' side of the school. In the bad weather the roads were empty.

"It looks deserted," I said.

"It isn't. Wait till you get inside."

The tires spun on a patch of ice as we climbed the driveway to Cottage Eight. We stopped next to a black Chevy, the only car in the parking area. Its windshield was coated with snow.

"That's Olsen's car. He has the shift before mine."

"It's brand new."

"Some of these guys work two shifts. They make a lot of money."

"Why don't you?"

He laughed. We sat for a moment, watching the building. Jean took out a cigarette. "The smell is pretty bad at first but after a couple of hours you don't notice it."

I could see small ways in which the building differed from the one my mother had entered. There was no box for the newspaper, no potted evergreens at the edge of the drive. Even in the darkness one could see that the front door needed painting. Some of the shutters were closed.

"None of these people are dangerous, are they?"

Jean finished his cigarette. "They're just feeble-minded. They can't take care of themselves."

We stepped out of the car. The air was cold and gusts of wind seemed to pass uninterrupted through my clothes. After a few steps the smell began, like a tangible line in space. Smells are hard to describe. This was a combination of pine, vomit, licorice, old urine, sweat, soap, and wet hair. Jean rang the bell and after a few moments the door opened.

I was prepared, of course, but prepared through my imagination, and I couldn't possibly have imagined the reality. First of all it was hot, really hot, like a furnace room. I began to sweat immediately. The smell was overpowering. It was useless to breathe carefully as I'd done outside; here the smell was so pungent and thick it seemed to have taken the place of air—a hot substitute filling my lungs, seeping into my blood, and making me its own creature. With the first deep breath I was no longer an air breather. I'd changed to another species.

It was noisy. A noise that raised the hair on the back of my neck. Far-out throats, tongues, and lips forming sounds that wound their independent way up and down the scale with no relation to anything. Whispering, mumbling, fake laughter and true laughter, bubbling sounds, short screams, bored humming, weeping, long roller-coaster yells—all of it in random dynamic waves like some futuristic orchestra. In this meaningless music were sudden cries of such intense human significance that I stood paralyzed.

It was as if all the saints, martyrs, and mystics of human history were gathered into a single building, each one crying out at the moment of revelation, each one truly

there at his extreme of joy or pain, crying out with the
purity of total selflessness. There was no arguing with
these sudden voices above the general clamor, they rang
true. All around me were men in a paroxysm of discovery,
seeing lands I had never known existed, calling me with a
strength I had never known existed. But they called from
every direction with equal power, so I couldn't answer. I
stood balanced on the pinpoint of my own sanity, a small,
cracked tile on the floor.

"They're a little noisy now. It's just before bedtime and
we let them blow off some steam."

I looked up and discovered a huge man standing in
front of me, smiling. Involuntarily I took a step backward.
He was all eyes, immense white eyes impossibly out of his
head, rushing at me. No, he was wearing his eyes like
glasses. Two bulbous eyes in steel frames. He turned his
head and the illusion disappeared. Thick lenses, that was all.
His bald head gleamed with sweat. His arm was as big as
my leg.

"I'm Olsen," he said.

"Where's Jean?"

"He'll be back in a minute."

There was movement behind his back. I watched from the
corner of my eye, afraid to look directly. A naked man
slipping into the room, hunched over like a beaten dog, a
shiny thread of spittle hanging from his jaw. He cruised
silently along the wall, limp fingers touching the plaster,
turned, and stopped, his shaggy head facing the blank wall
one inch away. Without even looking Olsen raised his voice
and said, "Back to bed."

The creature lifted one leg and touched his toes to the
surface of the wall as if it was a ladder he was about to
climb. Below the tangle of black hair in his crotch, his
veined penis and scrotum hung limply almost halfway to
the knee, against the inside of his thigh. It was as if they'd
been grabbed and stretched like soft taffy. His toes
scratched the wall. Olsen took a step toward him, leaning
over slightly, and clapped his hands smartly. "Back to bed!"
The creature scurried along the wall and disappeared
through an open doorway. For the first time I noticed
there were no doors. Doorways without doors. From each
darkened passageway the noises rushed at us. Suddenly,

the sound of a crash. Olsen knew just where it came from. "Back in a second," he said.

Alone in the room, I stood by the door, my hand touching the knob. I could hear Olsen shouting in another part of the building. Far back in the corridors half-visible figures were moving in the dim light. I supposed that Jean was with them.

An old man appeared, hesitating at the edge of the room. When he saw me he froze instantly, like a highly trained hunting animal. His watery blue eyes were fuzzy spirals and his cheeks sank into his head, making hollows the size of ping-pong balls. He wore a kind of diaper from which his skinny legs, all tendon and finely wrinkled skin, emerged, half bent with age. He took a step forward.

"Back to bed!" I said. "Back to bed!" For a moment he didn't move, then, leaning his head back, he opened his mouth and revealed two gleaming pink gums, toothless, looking like wet rubber. His thin shoulders shook with laughter. When his fuzzy eyes found me he shouted across the room.

"Sonny, I've been here since before you were born. I don't even belong here. I belong in a mental hospital. Everybody knows that." He turned and left the room.

I wanted to wait outside until Jean came back. There was a large brass lock high on the door. I turned what seemed to be the appropriate knob but the bolt didn't move. Examining the mechanism more closely, I heard a noise behind me.

Something was rushing down one of the corridors, something low and fast. No bullfighter ever waited for his foe more apprehensively. To my amazement I found myself giving a short, nervous laugh, a desperate guffaw in the teeth of my predicament. Zooming into the room was a flash of chrome-man, a monstrous human machine blurred with speed, bearing down on me like a homicidal hot-rodder. A man in a wheelchair, but what kind of man? His body was tiny, like a child's, his head impossibly huge, the size of a watermelon. Flailing at the wheels of his chair like a berserk rowboat enthusiast, he backed me into a corner and threw his hands into my face.

"See my pretty 'racelet?" he said in a high voice. "See my pretty 'racelet?"

Flinching, twisting to avoid the touch of his wild hands, I tried to slip past. He slammed his chair into the wall and trapped me.

"See my pretty 'racelet?"

"What? What do you want? What?" Reluctantly I looked him in the eye. His bland idiot's features seemed small in the gargantuan hydrocephalic head. All scrunched together in the cavity that was his face they stared out at me like a fish from a goldfish bowl.

"See my pretty 'racelet?" he said, still holding his arms up. In a tantrum of infantile frustration he drummed his heels against the bottom of the chair. "See! See!"

"He wants you to look at his bracelet," Jean said, grabbing the back of the chair and pulling him away. "This is Freddie. His nickname is pinhead."

"Pinhead, pinhead! See!"

"Go ahead," Jean said. "Just look at it."

Around the creature's wrist was a cheap chrome I.D. bracelet. He held his hand motionless when he realized I was looking at it. The word FREDDIE was engraved in block letters. I touched it with my index finger. "It's very pretty. Very nice."

"Pretty 'racelet?" Freddie said, calmer now.

"Yes. Very pretty."

"Pretty 'racelet?"

Olsen appeared from one of the corridors. His big feet clomped noisily on the tile floor. "Time for lights out?"

"Okay," Jean answered, rolling Freddie away. "Frank, you can go in the office." He pointed to an open doorway.

Freddie rocked back and forth in the chair. "Lice-out. Lice-out. Lice-out."

Olsen reached out and slapped his immense dome with an open hand. "Shut up, idiot." They rolled him down one of the corridors.

The office was a small room with a desk, a chair, and a cot. There was no door to close. I sat on the cot and watched the blank wall. As Jean and Olsen progressed through the building turning out lights, the screaming gradually subsided, falling to a steady murmur like the crowd noises in a movie. It was less nerve-wracking, but somehow more ominous. The mood in the building was changing from wildness to slyness. Plans were beginning to cook in countless heads, and as a novelty, a break in the routine, it seemed to me that I would be the focus. I jumped up nervously as Olsen came in. He looked down at me, his big white eyes embedded in their surrealistic lenses. "I'm going off now. I want to show you something."

I followed him out of the office, sticking close behind. We took a few steps into a hallway and stopped. In the gloom stray rays of light collected in his glasses like fireflies.

"The boys are harmless. They're scareder of you than you are of them, so you got nothing to worry about. I want to show you this guy so you know what he looks like. A couple of times he's grabbed a broom and snuck up behind somebody and belted them. If he ever tries anything all you got to do is look him in the eye and he backs down."

"Maybe it's better if he doesn't see me."

"He won't. He can't see past the light."

There was a snapping sound and a powerful flashlight beam showed us a glowing circle of green wall. We took a few steps and the beam spilled into a small room. With a flick of his wrist Olsen found the occupant, sitting on his bed, knees drawn up to his chest, rocking slowly back and forth. (In the South they call it hunkering.) He looked young, and strong—completely normal except for his nakedness and the fixed expression of anger on his face. His eyes blinked in the strong light but he didn't look away. The creaking of the bedsprings stopped as he held himself rigid. He seemed to be looking directly into my eyes in a contest of wills. Suddenly his head jerked forward and a glob of spittle curved through the air and fell at my feet.

"Tough guy," said Olsen. "Once he threw his own shit at me. But he'll never do that again."

My eyes were locked with the inmate's. "Did you punish him?"

"Punish him!" Olsen laughed. "I beat the living daylights out of him. He was in the infirmary for three days."

"Did he understand?"

"What?"

"Did he understand why you hit him?"

"He didn't throw no more shit so I guess he did."

"What's his name?"

"Gregory."

"Can we go back now?"

"He doesn't know how lucky he is. He's the only one in the building with a room of his own. Look." He flashed his light up the halls. Beds were set up along the walls of the corridor. People were sitting up in them watching us silently. Most of them fell back as the light struck them, like dominoes in a row. To the rest Olsen yelled "Lights out! Bedtime!"

"Can we go back now?"

Olsen had gone off duty and Jean and I were in the office.

"Lovely, isn't it," Jean said sitting on the edge of the desk.

"Is there any place with a door? I'd feel better with a door."

"No, but you'll be all right."

"What about that guy named Gregory?"

"He won't do anything. He's probably asleep. They go to sleep like *that*." He snapped his fingers. After a moment he raised his head and stared out the doorway. "Isn't it incredible the way some of them are hung? They've got equipment a horse would be proud of."

"Jean, I don't think I can make it."

"It's perfectly safe." He stood up. "I've got to make the rounds."

"I can't stay here."

"Well I can't take you back. You'll just have to."

"I'll sleep in the car."

"It's freezing out there."

"I'll take some blankets. It'll be all right."

He stood for a moment without answering.

"Please, Jean."

"Okay. Suit yourself. I've got to make the rounds." He started out, then looked back. "If it gets too cold out there you'd better come back in."

"I will. Yes. Thanks." Quickly I began to strip the blankets from the cot. Then, remembering, I rushed after him. "Jean! The lock! How do you work the lock?"

So for the rest of the winter I stayed in the cabin at night. I never got used to it, but in some ways the nights were better than the days. The nights were warm fantasies of terror, Technicolor nightmares. I recognized somehow that everything hapening to me alone at night in the cabin was of a low order of reality. My hallucinations, the fear itself, the entire drama came from inside my own head. I was *making* it all, and although it was terrifying, it was not, as were the days, cosmically threatening.

The days were emptiness, a vast, spacious emptiness in which the fact of being alive became almost meaningless. The first fragile beginnings of a personality starting to collect in my twelve-year-old soul were immediately sucked up into the silence and the featureless winter sky. The overbearing, undeniable reality of those empty days! The inescapable fact that everything around me was nonhuman, that in terms of snow and sky and rocks and dormant trees I didn't exist, these things rendered me invisible even to myself. I wasn't conscious of what was happening, I lived it. I became invisible. I lost myself.

At night I materialized. The outlines of my body were hot, flushed, sharply defined. My senses were heightened. I knew I was real as I animated the darkness with extensions of myself. If the sky was more real than I was, then I was more real than my phantoms.

But the days predominated. The flat sky. As the winter passed a sense of desolation invaded my mind. I wasn't afraid, it was too nebulous for that, but I was profoundly uneasy. Perhaps in the back of my mind was the fear that everything would go blank, that I would become the sky, without a body, without thought. I remembered the peculiarly impersonal quality of some of the screams in Cottage Eight.

In the spring I started going down to the school just to hang around, walking the four miles with a quarter in my pocket to get a milkshake at the soda fountain in the administration building. I roamed freely through the public rooms. In a scaled-down bowling alley I used to set up the pins for myself after each frame. Sometimes there were movies in the auditorium. I'd wait for a group of boys to come across the lawn behind their counselor and tag along at the end. I remember a conversation I had one day before a Gene Autry picture with a boy who attracted my attention because I thought he looked exactly like me.

"Who're you?" he asked. "Are you new?"

"No. I'm Mr. Fouchet's son."

"He takes our cottage at night sometimes. He's okay. He never hits you."

"Do the others?"

"Some of them."

(Whistles and applause as Mr. Miller, the director of the school, climbs on stage to make a few announcements before the picture. I laugh at the wildness of the audience. They're having a great time.)

"I'm going home next week," the boy says. "If you're around you'll see the car. It's a red Buick."

"We have a Ford."

"My pop's a policeman. He carries a gun."

(More whistles and cheers as the house lights go down and the picture begins. I watch the boy. There's no way to tell anything is wrong with him.)

The Southbury school affected me more deeply than I realized at the time. Most immediately it was a place in which being different was a good thing—I was different only because I wasn't feeble-minded. My general loneliness in the world was dramatized microcosmically, in terms favorable to myself.

I believed I was intelligent. For a long time that thought had been important to me. At the school I felt for the first time that my intelligence was worth something to someone else besides myself. Here was a huge organization, an immense, powerful world existing for the inmate, but existing for me as well. I was the other extreme! At last I'd found someplace where my only possession would be relevant! To picture myself as being aware of all this would be a misrepresentation. I wasn't vain. I didn't look down on the boys. In some ways I needed the school as much as they did, and I certainly felt closer to them than to the children at conventional schools.

But of course the Southbury School, except for one incident, was as uninterested in me as the world it represented. Which is as it should be. While I passed through the attenuated agonies of growing up, trying to get through to a psychologist in the library of the administration building, there were boys next door who were never going to grow up at all, boys who would starve to death without someone to feed them.

I was alone in the library reading *Life* magazine. A man stopped in the hallway and looked at me through the double glass doors. I watched him come in without raising my head.

"Hi," he said casually. "What are you reading?"

"Just this magazine."

"It's a good issue. I've read it myself." He spoke to me as if we were old friends. "You remember me, don't you?"

It came to me in a flash. He'd mistaken me for one of the boys. Perhaps the boy from the movies who looked so much like me. A bewildering array of emotions exploded simultaneously—confusion, embarrassment, a kind of childish love, apprehensiveness, but behind it all, as steady as the solid bar of sunlight across the polished table, triumph. The moment was at hand.

"Of course you're not really reading it, are you?" he said. "You mean you're looking at the pictures."

"No. I'm reading it."

"Don't you remember me? I'm Dr. Janetello."

I hesitated, trying to think up an answer, but he went on.

"Would you mind reading something for me?"

I looked down at the pages. "Members of the Eighty-second airborne reserves bail out over Colorado. Four thousand men took part in a mock attack . . ."

"That's enough," he said. On the table were two books I'd taken from the shelves. He picked them up. *"The Short Stories of de Maupassant* and *Pickwick Papers*. Do you read this too?"

"Yes. I liked *David Copperfield* so I thought I'd try this."

"How did you get in here?" he asked quickly. "Are you from Southbury?"

"My stepfather works here."

"You think it's clever to play me along like that?"

I didn't answer. It was going wrong. I looked up at his round face. A few beads of sweat were collected along his upper lip and his eyes suddenly seemed very small.

"Do you have permission to use the library?"

"No. I guess not."

He stood for a moment without saying anything, as if undecided whether to continue. Then he dropped the books on the table with a bang, turned quickly, and left the room. The double doors continued swinging long after he was gone.

5
Hate,
and a Kind
of Music

WHEN I was very young, six or seven at a guess, my father installed the family in a large apartment in a good neighborhood. Arranged by mail from the remoteness of a rest home in upper New York State, it was one of the last meaningful gestures he made toward us. My mother was glad to leave the tenement on Fifteenth Street. (An image from the very edge of memory: Late at night my mother stands in the doorway to Alison's and my room, her face hidden in shadow. "Quiet down now, children. I just heard the weather report and the temperature is over a hundred. Quiet down and go to sleep.") She was glad to leave the tenement, but worried by the knowledge that her husband was never coming back. At about this time she must have realized she was on her own. He would send money, visit once or twice a year for a day or two, but the hope that he would ever return as head of the house had been gradually relinquished. She was a courageous woman who refused to let life break her. A foreigner without friends or family, she had watched one life collapse, and where a weaker woman might have given up, she reorganized with the idea of building herself another.

The apartment on Eighty-sixth Street was to be a new start. My mother understood that it belonged to her, free and clear. She decided to take a boarder, as much for company as for the money it would bring in. She was already seeing Jean, but he hadn't started living with us yet, and the huge apartment needed animation. A woman named Daphne responded to the advertisement and took the front room. She stayed two or three years.

Daphne was recently divorced. She was from the Midwest, about my mother's age, with a pleasant good-humored face and dark hair. The tensions of breaking up with her husband made some of her hair fall out and for a few months she was terrified of losing it all. (Years later, under different circumstances, the same thing was to happen to me.) She earned her living as a therapist for deaf children, a difficult job I imagine she was good at, being gentle and patient by nature. On the basis of their common loss of husbands Daphne and my mother became fast friends. With only the sleeping children in the house they spent their evenings at woman talk, comparing notes on life, men, and the price of eggs, quietly and unhurriedly talking themselves into calmness, as if time would never run out.

Daphne left shortly after Jean moved in, undoubtedly not wanting to intrude on the new family. I have only the best memories of her, a delicate woman who always showed me consideration. She had a particularly nice way of touching my head, very lightly with her fingertips as she must have touched the deaf children.

Lots of people stayed in our house over the years, but most of them for short periods of time. Dull salesmen left quickly, aware of vague inadequacies in themselves, sensing a subtle invasion of their privacy. A sundry assortment of Jean's mildly nutty pals were given a few days or a week to prove themselves, all moving on when it became clear my mother found their interests irrelevant. She didn't share Jean's enthusiasm for clearly recognizable people, people with specialties. All Jean's pals had some dog-eared passport through life—one was an inventor, another a chess expert, another simply rebellious—sad, lonely men looking for some place to get out of the cold. Jean met them in cafeterias. Only Daphne and one other stayed for any length of time, and where Daphne had moved out rather than intrude, the other stayed on and on, becoming eventually as much a part of the family as any of us, if family is the proper word.

Donald came early and stayed late. He was around, off and on, until I left home at the age of seventeen. He even followed us to Florida once.

The rumor was that Donald had been a child prodigy, an image that must have haunted him, particularly since he still looked like one at the age of thirty-five. Not everyone could see it though; to most people his face was simply another bland, slightly chubby, anonymous American mask.

One had to look closely to see the face that lay underneath, the boy's face, the fifteen-year-old face trapped under the thin layers of fat. His eyes were intelligent and cold, changing very little when he took off his horn-rimmed glasses. He kept his lips compressed, perhaps to make them look less effeminate. His exceptionally strong hands were white and misleadingly soft-looking, and his body, his strange shapeless body, did nothing but fill its clothes without being fat or thin, or indeed anything else to call attention to itself. His appearance was unsettling because it said nothing. He was unmarked.

Donald was a musician, a pianist by trade, who worked most often as an accompanist for various singers because of his great skill as a sight reader. Privately he was interested in composition. He lived on what he earned, which wasn't much since he was always getting fired because of what my mother called "personality conflicts." She knew, as even the children knew, that Donald had personality conflicts for the simple reason that he was a bitter and sarcastic man, unable to get along with anyone except at the greatest effort. Even worse, he was unable to control a compulsive desire to hurt people, to hurt them for the pleasure of inflicting pain, deftly, with words, before they had time to defend themselves.

I remember Donald coming home one afternoon, his cheeks flushed and his hands dancing with nervousness. Describing a petty argument with a bus driver, he quoted himself to my mother with all the intensity of a small boy relating a schoolyard triumph. "So I said, 'Listen my friend, for a crummy thirty-five dollars a week no one expects you to be smart.'" (In the almost sexual heat of this kind of battle Donald's intelligence invariably deserted him.) My mother laughed nervously, not because she thought it was funny, but because her relationship with Donald forced her to laugh. He was the court jester. Donald to a slow waitress: "I'm going to report you. Don't you *dare* make a prissy face at me!" He often attacked people who risked losing their jobs if they answered back. People who might retaliate were dealt with more subtly, as we shall see.

My mother met Donald at a studio where she and Jean took singing lessons. The maestro, a man named Herbert, who knew almost nothing about singing and even less about music, had hung out his shingle on the basis of some vague acquaintance with physics and the production of sound. The accompanist was Donald, undoubtedly aware that Herbert was a fake and that neither my mother nor Jean had any talent. But he needed the money.

One can hardly imagine a scene more grotesque than that meeting, the beginning, as it turned out, of a life-long association. Jean, leaning over the piano croaking his heart out with enthusiastic abandon. My mother, a step or two away for the space she needed, mouth open and head tilted back, letting go her seemingly inexhaustible supply of loud sounds in a continuous ear-splitting stream, not so much like a soprano as a volcano. Donald pounding away for his daily bread, his overloaded ears numb with fatigue, and Herbert the impresario dashing back and forth in his Ezra Pound suit, waving his arms in meaningless gestures of exhortation, grabbing himself around the throat on the high notes, pounding his stomach on the low notes, his face twisted like a maniac's. I remember sitting in a large armchair, my feet off the ground, watching them. In those days there seemed nothing extraordinary about it, except the loudness. I couldn't possibly have known that it was all fake, a masquerade only slightly more complicated than my own solitary games in Central Park.

Donald moved in with us. Jean was hardly in a position to object, as my mother paid the rent, and in any case it was clear that those elements which would usually complicate the lives of three adults living in the same house were lacking in Donald's make-up. He was not, as far as I know, homosexual, but something much rarer, a person without sex. Whether he had any direct sexual urges at all, or whether he had them and totally repressed them or rechanneled them is conjectural. All that one could tell about Donald was the obvious fact that he was a person to whom physical love was as remote and insignificant as the canals of Mars. He was aware, of course, that sex played a part in other people's lives, but for him it was only something to joke about. Most of his sexual references were tainted with a peculiar infantilism. Camel cigarettes had an advertisement in which something called the T-zone was illustrated. Donald went around giggling about the pee-zone years after the ad died out. He was in the habit of washing his small cotton briefs by hand and hanging them around the bathroom on wire hangers, carefully spread out for proper exhibition. (See! I'm clean.)

Donald paid a small rent for his room, and for his inclusion in the family he played for my mother and gave the children piano lessons. He became my mother's flatterer and clown, a role he enjoyed. She was a strong and independent woman, qualities that he admired, and in addition she posed no sexual threat. She teased him about sex occasionally, but for the most part he was allowed to live as if it didn't exist. He liked to make her laugh. She laughed easily, at almost any deliberate witticism, and he felt free to make fun of whatever he wanted. He lived vicariously in her laughter, liking the warmth in her voice, liking the sudden and complete reduction of his own lonely and painful life into her all-encompassing, simple, unknowing laugh. She was, it seems clear, a mother to him.

I first began to recognize Donald as an enemy, and an enemy to be reckoned with, when he gave me piano lessons. He would sit nervously at the treble end, impatient and annoyed, as if he were about to leap up and catch a train. Whenever he spoke it was to make a barbed remark. At first his sarcasm didn't bother me, it was like a game, but as the weeks passed I became more and more uncomfortable, sensing that it wasn't a game at all, but the symptom of a deep and barely controlled anger.

I couldn't possibly have realized it at the time but of course he hated me with the clear, impersonal hate one has for a rival. I wasn't a romantic rival but, incredibly, a sibling rival.

Youth itself made him uncomfortable, more because he coveted the ancient scene of his own lost happiness than for the faint, barely flickering spark of lust it kindled in him. Always the threat of his strong hands—that was what he meant to me. He'd bare his clenched teeth and clamp his iron fingers around my arms as if he meant to squeeze them off, or sometimes, with a joke as camouflage, he'd grab my neck and shake me, his fingers carefully squeezing my throat. In those days my neck was skinny enough so that with the thumb and index finger of one hand alone he could almost encircle it. He always squeezed a little too hard, just past the point where it began to hurt. He wasn't satisfied until he saw in my eyes that he'd reached that point.

The farce of the piano lessons, which he must have hated as much as I did, was short-lived. Far from teaching me anything, the experience kept me away from the piano for a long time. When I finally started learning again I taught myself. (Many years later, during a summer vacation from college, I passed through New York on my way to a job as a pianist in a resort town in Delaware. Donald gave me a few words of advice. "You can't possibly keep the job so why take it at all?" In fact I did keep it, although at the time I could play in only two keys. It hardly mattered as my audience was always too drunk to notice.)

Donald was a clever and sensitive man. He knew that as long as he stayed on the good side of my mother he could say anything he wanted to Jean or to the children. His relationship with her was static, changing very little through the years. He made few mistakes.

The first, and least serious, was when he hit me. I was nine or ten years old and had forgotten to give him an important telephone message. We were alone in the house, standing in the living room, Donald trembling with rage. I didn't step back when he approached. No adult had ever struck me before, and I was completely taken by surprise. He did it quickly, with furtive speed, slapping me hard across the face with an open hand. I stared at him, amazed. (The cliché is true, it was as if I saw him for the first time.) His body shook for an instant in some minor spasm and his tight, pain-filled face looked down at me in anguish, expressing shame mixed with a wild and deep satisfaction. I stood stock still and he went away, words shooting from his mouth like steam from a leaky pressure-cooker. He told my mother about it, calling it discipline, but she knew her rights and told him that if anyone hit the children it would be herself.

The episode gave Donald a bad scare and he never struck me again. Years later he hit my little sister, the child of Jean and my mother, who received her first blow in life at the age of eighteen months, but again, despite my mother's disapproval, he got away with it.

Violence was uncharacteristic of Donald, though—in fact totally absent from his dealings with anyone besides children. The way he attacked Jean one Christmas Eve was much more his style.

Donald held the little glass swan in front of his mouth, talking quickly, his eyes shining. "It's supposed to be a test of lung power. You blow hard to push the water up the swan's neck." He blew into the tube, his cheeks swelling. "Nothing happens because I have my finger over this tiny hole in the back here." He pointed it out. "That's the trick."

My mother came in from the kitchen. "Well, the turkey's almost done."

"Have you got everything, now?" Donald asked me, looking down at the stuff on the table. "The puzzle works by squeezing the white dot on the corner. The others are self-explanatory."

"Yes."

My mother laughed. "Donald, you're incredible. Where'd you get it all?"

"A novelty store on Forty-second Street." He emphasized the word "novelty," savoring it as a special, ironically delicious tidbit. It was a mannerism of his to underscore his own words, flattering his listener's ability to read between the lines.

She laughed, looking down at the assortment of practical jokes. "You know what'll happen. Probably this year he'll make an effort." Donald's plan for Christmas Eve was possible only because Jean made it a point to be cynical about holidays, particularly religious holidays. "It's all a fraud," he would say about Christmas. "Commercialism. Big Business," and his voice would fall off. He was suspicious as well of the once-a-year imitation of happy domestic life in which we all participated. When Christmas came around he would just as soon have gone to the movies, leaving the whole pageant in my mother's hands, but of course he couldn't. He had to pretend he was father to the children, pretend to be pleased by gifts, pretend that Donald was his friend—all rather difficult as he was bad at pretending. The best he could do was to maintain a good-humored cynicism, to talk like George Bernard Shaw, but at the same time to let everyone know he was conscious of the comic overtones of his chosen role by lapsing every now and then into a delicately mechanical parody of himself. Donald knew that this was the way it would be, that Jean would be too preoccupied and vulnerable to retaliate.

At dinner Jean caught me looking at him several times, but he said nothing. Inside me a war was going on between excited anticipation and an amphorous sense of something being wrong. Over the turkey and wine Donald kept the conversation moving quickly, playing to my mother as usual. He looked at me occasionally, and once, for the first time I'd ever seen, he winked. I sat stunned. It was so out of character I began to have that worst of all feelings for a child, that more was going on than I could grasp.

After dinner we moved from the table to the other end of the living room for coffee. I held my breath as Jean dropped a nondissolving sugar lump into his cup, stirring slowly as he talked. But nothing happened. He sipped away without noticing.

The fake matches were equally unsuccessful. After two or three attempts to get a light he threw them on the table and pulled another book from his breast pocket without so much as a pause in the conversation. Donald, rambling around the room sampling the little bowls of sweets my mother had set out, seemed not to notice.

In our house it was the custom to open the presents on Christmas Eve, as in Denmark. An hour or two after dinner my mother gave the signal and Donald went to the tree, squatting over the brightly wrapped packages.

"All right everybody, this year you have to open mine first." He rummaged around and came up with a green box he tossed to Alison. As the rest of us watched she unwrapped it and held up a tray of scented soap.

"Thank you, Donald, yours is under . . ."

"No no no. We've got to go on. Here Frank!"

I caught the small package and unwrapped the sliding-letter puzzle Donald had explained to me. There was a card in his cramped writing: "Donald's Special I.Q. Test."

"You're supposed to make a word. Slide the letters around."

I looked down at the puzzle in my palm, the jumbled white letters in their black frame spelling out CGAMI. You were supposed to make AGICM, then press the white dot releasing letter M, slide it over and make MAGIC. I stared at it.

"Have you got the word yet?"

"I see the word."

I fooled with the letters until they made AGICM, then hesitated.

"I'm timing you," Donald said. "This is a contest. Five-minute limit. You've got three left."

I pushed the white dot and made the word. "Okay."

"Time: two minutes, fifteen seconds. Your turn, Dagmar." My mother took two and a half minutes and then it was Jean's turn.

"Here, I'll jumble them up." Donald mixed the letters and smiled.

"This is just your meat, darling," Jean said to my mother. "Like your crossword puzzles. Although why an intelligent person wants to waste time on . . ."

"Just try if you think it's so easy," Donald said, laughing.

Jean took the puzzle and bent over it.

"He didn't say it was easy. He just said it was a waste of time," I found myself announcing. Everyone looked at me.

"Listen to Judge Leibowitz," Jean laughed.

Irritated, Donald leaned forward, his watch in his hand. "Keep quiet, Frank. I'm trying to time him."

The room was silent as Jean pushed the letters around with his index finger. I looked up at my mother. She watched Jean's hands without a trace of expression. After a moment she lighted a cigarette, holding it awkwardly, blowing out the smoke uninhaled. In my lifetime I'd only seen her smoke once or twice before. It looked strange.

Alison busied herself by rewrapping her soap, crackling the shiny paper as she folded and sealed, working to make the package look exactly as it had before she'd opened it. She knew about the puzzle, but she paid no attention. It was as if the events in the room meant nothing to her, as if she was part of another family and was only in the room by accident. Her eyes downcast, she folded and sealed, folded and sealed, absent with neither pride nor shame, absent the way nuns are absent.

"Four minutes gone," said Donald.

"What is this?" said Jean. "I see the word but I can't get the M in front where it belongs. It won't go."

"You have to try different ways. Everybody else got it."

Jean looked up, his eyes moving quickly to each of us in turn, a tenuous, faintly puzzled smile on his lips. "There's

a trick to it." He put it on the table in a way that made it
clear he wasn't going to pick it up again. "Is there any more
coffee?"

"How about the presents?" I asked my mother. "Isn't it
time yet?"

"All right," she said. "But go see if there's any coffee
first."

"Yipee!" I jumped up from my chair and ran to the
kitchen. The pot was warm under my palm and about a
quarter full. I took a cup from the kitchen sink and was
about to fill it when Donald came in.

"Wait a second." He searched in back of one of the cup-
boards until he found what he wanted, a large coffee cup
I'd never seen before. He put it on the table. "Fill it."

I poured the coffee and put the pot back on the stove.

"All right," he said. "Take that in to him."

I stared at the cup, then at Donald. He started out, but
at the door he stopped and looked back, his white face set,
his eyes cold behind the glasses. "If you interfere," he said
slowly, "I'll break your neck."

Jean accepted the dribble cup without comment.
Throughout the excitement of the present-opening he
sipped at it slowly. Every now and then he would raise his
bent index finger and wipe the underside of his lower lip.
After a while, as my mother distributed gifts, I forgot about
him.

"What's this?" my mother said, holding up the glass swan
from the crumpled paper on her lap.

"Read the card," Donald said.

"Donald's Special Wind Test. To establish the existence
of your third lung," she read, laughing.

"Just blow and see how far the water rises in its neck."

She found the secret hole and covered it with the tip of
her finger, rather obviously, I thought, then turned the
swan around, pursed her lips, and blew.

"Nothing," said Donald. "You're not trying."

"I am!" She blew hard this time, her cheeks cracking.

"It moved a little!" Alison said.

"Let me try," said Donald.

We all tried, then my mother gave it to Jean.

He looked at it for a moment, turning it over carefully
in his long hands. Watching him, I felt my body tightening,

gathering itself the way it had in the woods in Florida as I ran toward the high-jump bar. He raised the swan to his mouth. For one literally breathless moment I thought he was going to put it down again, but he was only catching the rhythm of his breathing. He reached the top, bore down, and blew. The water rushed up the neck of the swan and streamed onto his face, a thin jet striking him on the bridge of his nose, running into his eyes, down his cheeks, and onto his shirt.

For a fraction of a second there was silence, and in that small full instant I changed, I aged. I understood hate for the first time. No movement, no sound, no distractions at that moment when the water hung from his face like ice. Hate was in the room, the air heavy with it, Donald's hatred for Jean, and my own instantaneously blind and bottomless hatred for Donald.

We all laughed. Empty, short laughter as if someone were poking our bellies. Laughter from shock.

Jean wiped the water out of his eyes, his head bent over. He wanted to know if there were any other surprises waiting for him and Donald said no, there weren't, it was all over.

It seemed logical to ask why my mother put up with him, but the full answer is beyond me. I know only that Jean became bored with singing very early on and they were left together with their music, practicing in the afternoons, giving an occasional recital for the experience, gradually improving their repertoire if nothing else. My mother had quickly reached the plateau of her ability. A height, it seems safe to say, few people would get dizzy contemplating.

Aside from the music they had nothing in common. Even in his function as court jester Donald was removed from her. She missed half his jokes, getting only the tone of malice which was her signal to laugh. He was a noise in the background to which in the end she paid little attention, either musically or humanly. He was her accompanist, a kind of slave. And yet for years they supported each other. He would say of her, "Dagmar? Dagmar's *mar*velous," and she of him, laughingly, unconsciously imitating him, "Well, Donald is just *Donald*."

In fifteen years I don't think either of them said anything that surprised the other. They had learned everything they wanted to know in the first few months. If there was a surprise it must have come later. Not in a word, or an opening of the heart, or any form of love, but in the knowledge that they gave each other nothing, for all the time they had. Can they have understood, as each approached a lonely old age, that they had denied each other's reality? Puppets holding puppet strings, each puppet a puppet-master, in deliberate ignorance, as if life were no more than a cycle of their separate fantasies, as if there were all the time in the world.

It's a big stage, empty except for the Steinway grand. Around me the noise is beginning to subside. I want another seat and turn to look up the long sloping orchestra for an empty place, but the auditorium is filled. As the house lights go down people begin to hush their neighbors. I feel my upper lip twitching at the corner of my mouth and cover it with my fist. Beside me an old man is asleep, his chin almost touching his protruding collar bone, his rumpled tweed jacket open to reveal a food-stained T-shirt.

Mr. Miller, the director, climbs onto the stage and speaks into the microphone. "And now boys and girls, a special treat. Mrs. Fouchet, whom we all know—at least most of us know her, don't we girls?" A smattering of applause from the girls' side. "Mrs. Fouchet is going to sings a few songs for us." More applause as Mr. Miller climbs awkwardly down to the orchestra and takes his seat in the front row. Silence.

Donald walks quickly from the wings and takes his place at the piano without looking at the audience. His hanging tails almost touch the floor. He bows his head, waiting.

I hear the faint swish of her gown. She is onstage! A rush of light and color, sequins, her heels clicking against the polished wood, her body moving in a blur of swirling clothes and incandescent air. A muted gasp from the inmates at the splendid sight of her, then silence. She stands next to the Steinway, one hand touching the wood. After a moment she looks at Donald, and then back at the audience.

Beside me the old man is awake, leaning forward to watch her, his jaw slack and his eyes blinking slowly. He

6

Please Don't Take My Sunshine Away

WE RETURNED to Florida early in the summer. My sister Alison stayed behind. She was only sixteen, but seemed to be very well organized and my mother felt sure she could look after herself. I was eager to go. When the old Ford finally pulled away from the curb I'd already been in the back seat for hours, examining road maps and drawing up time charts.

Once again we drove nonstop, to save money. When Jean asked me I'd rub the back of his neck or squeeze his shoulder muscles to get the stiffness out. If I was sitting in front while Mother slept he'd take the chance to give his foot a rest. Straddling the gear shift, I'd sneak the speed up to fifty-five, curling my toes against the accelerator, edging it down millimeter by millimeter so he wouldn't notice.

We kept a small bottle of smelling salts in the glove compartment, an old-fashioned brand with a border of twisted rose vines on the stained label. I made the mistake of taking a good sniff once, as if it were perfume, and felt my head explode with white fire. Jean used it when he felt himself getting sleepy.

At a small station in Delaware insects swirled around a naked bulb on a pole and a screen door creaked in the wash of traffic. The heavy trucks went by like ships, gleaming with lights, their flat exhausts splitting the air. Rumbling, long-distance monsters, they shook the earth, each one followed by a dancing kite tail of roadside trash.

At the apex of the immense blue dome a shapeless white sun streamed down through the air, locking the world into absolute stillness and silence. Heat. Wave after radiant wave passing through trees, palmettos, and deserted barracks as if they didn't exist, as if they were only images trembling on the air between sun and sand. Standing on the

slightly pitched roof, my hand shielding my eyes, I could
see three miles in every direction. My vision skimmed over
the neatly spaced buildings, then higher, over the tops of
the pine trees in a slow circle. Nothing moved. Far away,
the sea. At the horizon a motionless black spiral of smoke
hung slanting against the sky. The ship had been visible
earlier in the day. Now it was gone.

Climbing back to the peak of the roof through the still
air, I felt the film of sweat on my naked chest and shoulders evaporate in an instant of coolness. The Stanley
hammer I'd bought with my own money hung rakishly
from a loop on the side of my blue jeans and a carpenter's
apron half full of drawn nails bumped against my thighs
with a pleasant weight. Way down at the other end of the
roof Jean knelt at his work, bent over, his slender brown
back gleaming with sweat. Pulling at the tongs with his
long arms, he'd draw a nail, wincing at the sharp, incredibly loud screech of sound.

We had paid the federal government a small fee for the
right to scavenge lumber from an abandoned Army base
near Boca Raton. "Good, tough, seasoned boards," Jean
had said. "No shrinkage!" He held his hands in the air and
smiled at the simplicity of it, as if shrinkage was the one
great obstacle mankind had failed to overcome, the key
problem holding everyone back from the realization of his
dreams. Filled with awe at the power of ideas, as drunk as
any scientist or philosopher, he hardly noticed it was almost as much work to dismantle a building as to construct
one, or that we had to buy a truck to move the lumber. He
was happy, eager to work every day, even letting me join
him in the interesting jobs instead of standing on the side-
lines.

The boards on the roof were one by twelves, about ten
feet long. Nails were drawn with a special tool, after which
one could simply lift the board from the supporting studs
and slide it down to the edge of the roof. Like a seesaw
one end would drop out of sight while the other rose
gracefully into the air, pivoting away as the board fell with
a satisfying clatter onto the others below.

"Frank!"

I dropped on my stomach and let my head hang down
into the black hole where I'd removed some boards. Hold-

ing the edge of the plank to keep from slipping, I must have looked, from the inside, like Kilroy against the sky —curled fingers, head, curled fingers. "What?" On days when I did a man's work, removing half as many boards as Jean and occasionally more than my mother, I allowed a certain grown-up tone to emerge in my voice. "What is it?"

"Lunch," my mother said.

"I'll eat it up here."

"Well, tell Jean."

I stood up and yelled to him at the other end of the roof. "Lunch!" I waved unnecessarily, as if we were playing a game in which he was supposed to be even farther away. He stood up on his knees and put down the tongs. "Lunch!" He wiped the sweat from his forehead with the back of his arm and gave a little nod to show he understood. After a moment he went to the edge, swung onto the ladder, and lowered himself out of sight. I kept on working until Tobey came up.

Carrying a canteen of water and some sandwiches, he ran easily up the incline, his bare feet gripping the wood securely. "Wow! This is a spooky place. I went all around."

"Find anything?"

"Some old fire extinguishers. They're lots of them laying around. And a rusty old bed, and a broken-down piano that doesn't play."

"Where's the piano?"

"Over yonder." He gestured toward the center of the base. "A big spooky old room."

Straddling the peak of the roof, we unwrapped the waxed paper from the sandwiches. Tobey hung the canteen from a halfdrawn nail.

"What'd you get?" I asked, looking up.

"Ham."

"Me too. Shit."

"Don't you like it?"

"It's all this fat. I hate fat." I took the sandwich apart and began to pluck the white strips with my fingers. By the time I finished flinging the meat away onto the ground, there was almost nothing left. I ate the bread and margarine, still suspicious.

"Let's get her to make peanut butter and jelly tomorrow," Tobey said.

"She won't."

He opened the canteen, drank, and handed it to me. "What are those little pills they eat?"

"Salt," I said between swallows. "Salt pills because of sweating so much."

"Oh." He finished his sandwich, licked his fingers, and wiped them against his jeans. "Let's go."

Running down the wide, empty avenue between the barracks. Deserted buildings fall behind us as our toes drive into the hot sand, hundreds of dark buildings in long rows folding majestically on the periphery of vision, sealing off escape.

"Yipee!"

"Fuck the armeee!"

Rushing through the hot air, ripping it apart with speed, wind cramming our open mouths and ears, racing neck and neck, stride for stride in wild harmonious abandon. At the sweetest moment our legs give out, suddenly trembling, and we fall sliding into the sand, tumbling for the fun of it, rolling like dogs in the crystalline cloud.

I spit the dead grains from my mouth and shake my head. Looking up I see the twin lines of our footprints stretching back into a white glare. Hunched over in rapt absorption, Tobey picks at the calloused soles of his feet.

Pushing hard. The door swings easily and bangs against the inside wall. An enormous room, empty, the sun streaming in long bars across the wooden floor. My eyes search the corners, expecting something, but the place is bare. "Fuck the Army!" My voice resounds marvelously. "Up your mother's *ass* hole!" I stand as if waiting for an answer. The silence is oppressive and I run to the next building.

A fire extinguisher lies on its side on the floor. I pick it up to throw it across the room, but it's too heavy and all I can do is let it fall a few feet away.

"Hey Fraaaank!" Tobey calls from another building. I run outside and stand in the center of the avenue. I can't tell which building his voice is coming from. "Frank!" He calls again, waving from a doorway. "Over here."

"Find something?"

"Over here."

He takes me into a building that seems darker than the others. Some of the windows are broken and boarded up.

"Look at this."

A carving on the wall, lines chipped out with a knife, very elaborate and skillful.

"Wow!" I reach out and touch it. It's a woman, lying with her thighs spread apart and an immense disembodied phallus halfway inside her. She gazes over her breasts and belly at the viewer, eyes popping in a caricature of lust, tongue hanging. The detail is painstaking, down to the fine lines of pubic hair.

"Holy mackerel," says Tobey. "You think we can get it off the wall?"

"We'll need tools. We can do it tomorrow."

"Wouldn't it be great in the tree house."

"We can get it off there," I say, taking my hand away.

"It'll be safe in the tree house."

"We can't show it to anybody. Not even your brother."

"Hell, I wouldn't show it to him. He'd just take it. It's ours."

We step back to let the light fall cleanly against the wall.

"Wow."

"Holy mackerel."

Tobey gives a long, low whistle like a sharpy in the movies and we crack up simultaneously, moving around the room, bent over, laughing, and slapping ourselves.

Down the avenue in an easy trot toward the largest building. The sun is gone. Immense clouds from the ocean move swiftly overhead, their tops white and voluptuous, their undersides black with rain. (Florida weather is sudden and dramatic. I once saw a high cloud rain into a lower one, with no effect below.) The air smells peculiar, and in the filtered light, colors fade. Distant thunder as we run into the building.

An old gym. The hardwood floor had been taken up but the basketball backboards remain, a few strands of webbing hanging limply from the hoops. Our voices echo off the high roof.

"Find anything?"

"No. It's been cleaned out."

In a corner stands an old upright piano. The keys go down under my fingers but there is no sound. I open the top, and standing on a broken-backed chair, peer down into the strings. The hammers are there, like a line of soldiers, and the strings are rusty but taut. Carefully I lower my arm into the piano, get my finger behind one of the hammers and give it a gentle flip. A note sounds weakly.

"It works," I yell to Tobey. He is shimmying up the basketball pole.

Examining the front of the piano I find a small lever set into the wood. A corroded metal plate is readable after I rub it with spit. It says "Practice-Play." I push the lever slowly to the Play position and then strike a chord. The rooms fills with sound.

LEP-rosy (va-room), eee gods I've got Lep-rosy (va-room), there goes my eye-ball (plink), into your high-ball (plink-plink). . . .

Bump-a-dada, bump-a-dada, bump-a-dada, Just the way you look to-night.

Jada . . . Jada . . . jada jada jing jing jing.

Tobey sits on the basketball hoop high in the air. He stretches out his arms to show he isn't holding on. At just that moment an explosion rocks the earth. My chair trembles and the windows rattle in their frames. We wait breathlessly, Tobey with his arms still outstretched, myself motionless at the piano. A wall of water is falling from the sky, growing heavier with every instant of silence, gathering speed to drive deep in the sand. A drop on the drumlike roof. Another. And then, with a roar, the full load crashes down, shaking the building.

Tobey lowers his tail through the basketball hoop like a man sitting in a garbage pail. He hangs there for a second, then pulls himself up and drops silently to the floor. He yells something I can't hear.

"What?"

His lips move as he shouts. He wants to go out in the rain. I nod. He knows I'd rather stay with the piano so he doesn't wait, turning and running to the door which he throws open. Standing there, his body is a dark silhouette against the white lines of rain. He moves through the doorway and the white lines fall behind him like a curtain.

At the window I watch him running down the avenue, his jeans already black and soaking, his bony shoulders shining with epaulets of spray. He trots, slows down, staggers, his arms straight up as if the rain were a rope he could climb.

Turning slowly, head lifted and mouth open to catch the drops, his back bends like a smooth, stringless bow.

Evening is approaching and the sky has cleared. Yellow light skims over the tops of the pine trees and strikes the side of the barracks, making the wet boards steam lazily. Fat drops of water sparkle with prismatic colors as they drop from the eaves to the pocked sand.

"One more load," Jean says to us as he stands over the stacked lumber. "All right, Dagmar." They lift four or five boards and move, in step, toward the truck.

"Let's take seven this time," Tobey says.

We count seven boards and scrabble for a grip. My fingers hurt when he picks up his end. Finally we lift them away.

"Too many," I say without breathing.

"We'll make it."

Our heels digging into the wet sand, we sidestep to the truck. Every nuance of Tobey's movement is transmitted to me across ten feet of boards.

"Watch it!"

"Look out!" we yell, enjoying the sight of Jean and Dagmar scurrying out of the way.

"Don't take so many," Jean says. "It only makes it harder. Why knock yourself out?" We don't explain that each time we've added deliberately another board, searching for the limit. We know it's harder, but it's more fun.

I put my end on the truck with relief and run to help Tobey. Jean joins us and we push the boards forward, sliding them in over the others.

"Okay. That's it," Jean says, taking off his apron.

"Can we ride on the running boards?"

"Not on the highway."

"Just till we get there."

"All right. But you have to get in back at the highway."

Tired, my mother leans against a fender for a moment of rest. She is two months pregnant.

The truck bumps along down the narrow coral road, chasing its own shadow. I see my head and shoulders racing along the surface of the road, rippling like wash on a line. As we pass an overhanging branch Jean spins the wheel to climb onto the crown and I press against the hot

cab. The needles whip by, just touching, stinging my back.
The wind washes it away in an instant.

On the other side Tobey extends his arm over the top
of the roof. I reach out and take his hand. As the woods
fall back and the truck picks up speed we lean out palms
locked together, free arms triumphantly in the air like
trick riders standing on the backs of horses. The wind roars.

"But *dar*ling," he almost yelled at her, "don't you see what
I mean?"

Mother and Jean were having an argument about Carl-
ton Fredericks, the soap-opera nutritionist, and it was clear
that if I waited around for supper I'd miss my ride to the
fair. I slipped out of the house on tiptoes, carefully closing
the screen door behind me, wincing as the spring creaked.

It was good to be out. It was always good. Their voices
faded away as I walked up the moonlight road toward
Tobey's. Every now and then a dog barked—close by,
from across the road, from the fringes of the woods. Yard
dogs, talking over great distances like telegraphers at sea,
waiting, cocking their heads to listen to the silence,
haunches trembling for the answering yip or the long,
atavistic howl. Steel guitars came from a kitchen radio,
slippery tremolos drifting out across the warm air like slow
birds. I counted my change in the moonlight. Seventy-three
cents.

As Tobey's house came into view I broke into a run. In a
yellow window I could see his mother washing up after
dinner, her body rocking gently back and forth as she
shifted her immense weight from one leg to the other.
Popeye, the old dog, jogged halfway across the yard to
investigate me. Popeye was blind so you had to tell him
who you were.

"It's me 'peye. Just me."

Tobey's father was sitting in front of the house, reclining
in a tattered deck chair we'd found at the dump. He was
drinking from a wine bottle, holding it up in the bright
moon after each slug to see how much was left. "Evening,
boy."

"Evening, sir." I stood before him for a moment, waiting for him to speak. It was a tradition and he got annoyed if you didn't honor it. Having seen him mean drunk
on more than one occasion, I always did. (The quietest

thirteen-year-old boy in the world is the boy who finds a raving, half-blind, red-necked, out-of-work hillbilly house-painter between himself and the door.)

"You coming with us to the fair?"

"Yes sir. If I can."

He took a drink and smiled, his mouth stained with wine. "Course you can. Course you can," he said. "You're a good boy."

"Is that Tobey taking a shower?" Someone was in the stall by the outhouse.

"That's Sean."

We heard the rattle of a pail and then a splashing sound. "Shee-ut! It's cold."

"Sean!" The old man's voice rose suddenly, like a load of coal dumped in a chute. "Hush up your mouth!"

"Well, it's *cold,* Pa."

Not bothering to answer he slumped down in the deck chair. "Go on, boy," he said to me. "Tobey is inside."

At just that moment the screen door opened and Mrs. Rawlings threw out a basin of water. It flashed through the air and struck the ground where the light spilled from the window. A thousand gleaming flies lifted from the greasy sand the instant the water hit, and fell back the instant afterward, like a green blanket.

"Well, look who's here," she said, smiling. "Ready to go to the fair?"

"Yes ma'm." I followed her into the house, my head down, watching her elephant legs. I smelled a cake in the kerosene oven.

"You boys go in back now so you won't be underfoot," she said, wiping the oilcloth on the table. "I've got to get ready."

"Is the cake for tonight?" I whispered as we pushed through the curtain.

"I think so," Tobey said.

We sat on Tobey's bed and played cards in the flickering light. The house was one room, divided by a dark curtain strung up on a length of wire stretched from wall to wall about six feet high. The kitchen, dining table, and chairs were on one side, and the beds on the other. There were four beds, taking up almost every inch of space. One had to turn sideways to walk between them. Tobey, his older brothers, Sean and Pat, and of course Mr. and Mrs. Rawlings all slept there. Their clothes and personal belongings were neatly crammed into open shelves high on the walls. The family shotgun hung on two nails over the only window.

"Gin."

"Oh shucks. I was almost there."

"All right now, come out here while I get dressed." Mrs. Rawlings pulled the curtain back and waited. "Just one piece each," she said. "No snitching when I ain't looking."

"Ahh," Tobey sighed. "Coconut."

On the round table were two plates of cake, and resting on the stove the mother lode, fresh icing rippling down its sides.

"Ma. You didn't wash the bowl?"

She laughed from the other side of the curtain. "No, honey. It's there on top of the icebox."

Sean pushed through the door, dressed in jeans and a freshly laundered shirt. The cuffs were folded back twice to show his muscular forearm. His wet hair was slicked back over his head, revealing a pale white band at the top of his brow.

"The bowl's ours!" Tobey said.

"Hell, you're welcome to it." He sat down by the old radio (tall, with carved wood, like a miniature cathedral) and fiddled with the dial till he got some music. Then, suddenly impatient, he turned it off and went to the door. "Pa, when are we going? It's getting late."

The old man didn't answer. Tobey and I ate our cake and listened to Mrs. Rawlings moving softly on the other side of the curtain.

She stood at the side of the road, her plastic purse hanging from folded hands. A small straw hat was placed straight on her head, pinned to her hair with two long needles like antennae. She wore a print dress she'd made from twenty-pound flour sacks.

The old man, Sean, Pat, and I stood behind the old De-Soto, leaning up against it like the victims of a police frisk. "Be sure it's in second," Mr. Rawlings yelled over the rear fender.

"I know what to do, Pa," Tobey answered from inside.

"And don't turn the ignition on until we get up some speed!"

"I know, I know," he said.

"And don't talk back to your pa!"

Pat, the eldest brother, a big, gentle man who always spoke softly, turned to me. "There ain't too much room back here, Frankie. See if you can get a purchase up there on the doorpost."

I ran to my position. Through the window Tobey looked absurdly small behind the wheel. He had to crane his neck to see over the hood. His white teeth gleamed in the moonlight as he smiled.

"All right now . . . HEAVE!"

The car began to roll immediately, coral crunching under the tires as it picked up speed. Soon I found myself running just to keep up. After twenty or thirty yards the old man yelled, "Now!"

Tobey snapped out the clutch and the car pushed back at me, almost knocking me over. The engine coughed, died, coughed, and caught. I heard him cry "yipee" as he pulled away in a sudden burst of power, rear tires spinning and engine roaring. In a split second he was far up the road, without lights, shifting into third.

Breathing heavily, I came to a halt. Ten yards behind me the three men stood in the middle of the road, bent over, half-bent, their arms hanging at their sides. And behind them, way back in the distance where we'd started, Mrs. Rawlings took a step forward to look after us.

"Where in hell does he think he's going?" the old man asked, but he wasn't angry.

We could barely fit in the car. The springs sank alarmingly as Mrs. Rawlings eased herself into the front seat, making the old DeSoto look as if it was headed for the center of the earth, but things straightened out when Sean and Pat got in back. Tobey sat on my lap and we were off.

It didn't take long to drive through Chula Vista. Doc's grandiose plans notwithstanding, the neighborhood had failed to grow. Very few houses ever reached completion and most people lived in a state of impermanence, as if afraid to commit themselves. (Perhaps that was the key. Chula Vista looked like a failure, there was the feeling the whole place could be knocked down and carted away in a single night. The people were poor. What little money they had couldn't be risked on a failing venture. More important, they couldn't risk their energy. These people breathed failure, moving from town to town in an endless cycle of disillusionment. They had learned to hold back, to never put too much of themselves in any one place because when the road was built, or the schoolhouse painted, or the forest cleared, or the oranges picked, they might have to move on.) They didn't want to waste themselves, and so they lived in frame shacks with tarpaper walls, or concrete pillboxes without glass in the windows. There was even a five-room house without a roof. The family lived at one end under an Army surplus tent. They lived in trailers, lean tos, and quonset huts, and the years slipped by.

Down Dania Boulevard, the DeSoto creaking like a hay wagon. I could see the rusted-out front fender waving in the wind. Every now and then a big Buick or Caddy would rush up behind us, lights flashing, and whip by as if we were standing still. Big, thick-necked men, holding their broads, speeding down to Miami and the dog track and the Fronton. An Olds fishtailed past at ninety-five and we saw a blonde head dip down. Sean opened a bottle of wine. "You just know she's blowing him," he said softly to Pat.

Tobey and I watched the tail lights disappear in the distance.

"Let me have some," Tobey whispered, making a grab for the bottle.

Sean held it back. "Well, looky here!" he said in mock surprise.

"Just one. I won't take much."

"What'll you give me?"

"Aw, Sean, come on."

Tobey took the bottle and raised it to his lips. I watched his Adam's apple moving like a piston, once, twice, three times. Sean reached for the bottle but at just that moment Mrs. Rawlings turned around and froze everybody. All breaths were held. Quick as a flash she reached back and snatched the bottle, glaring at Sean. "You giving wine to those children?"

There was no escape for Sean. Caught between Pat on one side and Tobey and me on the other, he just looked down at his shoes. Mrs. Rawlings raised her tree-trunk arm to the roof of the car. Her five fingers were spread like a star. A faint grunt escaped her lips as she drove the whole weighty load straight down on top of Sean's unsuspecting head. A tremendous blow, traveling down his backbone and compressing the entire back seat with stunning force.

It took a moment for Sean to reorient himself. "Aw, Maw," he said.

Mrs. Rawlings rolled down her window and threw out the wine bottle.

"Aw, Maw!" he said again, slightly bewildered at the speed with which events had transpired. "It was almost full."

Mrs. Rawlings didn't answer. She raised her head to watch the road and never looked back. Pat laughed quietly, without a trace of malice.

A perpendicular column of blue light descended from the sky to the parking field, striking the earth behind a screen of silhouetted automobiles, spreading a pool of white radiance, a vague open-topped dome of light in the air above us. Insects drifted through like snowflakes, disappearing at the perimeter.

"Now make sure you know where the car is," Mrs. Rawlings said. "We'll meet here at midnight." She saw Sean rushing off. "Sean! Did you mind me?" He was gone before she could stop him. "That boy," she said sadly.

The old man took out his change purse. "How much money have you got?"

"Sixty cents," Tobey answered.

"Frankie?"

"Seventy-three cents, sir."

He counted some change and held it out to us. "That makes a dollar and a half each. And don't spend it all in one place."

"Thank you!" we yelled together.

Pat gave us each a quarter, and just before we took off, Tobey's mother held out two silver coins. "That's eating money," she said. "And you ain't getting any more so don't spend it on those bumper cars like last time."

"We won't, Momma. Thanks."

"Thank you, ma'm."

"All right, boys. Have a good time and stay out of trouble. We'll see you later." She moved off on her husband's arm, smiling, one hand unnecessarily holding down her hat (as if he were sweeping her away in a waltz or a polka, as if only now, at the last moment, could she control her appearance before giving up to the madcap whirl of the evening), her buttocks rolling like ships at sea.

On the fairway Tobey and I darted through the crowd like needles through a tapestry, turning, pausing, deftly insinuating ourselves across the slow movement of the parade.

The bumper cars! Waiting on line we draped ourselves over the wooden railing and surveyed the scene. On the steel floor small cars raced into the distance, took a curve, and raced back, each with a long pole to the shiny roof trailing sparks of power. Most of the drivers were children, but here and there an adult could be seen, or a young couple crammed in together, giggling, trying to avoid collisions. WHOMP! We laughed as a kid in overalls caught a teen-aged girl broadside and spun away before she could retaliate. WHOMP! Someone else hit her. This time she straightened out and gave it some speed, accelerating nicely.

"That one looks good," I said. "Number Ten. I hope she gets out." There were small but critical differences in the power of the cars. It was important to get the faster ones.

"Thirty-eight," Tobey said. "And that blue one, Ninety-nine."

When the boy came around we each bought a ribbon of tickets. The air was full of ozone, a thin, sharp, white smell in the back of one's nose. A whistle blew and the power was cut. All over the floor cars rolled to a stop.

"She's getting out," I yelled as the crowd pushed up behind us. "Number Ten! I've got Number Ten."

"Ninety-nine! In the back."

As the floor cleared the boy swung open the barrier and stepped to the side. With a tremendous roar fifty kids rushed out onto the steel track, fanning out from the narrow gate in all directions like water from a split hose. Someone was at my side, racing me to Number Ten, but at the last moment (when he was slowing down) I leaped into the air and landed with both feet in the cockpit, my hands grabbing the pole for support. Laughing, I slithered down into position and watched him run off for another car.

The controls were simple. An accelerator and a steering wheel. I spun the wheel, testing the amount of play. It was fairly tight. Waiting, I tried to find Tobey, but the view was obscured.

At last every kid had a car. The barrier was closed and a whistle sounded. I pressed the accelerator to the floor as somewhere out of sight the power was turned on. My car began to move. The sound in that vast room filled with cars was not unlike the powerful noise of a subway train as it pulls away from the platform. Dozens of cars moved at top speed around the track, dodging in and out as the drivers attempted to get the feel of their vehicles. I bent back my head, sighting up the pole to watch the metal tongue sliding across the roof, sucking power.

Confident, after a few experiments, that my car was one of the best on the floor, I took off to look for Tobey, side-swiping a few kids along the way just for the hell of it. "One Way Only!" said a sign on the wall, "No Head On Collisions." Tobey was waiting for me at the edge of the curve. He'd got the car he wanted, the blue one. I pulled up beside him.

"Okay?"

"Okay!"

"Who do we get?"

"Watch it!" Tobey was struck by a giggling girl who made no attempt to control her vehicle. She'd been pushed into Tobey by a fat boy in a Tom Mix T-shirt. "Him!" Tobey yelled. "Tom Mix!"

Our strategy had been worked out the previous year. The only question was who went first. Toby took off, and after skirting the helpless girl, I counted to ten under my breath and followed. Elbows out, back curved over the wheel, Tobey pursued the fat boy, slowly closing the gap. We went an entire lap before Tom Mix made his move. He went to the outside, figuring to cut across and catch the giggling girl from behind. Tobey anticipated this and raced down the rail, turning at the last moment to cross paths with plenty of speed. At exactly the same time I aimed for the spot where it seemed to me Tom Mix would end up, collecting maximum speed on the long straight run.

It worked perfectly. Tobey closed in, his head bent down. At the last instant Tom Mix saw him coming and tried to turn away, but it was too late. FA-BOOM! Tobey caught him solidly on the left fender, spinning the car a quarter turn, reversing his wheels, and bringing him to a halt. Tom Mix spun the steering wheel frantically, trying to straighten himself out and get started again. He'd been

prepared for Tobey, but as I barreled in, teeth clenched,
straight-armed, I could see he didn't expect me. His body
was loose. Innocent. FA-BAM! A marvelous, straight-on
hit, jolting him in his seat, shaking his fat like Jello.

We were invincible! Gasping, choking with laughter too
wild and sweet to come out, our brains bursting with excitement, we drove off to new conquests.

It was getting late. The crowds had thinned out and along
the fairway most of the stalls were closing down for the
night. Tobey and I sat on the guard rail of a darkened
carousel eating hot dogs, automatically waving away the
flies.

"How much have you got left?"

"Thirty-five cents," I said.

"I've got a quarter."

"I guess it's almost midnight."

Tobey jumped down from the fence and ran to ask
someone what time it was. Tired, I walked after him.

"Ten of," he said when I reached him.

"Well, let's mosey on down."

We ambled along the littered promenade in the general
direction of the parking field, checking the sandy ground
for dropped coins. Tobey bent over and picked up a small
felt pennant on a stick. DANIA-FLA. on a background of
orange blossoms. "For the tree house."

We stopped in front of a freak show to look at the
posters. The alligator man. The duck woman. The armless
wonder. Special attraction! The man without a face.

"I saw it last year," Tobey said. "It's a fake."

"They say he's got alligator skin."

"He's painted up. He lies around in a pit full of sawdust
with these big hunks of raw meat. But he doesn't touch the
meat or anything. It's a fake."

"You mean he's just like us only painted up?"

"Well, no," Tobey said, pausing. "He don't have no
arms. His hands sort of grow out of his shoulders."

"What?"

"Like little baby hands. But they're dead. He can't move
them."

"Didn't it make you feel funny to look at him?"

"I didn't like it. He just lay there in the sawdust, real
still, like he was dead, with his head turned away. And we

all walked by. If he'd really been an alligator man, well then okay, but it was a fake and I didn't want to look." He turned away from the poster. "Let's go."

At the edge of the fair a small booth is still open, its lights shining out into the empty air. A big man in a purple jacket sits on a stool behind the counter drinking a container of coffee. As we approach he pauses momentarily, looks at us over the rim of the container, and then continues drinking as if he hadn't seen us.

We stop twenty feet away to examine the game. It's a ring toss. Ten cents a throw and the prizes are on the walls. Pennants, funny hats, candy boxes, two live canaries, china dolls, stuffed animals, canned hams, ukuleles, toasters, radios, silverware. Tobey nudges me. "Look there, on the back wall." I whistle softly. Mounted on a wooden plaque, with a belt and holster hanging next to it is the grand prize, a silver revolver.

"Wow," Tobey whispers as we move forward.

"It's beautiful. Look at the carving on the handle."

"With a holster and everything."

The big man hasn't looked at us, or moved a muscle.

"How do you win the gun?" Tobey asks.

"Two out of three tosses on the red peg," he says expressionlessly.

We look at the back wall. Recessed into a lighted chamber under the pistol is a red peg, angled backwards under a sloping roof. I give Tobey a nickel. "We can both try."

"Okay. Give me three, please."

It's as if the man is blind. He stares fixedly out into the darkness. Bright lights shine behind his head. He leans forward slightly, collects the change with one hand, and brings up three rings from under the counter with the other, all in one smooth movement, without looking down or changing position on the stool.

Tobey takes aim and throws a ring. It strikes the wall and falls onto a shelf below. "Too high," he says, and throws again. The second ring is too low. "Shucks," Tobey says. "Well, for one I get a radio." He throws the last ring. It strikes the recessed enclosure straight on, but doesn't fit and falls away. "Did you see that?" he asks me.

"It won't go that way. You have to lob it in at an angle so it'll fit."

"I'm going to ask Momma for another thirty cents. I'll be right back." He runs off into the darkness.

I stand for a moment, studying the red peg. My heart beats quickly because of the discovery of throwing at an angle. It'll still be difficult, the ring must enter the enclosure at exactly the right tilt. Once inside, it must fall on the peg by its own weight. I remind myself to throw softly so it won't bounce off the back wall.

"I'll take three."

Once again he leans forward in the smooth gesture, slapping the rings on the counter near my hands. Behind me, far away, I can hear cars starting up on the parking field.

The edge of the counter presses against my stomach. I toss the first ring, giving a faint flick of the wrist at the last instant to keep it from turning over in the air. It sails into the enclosure as if guided by an invisible hand. I can hardly believe my eyes. It falls slowly toward the peg, strikes, and leans. I duck down my head and shield my eyes from the bright lights. Yes! It covers the top of the peg! Another good toss could knock it over.

Three feet away the man sits absolutely without movement. I can hear his breathing. He hasn't looked up, or back at the red peg. It's as if I'm not there.

Picking up the second ring I know I'm going to win. Nothing can stop it, as if it's already happened, as if time were running backward. A peculiar, giddy feeling comes over me. A lightheadedness, strangely familiar. I throw the second ring. It misses and falls away. I shrug, blinking, as if something annoying had happened around me, some minor irritation interrupting my concentration. I feel like asking for the ring back even though I know it makes no difference. The third ring is in my hands. I lean forward, aim, and throw. It goes into the enclosure, as I had known it would, falls onto the peg, and knocks the other loose underneath itself. I've won. Two rings over the red peg. I look at them for a moment. An immense calmness lies over my soul. Then I look up at the revolver.

"I've won."

The man doesn't move.

"I've won. Look."

He turns around and looks back at the peg. Then he gets off the stool and walks back and takes the rings off the peg and drops them with the others on the shelf. He comes back and stands in front of me, gazing out over my head. "You missed."

"What?"

He says nothing.

For a moment I don't know what to do. I stand there looking up at him. His face is white and hard.

"But I won," I say.

Slowly he lowers his head and looks at me. His eyes are dark under thick black eyebrows. He lifts his arm from behind the counter and extends it to me. As if in a dream I reach out to shake hands.

Gently but firmly he takes my wrist, bends, and spreads his knees a fraction of an inch, and slowly rubs my palm under his balls.

The arc light had been turned off, and without a landmark it took me some time to find the car. I wandered around the field for five or ten minutes, not really looking, trying to calm down. Eventually I came on the DeSoto. Pausing behind a pick-up truck I wiped my eyes carefully on the sleeve of my shirt and took a couple of deep breaths.

"Hey!" Tobey was sitting on the running board, his chin in his hands.

"Hey!" My voice sounded strange.

"Pat says Sean went off somewhere. With some girl. Pa wants to go without him but Momma says we should wait."

I opened the back door and climbed into the car. Pat was asleep. I sat in the corner and pressed myself against the wall, my eyes closed.

"I don't give a hot damn," the old man said. "I ain't gonna wait no longer. He's gone, woman."

"Well, five minutes more."

"God-damn women fussing over every little thing."

We waited ten minutes, and when Sean still hadn't appeared the old man started the engine. "Come on, boy," he said to Tobey. "He ain't coming back."

Tobey got in beside me. I kept my eyes closed, pretending I was asleep. Lights flashed across my eyelids as we reached the main road.

Halfway home I opened my eyes to see where we were. Tobey saw me looking out the window. After a minute or two he asked, "What's wrong?"

"Nothing," I said, and settled down as if to go back to sleep.

Chula Vista was dark, but the lights were still on at my house. Mr. Rawlings stopped at the corner and let me out.

"See you tomorrow," Tobey said.

"O.K." I waved and started for the house. The moon had set and all the stars were out, thousands of them spread over the black sky all lacework. It was a quiet, windless night.

Their voices carried on the still air. I heard them, arguing away in the same tones as when I'd left, Jean's slightly hoarse rising sentences, Mother's rich contralto falling sentences, back and forth, back and forth, like animals pacing their cages.

I pushed open the screen door and started for my bed.

"Frank? Is that you?" my mother called from the other side of the curtain.

"Yes."

"Wash the dishes before you go to bed."

7
Shit

SOON after the incident at the fair the day-to-day pattern of my life changed considerably. Tobey, with whom I'd usually spent every waking moment, was forced to go to work with his father, probably at his mother's insistence, to keep the old man from drinking on the job. This, in itself, was not extraordinary—sons often worked as their fathers' assistants. Tobey had done it for short periods a number of times during the summer, and so had I, working with Jean on the construction of a schoolhouse as well as on the duplex on our own property. But this time the job was a long one, destined to last till the beginning of school, and far enough away (twenty miles) so that Tobey left early and came back late. I couldn't go along because Tobey was ashamed.

For a while I continued to roam the woods, going to our old haunts as if he were still with me. But without company the days grew long and the emptiness of the woods uncomfortably reminiscent of the winter sky in Connecticut. Pedaling aimlessly along an overgrown road far from civilization, I would suddenly be struck by the utter desolation of the scene around me. Landscape we had raced through, singing songs, laughing on our way to the quarry, the guava tree, or the deserted shack—the same landscape now struck straight through to my heart. It wasn't a fear of bogeymen, or the dark, or even of the unknown in the usual sense of the word, it was the simple existence of the woods that scared me, the fact that it was all there, other than me, and much stronger than me. Gradually my area of operations narrowed from a five-mile to a one-mile circle, and eventually, as torpor overwhelmed me, to the immediate environs of the house.

I was trapped—forced by some nameless and unconscious unease to spend my time at exactly that place where

I was bound to be most unhappy. Jean's and Dagmar's arguing voices—tireless (in a sense it was as if *only* their voices argued; they became their voices), their ever increasing propensity for giving me pointless, dull, and occasionally humiliating chores to get me out of the way, their unbroken disapproval, set by now so deeply in their minds that it became the actual fabric of life for all of us, unquestioned by us, as if there were no alternative—these things, petty as they were, made me unhappy.

I had nothing else, after all. An adult recognizes petty problems for what they are and transcends them through his higher preoccupations, his goals—he moves on, as it were. A child has no choice but to accept the immediate experiences of his life at face value. He isn't moving on, he simply is. Children agonize over an overdue library book or an accidentally broken gas meter with all the emotion that an adult experiences at the threat of prison. The dominating elements of life at home were anger, boredom, and disapproval. Unlike Jean and Dagmar I had nothing else. My defense was to retreat. I became vague around the house. I didn't see things. I didn't hear things. In a way I suppose I went to sleep.

We had three dogs. Dansker, a tawny boxer, Penny, a nervous, intelligent fox terrier, and Flossie, the clown, a bumbling, loose, droopy-eyed hound dog. Jean, undoubtedly responding to deeply buried memories of plantation life in aristocratic Louisiana, had built an elaborate kennel for them. A kennel so elaborate, in fact, with its three snug warrens and cement runway, that in many ways it seemed preferable to the main house. There was a drawback, though. I had to keep it clean.

Penny was all right. She took neat, lady-like shits, usually firm, in the corner of the runway up against the fence. One pass of the shovel and everything was okay. The other two were less controlled. Dansker's breeding might have shown if it hadn't been for the example of Flossie depositing her formless turds with innocent self-abandon wherever they fell, fouling clean areas as well as dirty ones without the least sense of ritual or responsibility, without, in fact, the slightest indication in her eyes (I had watched her, crouched, pointing her rectum to the ground) that anything happening at the other end was of any importance whatever. She was such a blissfully stupid dog, like a brontosaurus, with its split nervous system and stunning idiocy. She crapped incessantly, expressing in this, as in everything else she did, the fact that something was seriously wrong with her. Not sickness (she was wonderfully healthy), or bad training, but some inbred genetic catastrophe, some hidden anatomical uniqueness making her not so much a dog as like a dog. Only in a world of abundance could she have existed at all. Half the food passed through her body untouched by the chemistry of digestion.

Every evening at sundown I opened the gate, blocked their exit with my shovel, and slipped inside. (At least once I must have paused, leaned back against the chicken wire, and looked out at the immense wilderness surrounding us, the endless miles of sandy woods spreading out in every direction, where all the dogs in Chula Vista could crap for a thousand years without making a mark, where even I, Indian-style, gazing at a hawk in the sky or a line of ants climbing bark, had released my cigars since time out of mind.) The dogs would gather round, sniffing my feet and pressing against my legs. In her mindless enthusiasm Flossie had knocked me down more than once. As soon as I started pushing the shovel they would run into their houses as if ashamed of themselves.

First a tour around the edge, up against the fence, shaking the shovel every now and then to equalize the load. At the slightest breeze I would stop, raise my head, and fill up with clean air. Once around, and I was back to the gate. Outside, I'd carry the load downwind, walking slowly to avoid accidents. In a corner of the lot I'd drop it on the sand, dig a hole (cleaning the shovel in the process), and go back for more. With the second load the worst was over. I buried it with satisfaction. Then I hosed down the runway (we had running water by then), the shovel, and of course my feet.

Jean had accused me of getting sloppy with the shovel and leaving too much for the hose. It was true that around the perimeter of the kennel, just outside the chicken wire, a great deal of shit had collected in the sand, and it was also true that on hot days it smelled pretty bad, but I sprinkled a few handfuls of lime every week and never let it get entirely out of control.

"It stinks," Jean said one sweltering day.

"I don't smell anything."

What could he do? Take over? He gave me a pained look and walked away. Anyway, he'd pretty much given up the plantation image. In his mind the kennel had fallen into that large, familiar, and uninteresting category of Pure Ideas Destroyed by Impure Reality. Perhaps never before had there been so clear an example.

She was calling me. I couldn't see, but I knew she was standing in the front yard projecting her mezzo across the road into the woods, unaware that I was thirty yards away, safe in Flossie's house. I'd been there for hours, dozing through the noon heat with the dogs, whispering to them, holding them against me. Her voice was meaningless. My name was meaningless. Sounds from out there barely reached me, lapping at the edge of consciousness like noise from distant radios. For weeks I'd been slipping away, not into the woods as they thought, but down on my hands and knees into Flossie's warren, a wooden box six by three by three.

Sunlight filtered through the cracks between the boards, striating my skin, strapping Flossie against my legs with white bands. Dansker and Penny were asleep next door, sighing every now and then like old horses, or occasionally twitching in their dreams, scratching their hard nails against the cement. It was past noon and the temperature was over a hundred. The air was heavy and motionless, dust motes frozen like specimens in glass. I stared at the bleached hairs on my arm.

It was a microcosmic world, closed on all sides. Within it my body was so large as to be meaningless—the way the sky is large outside—an immense thing so vastly out of scale it could be forgotten. A fingernail was huge, one hair a complete and engrossing entity, the cement under my head like a close-up of the surface of the moon. Paradoxically the smallness of everything gave me the sensation of great space, I suppose because in some way I became as small as the things I contemplated: a flake of silica, a sand burr, a detail in the grain of a wallboard.

When I was in college I had a powerful phonograph at the head of my bed. In the afternoons I would lie down with my ear a few inches from the speaker, listening to records. The effect was odd, and unexpected. Invariably I was driven into a halfsleep, literally beaten into unconsciousness by the tremendous noise pouring through my ears, as if my overloaded mind had to turn itself off. Something like that happened in Flossie's warren. *Images* drove me under, images too strong to let through full force. Contemplating minutiae magnified, I drifted through the hours wrapped in a cloud of absent-mindedness. Faintly dizzy, half-asleep, and beyond time, I slipped gradually out of the world.

A buzzing inside my head. My body is far away, much too far to respond to my wishes. I stare at my fingers curled on the floor. Immense, swollen fingers, weighty as sandbags. They are dead. I see nothing except exactly what I am looking at, as if I were watching the world through a tube. When I shift my glance to the floor a few inches below my hand, my thumb and index finger disappear.

It occurs to me that if I want to come back I'd better do it now because in a few moments it'll be too late. Instantly I relax, letting myself be swept away. I don't want to come back. The buzzing increases, swallowing me, drowning me until a mysterious change of frequency occurs and I come through into the clear, up above the buzzing into a silent, calm world, my heart bursting with happiness.

Paradise! Light! Air! I am extended over vast spaces like a pure white cloud, drifting freely, roiling exuberantly in the sunlight high above the earth. I sail through the blue! I am everywhere!

Or I lie on my stomach, my chin propped in my hands, watching elaborately plumed birds strutting by the side of a clear stream, ruffling their brilliant feathers with pompous arrogance. Suddenly two of the birds rush at each other in the air. Quick as a wink one of them is gone. Swallowed. A single yellow feather drifts down to settle on the moss. I laugh, delighted by the purity of it. I am aware of beauty flooding me like a balm, illuminating my insides, making me clean.

From the corner of my eye I see a bird approaching me, gingerly stepping through the flowers, lifting its pronged feet high in the air. A miniature face peers at me from behind its wing. Out steps a tiny woman, smiling radiantly.

She is five or six inches tall, and her face is neither beautiful nor ugly, but like a child's drawing contains only those essentials necessary to make it recognizable. Instantly I realize she is the embodiment of all beauty. Her smile becomes more radiant, dazzling me. She is pleased by my recognition of her. My brain spins. It is all true! There is beauty beyond what I can imagine! There is a force somewhere that knows of my uniqueness and has judged me deserving, revealing itself. She nods, reading my thoughts, and somehow lets me know her own happiness at releasing me from ignorance. Everything is changed! I'll never be ashamed again!

"Don't worry," she says. "We know you. We've been watching you. You're a good boy."

Together we levitate in the air, ascending through brightness into darkness. I sense she is leaving me.

"Where are you?"

"I'm here."

"When will I see you again?"

"When the time is right."

"Goodbye." I send my voice into the darkness. "Goodbye."

Or I am a running dog—a lean black dog chasing Flossie through the woods. Effortless speed. My paws barely touch the sand as I streak past the underbrush. I could go on all day, never tiring, never stumbling. Flossie's white hindquarters flash against the green, leaning first to the left and then to the right as she cuts in and out between the trees. Her shanks tremble as she clears a fallen log. Powerful limbs propel me high into the air. I'm almost on her. Coming down, I'm right in stride, all four feet close together, back legs snapping out the instant they strike the ground. She's tiring. I nip the soft flesh beside her backbone. Now her whole body quivers even as she runs. I push with my shoulder, breaking her stride, and leap on her back.

Stillness. We are in a clearing. The sand is hard and hot from the sun. She whimpers under me.

"Frank! Frank!"

A voice. Far away.

"Fraaaank!"

Repeated into meaninglessness, it ceases to be my name. Only an odd sound. Strange floating voices calling out. Voices that don't expect to be answered, like the voices of ghosts.

"Fraaaank!"

Why are they calling? Whom are they calling?

I remember waking up one night in my bed. The instant my eyes opened I was totally awake, aware of the stillness of the house and the hard white moonlight pouring in through the screen door in the kitchen. Lifting my blue jeans from the floor I crept quietly out of the house and stood naked in the yard, shaking them in case a scorpion had climbed into the material for warmth. The moon bathed my body like cool water, making my skin pale and showing up dozens of small scabies scars on my chest and arms. I touched them abstractedly with a fingertip, faintly sad that they were almost gone. (The disease itself had been uncomfortable, too itchy, but the marks amused me. Any kind of body occurrence was a source of satisfaction. I'd charted the course of a worm under the skin of my foot for weeks before it finally died.) I slipped on the jeans and went to the kennel.

They weren't asleep. Gathered at the door, their tails wagging, they seemed to understand the need for silence. Flossie swallowed a yelp as I entered. Like a skinny Buddha on the concrete floor I let them surround me, dealing out equitable love to them all, nodding my head to avoid their wet kisses. But after a few moments they left me and rambled nervously around the runway.

Something was wrong. They were worked up. Penny stood with her muzzle against the chicken wire, her body shaking and her ears laid low. Dansker paced around the fence like a caged lioness, stopping every few strides to lift her head and sniff the air. Even Flossie was behaving strangely, starting off for a corner of the kennel only to stop in midstride for no apparent reason and shy off in another direction. I kept quite still and watched them, aware now of a certain alertness in myself. It was as if we were waiting for something.

On the other side of the fence white sand stretched away into the distance. Smooth and luminous as a field of snow it ran out to the edge of the woods, stopping abruptly at a line of absolute blackness under the trees. In bright suspension up above were the staggered tops of the pines, moon-lit, like floating Christmas trees. Two or three stars gleamed weakly near the horizon. Nothing moved.

As if responding to an inner signal, a command that only she could hear, Dansker broke and ran directly at the fence, leaping up at the last moment to crash heavily against the wire. She fell to the ground, backed up, and jumped again, this time a little higher. Wincing involuntarily as she hit the concrete, I started toward her. I took one step—one step that she saw from the corner of her eye—and stopped. Her upper lip slid back and the short hair on the back of her neck rose straight into the air. Unable to believe that a dog I had slept with, wrestled with, ridden like a horse, and separated from fights with my bare hands would ever attack me, I took another step. She opened her mouth, cocking her head to one side, and faked an attack, lunging forward with terrific speed and stopping only at the last moment. Snarling—a sound so utterly feral I wouldn't have believed it possible in a tamed animal—she watched me carefully, ready to leap. I backed away, my eyes holding hers. (Or perhaps hers holding mine?) Flossie and Penny were in separate corners, very still, leaning against the wire. They watched me sideways, their heads low.

When I felt my back touch the wall I lowered my arms and stood quietly. Again and again Dansker ran at the fence, jumping higher with each attempt. It seemed to me she was taking a lot of punishment in the falls but it didn't faze her. After a dozen tries she made a magnificent, soaring leap that took her almost to the top. Hind legs scrabbling frenetically, her unsheathed nails caught the chicken-wire at the last possible instant. With one awkward, twisting, desperate thrust she was up and over, falling through the air to the sand on the other side and away like a jack rabbit.

Flossie and Penny went simultaneously insane, running at the fence with complete abandon. They seemed to know they hadn't a hope of getting over and threw themselves against the wire as if to beat it down with the weight of their bodies.

After a moment's hesitation I went over and opened the gate. Still they threw themselves at the fence.

"Hey Flossie! Penny! This way."

They turned, saw the open gate, and made a dash for it, their hind legs slipping out from under them. Streaking past my feet they hit the sand and leaned into a wide turn, running full tilt toward the woods. Flossie looked like a greyhound, her body folding with each stride as if her spine were one long hinge with the pin in the middle, opening and closing, opening and closing as she ran, her white paws barely touching the ground. Nearing the woods they seemed to run faster. One moment they were there, and the next they were gone, swallowed by the blackness under the trees.

I walked out across the sand, following their path for twenty or thirty yards, and then stopped. My shadow was ink black. Kneeling down, I raised my arm to make a swan and watched its beak open as I moved my thumb. My hands flapping, I did an eagle, then an alligator with teeth (very tricky) and a devil's head. Drawing patterns in the sand, I combined them with the shadows. Finally bored, I sat back on my heels and watched the woods.

After an hour or two I lay down. In the morning the sun would wake me while the others still slept.

The dogs returned three days later. I found them gathered in the yard one morning, wagging their tails, slinking sheepishly away as I approached, all three of them mewing pathetically in an orgy of self-abasement. When they understood I wasn't going to beat them they leaped on me joyfully, licking my neck and arms and tugging at my jeans. I took them out to the kennel and fed them, picking off the sand burrs while they ate. Except for ravenous hunger and a few scratches they didn't seem any the worse for wear.

It wasn't the same after that. For some reason the kennel didn't appeal to me any more. I don't think it was so much Dansker's behavior (she was a dog after all, and I knew any dog would regress if pushed hard enough) as it was the mysteriousness of what had happened. Why had they been so eager to get out? I realized I would never know, and my inability to share their most passionate moments disillusioned me. They had their own cabal from which I was excluded, and try as I might I would never really understand them. The discovery that the dogs, like humans, could not be taken for granted was hard for me.

My bike had grown rusty from neglect. I oiled the pedals and the seat springs, crammed cup grease into the axles, and pumped the tires to sixty pounds. To hell with Chula Vista! It was only seven miles to town, and nine to the beach. I went into the house and put on a shirt. Stealing sixty cents from my mother's change purse seemed the most natural thing in the world, although as far as I can remember it was my first theft. I did it dreamily, automatically, as one cleans one's nails.

Pedaling down the empty coral road toward the highway I swerved in and out to avoid potholes, or jerked the front wheel in the air when forced to cross them head on. The fenders rattled constantly, making a tremendous racket, but I knew they wouldn't come off. It was a strong, well-built bike, a lightweight with thin tires, designed for speed. I didn't bother to look up the side roads for rabbits. At the highway I turned right, savoring the sudden smoothness of the asphalt, and bending over the handlebars to cut wind resistance, settled down into a slow, steady rhythm.

The road cut straight through the woods for about a mile, without a single curve or landmark. I marked my progress by familiar sights—a rusted-out mailbox half buried in the sand, a peculiarly twisted pine tree, or an old tire. Halfway to the railroad tracks a Dr. Pepper sign hung crookedly from a telephone pole, its peeling surface pock-marked with .22-caliber holes.

At the crossing of the Atlantic Coast Line civilization began. The man who tended the barrier lived in a small frame house close to the tracks. Set down in a slight depression, it had a peculiar fascination after the long ride through the pine wastes. Lush tropical plants with wide, dark-green leaves surrounded the building. Shade trees closed in from three sides and hung over the roof, hiding everything in unnatural darkness. Burst seedpods and fallen vegetation stained the dingy white walls, dripping down the clapboard like ivy in streaks of green and black. Beads of moisture clung to every surface. Very rarely the wife could be seen moving about on the lawn with a hose. She was fat and gray-haired and never looked up as I passed, as if deafened by the trains. It was vaguely sinister.

The tracks themselves were crossed in a single fender-rattling instant. Trains were rare. If one came I'd always wait and watch it go by, sometimes placing a penny on the tracks to be flattened, or a stick between the ties to be knocked over. When the train had gone stillness would reclaim the world. I'd look down at the rails, gleaming in the sun, perfectly static, and the sand on the ties, and the flattened penny till it seemed impossible the train had ever existed.

A short spur led to the deserted factory, its cantilevered loading platforms hanging empty and weatherbeaten over the rusty tracks. I'd explored it many times, climbing in through some loose boards. There was nothing inside but a few piles of burlap bags and the smell of chemical fertilizer.

Now the road began to curve and houses appeared on either side—houses with lawns, driveways, and hedges. Sprinklers turned, throwing spray into the air and dark half-moons on the sidewalk. In the quiet and coolness pedaling seemed easier. Sitting straight I followed the smooth curves effortlessly, my arms hanging at my sides. A group of kids playing on the sidewalk stopped to watch me go by, automatically falling silent until I was past. They took me for a redneck. I heard their voices starting up behind me once I was out of sight.

Mile after mile of well-kept houses slipped by. At the first gas station I stopped for a Coke and checked the tire pressure. I liked gas stations. You could hang around as long as you wanted and no one took any notice. Sitting on the ground in a shady corner with my back against the wall, I took small sips at the Coke and made it last.

Is it the mindlessness of childhood that opens up the world? Today nothing happens in a gas station. I'm eager to leave, to get where I'm going, and the station, like some huge paper cutout, or a Hollywood set, is simply a façade. But at thirteen, sitting with my back against the wall, it was a marvelous place to be. The delicious smell of gasoline, the cars coming and going, the free air hose, the half-heard voices buzzing in the background—these things hung musically in the air, filling me with a sense of well-being. In ten minutes my psyche would be topped up like the tanks of the automobiles.

Downtown the streets were crowded with shoppers. I cut in and out between the slow-moving cars, enjoying my superior mobility. At a red light I took hold of the tailgate of a chicken truck and let it pull me a couple of blocks. Peeling off at the foot of Los Olas Boulevard, I coasted up to the bike rack in front of the Sunset Theater.

It cost nine cents to get in. I bought my ticket, paused in the lobby to select a Powerhouse candy bar, and climbed to the balcony. The theater was almost empty and no one objected when I draped my legs over the seat in front. On the screen was a western, with Randolph Scott as the sheriff. I recognized a cheap process called Trucolor and hissed spontaneously, smiling foolishly at the empty darkness around me afterwards. Except for the gunfights the film was dull and I amused myself finding anachronisms.

The feature was better, an English movie with Ann Todd as a neurotic pianist and James Mason as her teacher. I was sorry when the house lights came on.

Outside, blinking against the sun, I left my bike in the rack and wandered down the street. Something was happening in front of the dime store. I could see a crowd of kids gathered at the doors and a policeman attempting to keep order. I slipped inside behind his back. The place was a madhouse, jammed with hundreds of shrieking children, all pressing toward one of the aisles where some kind of demonstration was going on.

"What's happening?" I asked a kid as I elbowed past.

"It's Ramos and Ricardo," he shouted. "The twins from California."

I pushed my way to the front rank and looked up at the raised platform.

There, under a spotlight, two Oriental gentlemen in natty blue suits were doing some amazing things with yo-yos. Tiny, neat men, no bigger than children, they stared abstractedly off into space while yo-yos flew from their hands, zooming in every direction as if under their own power, leaping out from small fists in arcs, circles, and straight lines. I stared open-mouthed as a yo-yo was thrown down and *stayed down*, spinning at the end of its string a fraction of an inch above the floor.

"Walking the Dog," said the twin, and lowered his yo-yo to the floor. It skipped along beside him for a yard or so and mysteriously returned to his palm.

"The Pendulum," said the other twin, and threw down a yo-yo. "Sleeping," he said, pointing to the toy as it spun at the end of its string. He gathered the line like so much loose spaghetti, making a kind of cat's cradle with his fingers, and gently rocked the spinning yo-yo back and forth through the center. "Watch end of trick closely," he said smiling, and suddenly dropped everything. Instead of the tangled mess we'd all expected the yo-yo wound up safely in his palm.

"Loop-the-Loop." He threw a yo-yo straight ahead. When it returned he didn't catch it, but executed a subtle flick of his wrist and sent it back out again. Five, ten, twenty times. "Two Hands Loop-the-Loop," he said, adding another, alternating so that as one flew away from his right hand the other flew in toward his left.

"Pickpocket," said the other twin, raising the flap of his jacket. He threw the yo-yo between his legs, wrapping the string around his thigh. As he looked out over the crowd the yo-yo dropped, perfectly placed, into his trouser pocket. Laughing, the kids applauded.

I spent the whole afternoon in one spot, watching them, not even moving when they took breaks for fear I'd lose my place. When it was over I spent my last money on a yo-yo, a set of extra strings, and a pamphlet explaining all the tricks, starting from the easiest and working up to the hardest.

Walking back to the bike I was so absorbed a mail truck almost ran me down. I did my first successful trick standing by the rack, a simple but rather spectacular exercise called Around the World. Smiling, I put the yo-yo in my pocket and pulled out the bike. I knew I was going to be good at it.

8
A Yo-Yo
Going Down,
a Mad Squirrel
Coming Up

THE common yo-yo is crudely made, with a thick shank between two widely spaced wooden disks. The string is knotted or stapled to the shank. With such an instrument nothing can be done except the simple up-down movement. My yo-yo, on the other hand, was a perfectly balanced construction of hard wood, slightly weighted, flat, with only a sixteenth of an inch between the halves. The string was not attached to the shank, but looped over it in such a way as to allow the wooden part to spin freely on its own axis. The gyroscopic effect thus created kept the yo-yo stable in all attitudes.

I started at the beginning of the book and quickly mastered the novice, intermediate, and advanced stages, practicing all day every day in the woods across the street from my house. Hour after hour of practice, never moving to the next trick until the one at hand was mastered.

The string was tied to my middle finger, just behind the nail. As I threw—with your palm up, make a fist; throw down your hand, fingers unfolding, as if you were casting grain—a short bit of string would tighten across the sensitive pad of flesh at the tip of my finger. That was the critical area. After a number of weeks I could interpret the condition of the string, the presence of any imperfections on the shank, but most importantly the exact amount of spin or inertial energy left in the yo-yo at any given moment—all from that bit of string on my fingertip. As the throwing motion became more and more natural I found I could make the yo-yo "sleep" for an astonishing length of time—fourteen or fifteen seconds—and still have enough spin left to bring it back to my hand. Gradually the basic moves became reflexes. Sleeping, twirling, swinging, and precise aim. Without thinking, without even looking, I could run through trick after trick involving various combinations of the elemental skills, switching from one to the other in a smooth continuous flow. On particularly good days I would hum a tune under my breath and do it all in time to the music.

Flicking the yo-yo expressed something. The sudden, potentially comic extension of one's arm to twice its length. The precise neatness of it, intrinsically soothing, as if relieving an inner tension too slight to be noticeable, the way a man might hitch up his pants simply to enact a reassuring gesture. It felt good. The comfortable weight in one's hand, the smooth, rapid descent down the string, ending with a barely audible snap as the yo-yo hung balanced, spinning, pregnant with force and the slave of one's fingertip. That it was vaguely masturbatory seems inescapable. I doubt that half the pubescent boys in America could have been captured by any other means, as, in the heat of the fad, half of them were. A single Loop-the-Loop might represent, in some mysterious way, the act of masturbation, but to break down the entire repertoire into the three stages of throw, trick, and return representing erection, climax, and detumescence seems immoderate.

The greatest pleasure in yo-yoing was an abstract pleasure—watching the dramatization of simple physical laws, and realizing they would never fail if a trick was done correctly. The geometric purity of it! The string wasn't just a string, it was a tool in the enactment of theorems. It was a line, an idea. And the top was an entirely different sort of idea, a gyroscope, capable of storing energy and of interacting with the line. I remember the first time I did a particularly lovely trick, one in which the sleeping yo-yo is swung from right to left while the string is interrupted by an extended index finger. Momentum carries the yo-yo in a circular path around the finger, but instead of completing the arc the yo-yo falls on the taut string between the performer's hands, where it continues to spin in an upright position. My pleasure at that moment was as much from the beauty of the experiment as from pride. Snapping apart my hands I sent the yo-yo into the air above my head, bouncing it off nothing, back into my palm.

I practiced the yo-yo because it pleased me to do so, without the slightest application of will power. It wasn't ambition that drove me, but the nature of yo-yoing. The yo-yo represented my first organized attempt to control the

outside world. It fascinated me because I could see my
progress in clearly defined stages, and because the inti-
macy of it, the almost spooky closeness I began to feel
with the instrument in my hand, seemed to ensure that
nothing irrelevant would interfere. I was, in the language
of jazz, "up tight" with my yo-yo, and finally free, in one
small area at least, of the paralyzing sloppiness of life in
general.

The first significant problem arose in the attempt to do
fifty consecutive Loop-the-Loops. After ten or fifteen the
yo-yo invariably started to lean and the throws became
less clean, resulting in loss of control. I almost skipped the
whole thing because fifty seemed excessive. Ten made the
point. But there it was, written out in the book. To qualify
as an expert you had to do fifty, so fifty I would do.

It took me two days, and I wouldn't have spent a moment more. All those Loop-the-Loops were hard on the
strings. Time after time the shank cut them and the
yo-yo went sailing off into the air. It was irritating, not
only because of the expense (strings were a nickel each,
and fabricating your own was unsatisfactory), but because
a random element had been introduced. About the only
unforeseeable disaster in yo-yoing was to have your string
break, and here was a trick designed to do exactly that.
Twenty-five would have been enough. If you could do
twenty-five clean Loop-the-Loops you could do fifty or a
hundred. I supposed they were simply trying to sell strings
and went back to the more interesting tricks.

The witty nonsense of Eating Spaghetti, the surprise of
The Twirl, the complex neatness of Cannonball, Backwards round the World, or Halfway round the World—I
could do them all, without false starts or sloppy endings.
I could do every trick in the book. Perfectly.

The day was marked on the kitchen calendar (God Gave
Us Bluebell Natural Bottled Gas). I got on my bike and
rode into town. Pedaling along the highway I worked out
with the yo-yo to break in a new string. The twins were
appearing at the dime store.

I could hear the crowd before I turned the corner. Kids
were coming on bikes and on foot from every corner of
town, rushing down the streets like madmen. Three or four
policemen were busy keeping the street clear directly in

front of the store, and in a small open space around the doors some of the more adept kids were running through their tricks, showing off to the general audience or stopping to compare notes with their peers. Standing at the edge with my yo-yo safe in my pocket, it didn't take me long to see I had them all covered. A boy in a sailor hat could do some of the harder tricks, but he missed too often to be a serious threat. I went inside.

As Ramos and Ricardo performed I watched their hands carefully, noticing little differences in style, and technique. Ricardo was a shade classier, I thought, although Ramos held an edge in the showy two-handed stuff. When they were through we went outside for the contest.

"Everybody in the alley!" Ramos shouted, his head bobbing an inch or two above the others. "Contest starting now in the alley!" A hundred excited children followed the twins into an alley beside the dime store and lined up against the wall.

"Attention all kids!" Ramos yelled, facing us from the middle of the street like a drill sergeant. "To qualify for contest you got to Rock the Cradle. You got to rock yo-yo in cradle four time. Four time! Okay? Three time no good. Okay. Everybody happy?" There were murmurs of disappointment and some of the kids stepped out of line. The rest of us closed ranks. Yo-yos flicked nervously as we waited. "Winner receive grand prize. Special Black Beauty Prize Yo-Yo with Diamonds," said Ramos, gesturing to his brother who smiled and held up the prize, turning it in the air so we could see the four stones set on each side. ("The crowd gasped . . ." I want to write. Of course they didn't. They didn't make a sound, but the impact of the diamond yo-yo was obvious.) We'd never seen anything like it. One imagined how the stones would gleam as it revolved, and how much prettier the tricks would be. The ultimate yo-yo! The only one in town! Who knew what feats were possbile with such an instrument? All around me a fierce, nervous resolve was settling into the contestants, suddenly skittish as racehorses.

"Ricardo will show trick with Grand Prize Yo-Yo. Rock the Cradle four time!"

"One!" cried Ramos.

"Two!" the kids joined in.

"Three!" It was really beautiful. He did it so slowly you would have thought he had all the time in the world. I counted seconds under my breath to see how long he made it sleep.

"Four!" said the crowd.

"Thirteen," I said to myself as the yo-yo snapped back into his hand. Thirteen seconds. Excellent time for that particular trick.

"Attention all kids!" Ramos announced. "Contest start now at head of line."

The first boy did a sloppy job of gathering his string but managed to rock the cradle quickly four times.

"Okay." Ramos tapped him on the shoulder and moved to the next boy, who fumbled. "Out." Ricardo followed, doing an occasional Loop-the-Loop with the diamond yo-yo. "Out . . . out . . . okay," said Ramos as he worked down the line.

There was something about the man's inexorable advance that unnerved me. His decisions were fast, and there was no appeal. To my surprise I felt my palms begin to sweat. Closer and closer he came, his voice growing louder, and then suddenly he was standing in front of me. Amazed, I stared at him. It was as if he'd appeared out of thin air.

"What happen boy, you swarrow bubble gum?"

The laughter jolted me out of it. Blushing, I threw down my yo-yo and executed a slow Rock the Cradle, counting the four passes and hesitating a moment at the end so as not to appear rushed.

"Okay." He tapped my shoulder. "Good."

I wiped my hands on my blue jeans and watched him move down the line. "Out . . . out . . . out." He had a large mole on the back of his neck.

Seven boys qualified. Coming back, Ramos called out, "Next trick Backward Round the World! Okay? Go!"

The first two boys missed, but the third was the kid in the sailor hat. Glancing quickly to see that no one was behind him, he hunched up his shoulder, threw, and just barely made the catch. There was some loose string in his hand, but not enough to disqualify him.

Number four missed, as did number five, and it was my turn. I stepped forward, threw the yo-yo almost straight up over my head, and as it began to fall pulled very gently to add some speed. It zipped neatly behind my legs and there was nothing more to do. My head turned to one side, I stood absolutely still and watched the yo-yo come in over my shoulder and slap into my hand. I added a Loop-the-Loop just to show the tightness of the string.

"Did you see that?" I heard someone say.

Number seven missed, so it was between myself and the boy in the sailor hat. His hair was bleached by the sun and combed up over his forehead in a pompadour, held from behind by the white hat. He was a year or two older than me. Blinking his blue eyes nervously, he adjusted the tension of his string.

"Next trick Cannonball! Cannonball! You go first this time," Ramos said to me.

Kids had gathered in a circle around us, those in front quiet and attentive, those in back jumping up and down to get a view. "Move back for room," Ricardo said, pushing them back. "More room, please."

I stepped into the center and paused, looking down at the ground. It was a difficult trick. The yo-yo had to land exactly on the string and there was a chance I'd miss the first time. I knew I wouldn't miss twice. "Can I have one practice?"

Ramos and Ricardo consulted in their mother tongue, and then Ramos held up his hands. "Attention all kids! Each boy have one practice before trick."

The crowed was silent, watching me. I took a deep breath and threw, following the fall of the yo-yo with my eyes, turning slightly, matador-fashion, as it passed me. My finger caught the string, the yo-yo came up and over, and missed. Without pausing I threw again. "Second time," I yelled, so there would be no misunderstanding. The circle had been too big. This time I made it small, sacrificing beauty for security. The yo-yo fell where it belonged and spun for a moment. (A moment I don't rush, my arms widespread, my eyes locked on the spinning toy. The Trick! There it is, brief and magic, right before your eyes! My hands are frozen in the middle of a deaf-and-dumb sentence, holding the whole airy, tenuous statement aloft for everyone to see.) With a quick snap I broke up the trick and made my catch.

Ramos nodded. "Okay. Very good. Now next boy."

Sailor-hat stepped forward, wiping his nose with the back of his hand. He threw once to clear the string.

"One practice," said Ramos.

He nodded.

"C'mon Bobby," someone said. "You can do it."

Bobby threw the yo-yo out to the side, made his move, and missed. "Damn," he whispered. (He said "dahyum.") The second time he got halfway through the trick before his yo-yo ran out of gas and fell impotently off the string. He picked it up and walked away, winding slowly.

Ramos came over and held my hand in the air. "The winner!" he yelled. "Grand prize Black Beauty Diamond Yo-Yo will now be awarded."

Ricardo stood in front of me. "Take off old yo-yo." I loosened the knot and slipped it off. "Put out hand." I held out my hand and he looped the new string on my finger, just behind the nail, where the mark was. "You like Black Beauty," he said, smiling as he stepped back. "Diamond make pretty colors in the sun."

"Thank you," I said.

"Very good with yo-yo. Later we have contest for whole town. Winner go to Miami for State Championship. Maybe you win. Okay?"

"Okay." I nodded. "Thank you."

A few kids came up to look at Black Beauty. I threw it once or twice to get the feel. It seemed a bit heavier than my old one. Ramos and Ricardo were surrounded as the kids called out their favorite tricks.

"Do Pickpocket! Pickpocket!"

"Do the Double Cannonball!"

"Ramos! Ramos! Do the Turkish Army!"

Smiling, waving their hands to ward off the barrage of requests, the twins worked their way through the crowd toward the mouth of the alley. I watched them moving away and was immediately struck by a wave of fierce and irrational panic. "Wait," I yelled, pushing through after them. "Wait!"

I caught them on the street.

"No more today," Ricardo said, and then paused when he saw it was me. "Okay. The champ. What's wrong? Yo-yo no good?"

"No. It's fine."

"Good. You take care of it."

"I wanted to ask when the contest is. The one where you get to go to Miami."

"Later. After school begins." They began to move away. "We have to go home now."

"Just one more thing," I said, walking after them. "What is the hardest trick you know?"

Ricardo laughed. "Hardest trick killing flies in air."

"No, no. I mean a real trick."

They stopped and looked at me. "There is a very hard trick," Ricardo said. "I don't do it, but Ramos does. Because you won the contest he will show you. But only once, so watch carefully."

We stepped into the lobby of the Sunset Theater. Ramos cleared his string. "Watch," he said, and threw. The trick started out like a Cannonball, and then unexpectedly folded up, opened again, and as I watched breathlessly the entire complex web spun around in the air, propelled by Ramos' two hands making slow circles like a swimmer. The end was like the end of a Cannonball.

"That's beautiful," I said, genuinely awed. "What's it called?"

"The Universe."

"The Universe," I repeated.

"Because it goes around and around," said Ramos, "like the planets."

I pedaled out Los Olas Boulevard toward the beach, gliding along the empty sidewalk under the towering royal palms. At the drawbridge I disregarded a "No Bicycles" sign and zipped over at full speed. Even if the bridge-keeper had seen me I'd be gone before he got out the door. I took a right at Lotus Drive and coasted down to my cousin Lucky's house.

"Hey, Lucky!"

No answer. I pulled open the screen door and walked through the kitchen, dining room, and living room on my way to the front porch. From there I could see him out on the sea wall, spearfishing, a long gig held above his head as he walked along, his lean brown body bending slightly over the water.

"Hey, Lucky," I shouted, trotting out to him.

He didn't look up, but froze suddenly, staring down into the water. Just before I reached him he threw the gig. I knew perfectly well he hadn't seen a fish. There was a studied calmness, unlikely if he'd had a real target, and his

throw was subtly overdramatized, like the movements of
Olympic athletes. He was playing, which seemed perfectly
natural to me, but he covered it up because he thought he
was too old. Without actually thinking about it I understood, and never called him on his white lies. Lucky was always in rehearsal for great, unspecified trials ahead. I liked
him.

"Shit," he said. "A mullet big as Shadow." (His dog.)
Pulling the string hand over hand to retrieve the gig he
peered into the water, feigning frustration. "Almost got
him."

"Maybe he'll come back in."

We ambled along the sea wall.

"Two girls moved into one of Schmidt's cottages yesterday. Secretaries from up North on vacation."

"I got a yo-yo since I saw you," I said.

"Judy and Cissie. Judy's tits are so big she has to watch
it going around corners. The other one has red hair down
to her waist. I saw her take it down last night."

"What do you mean you saw her?"

"Just what I said." He gazed down into the water.

I waited a moment, but he would say no more. "How?"
I felt a slight stiffening in my neck and my ears grew
warm. I wasn't at all sure I wanted him to answer.

"You'll find out." He hefted the long gig in the air, toss-
ing it lightly to change his grip. "Maybe."

"Look at the crab!" A small white crab was pulling at a
pop bottle on the sandy bottom. "You going to hit him?"

He shook his head. "I hate those ugly shit-eaters. The
only thing worse is a land crab."

"Or a snake."

"I don't mind snakes," he said.

"I won a yo-yo contest at the dime store today."

Once again he stopped, crouching, and motioned me
back with his free hand. "Hold it, hold it."

"The mullet?"

After a moment he straightened up. "No. Just some sea-
weed. The hell with it."

We cut back across the neighbor's lawn, feeling the short
tough grass between our toes. Lucky walked quickly. "The
girls went up to the beach."

"How old are they?"

"Twenty or twenty-one."

"What do you call them girls for, then?" I said. "They're not girls."

"Well, whatever they are they went to the beach and that's where I'm going."

"Can you lend me a dime? I'll have enough for a banana split at Ray's."

"I guess so. Daddy gave me two bucks yesterday for cleaning his reels."

We dropped off the gig in Lucky's room, drank a glass of milk in the kitchen, and started for the beach. It was only a few blocks so I left my bike. I did a few tricks as we walked along.

"Hey. That's pretty good. Let me try." He threw a few times, trying for a Loop-the Loop.

"I won a contest at the dime store," I said, pulling out Black Beauty. "They gave me this. You can't buy them."

We walked for a while, yo-yoing together, until I felt his hand on my arm. "There they are," he said under his breath, "coming right at us." He undid the yo-yo and gave it back to me. The two girls strolled toward us unhurriedly, white towels draped over their shoulders. "My God," Lucky said distantly, like a man talking in his sleep, "will you look at the boobs on her." I could feel him gathering himself. Nervous energy radiated like an electrical aureole around his body.

"Hi there!" he said in a totally false voice. "How's the water?"

"Hi," said Boobs. "Well, it's just great." They paused without committing themselves, as if just for a moment to catch their breaths.

"We're just going up for a swim ourselves," Lucky improvised. It occurred to me that he had the proper fatuous grown-up tone, but that he was saying everything too fast. The words leaped out of his mouth like machine-gun bullets.

"Who's your little friend?" asked Redhair.

"Oh, that's my cousin Frank," Lucky said quickly, like a tourist guide pointing out some dull local landmark. Staring at my toes I felt a mild anger whipping around in my heart. I might have been skinny, but I certainly wasn't little. I was five feet eight. "He's from up North too, and I sort of look after him."

Lucky was only two or three years older than me, but the process of physical maturation, only just begun in my case, had wreaked most of its changes in him. He was six feet tall, well muscled, and his voice was a smooth baritone. Had I been a little more aware of such things I would have realized that like almost all the Fouchet men he was exceptionally attractive to women.

"Well," said Boobs, moving away. "See you later. C'mon Cissie. I want to get this sand off me."

"Bye," said Lucky, with a little fluttering wave. "See you later, girls."

I tapped him on the arm. "So you look after me, do you?"

"Oh, what the hell," he said weakly.

"Hi there!" I mimicked the weird voice he'd used. "How's the water?"

"Do you realize," said Lucky, moving closer as if afraid of being overheard although we had the sidewalk to ourselves. "Do you realize that in a very few minutes little Miss Titties will be ever so gracefully slipping out of her teeny little bathing suit? Do you realize that her immense, glistening knockers will pop out like a pair of well-oiled basketballs? Do you realize that probably at this very moment she's dancing along to the shower with every last bit of razzamatazz flapping around in the open air?"

I threw my yo-yo nervously. That kind of talk had a strong effect on me. "I wouldn't mind dancing right along with her," I said, aware that I'd struck a good balance between the sort of wisecrack one was supposed to make, and my true feelings—that to be there with her, to hold her and have her like it because I was a man, to learn the mystery from her, to die inside her would be, in no uncertain terms, the best possible thing that could happen. Literally heaven on earth. Even the thought made my hands tremble. My dry throat swallowed nothing.

"You know why girls shouldn't drink beer on the beach?" he asked.

"No. Why?"

"They'll get sand in their Schlitz."

Laughing, we went into Ray's and ordered banana splits.

While Lucky took a workout, swimming parallel to the shore in a steady blind crawl down to the last hotel and back, I lolled in the warm sea, my legs dangling weightless in the sunny green water. I didn't believe in exercise, conscious exercise to build one's muscles. As a skinny kid, a kid so skinny total strangers would come up to me on the street and offer to buy me milkshakes, I had long ago learned to put up with my freak's body. The situation was embarrassing, ridiculous, sometimes unbearable, but I knew it couldn't be changed. Set very deeply in my mind was the idea that any program of self-betterment would be doomed from the start. To change from weakling to strongman, from C student to A student, from bad boy to good boy! I not only believed it couldn't be done, but even that it wasn't worth doing. Success would have made me another person, or an actor hiding the past. And I wouldn't succeed, I would fail. Failure was dangerous, threatening my only reliable source of strength, my pride. I was proud, and God knows why. I had no reason to be. I'd picked it up somewhere and it held me together. Better simply to live in my absurd body and not think about it.

One could always drift in the warm cloudy water, hearing the cries from the beach skipping out like stones over the soft roar of the breakers, watching the immense clouds, feeling the sun on wet hair. There was always the knowledge of one's shadow, an extension of oneself slanting down in a long dark bar, a black column sliding into the depths and into the darkness.

I spent the last few days before school in the woods, attempting to re-create the trick Ramos had shown me in the lobby of the Sunset Theater. I'd broken it down into three steps, the world, the solar system, and the galaxies, the sum of which was The Universe. The world and the solar system were within my abilities, but in the galaxies stage the yo-yo would run out of gas or the string would tangle. My strategy was to go back and practice the simple Cannonball for duration, snapping my throws out more and more evenly, trying for perfect balance so the string wouldn't touch the inner walls of the yo-yo. At the same time I speeded up the first two stages, attempting to feel The Universe not so much as three separate maneuvers but as one continuous rhythmic statement. Progress was slow but steady, and had I not been interrupted by the opening of school, I might have learned it in a week.

A sad fact about school was the prolonged separation from Tobey. I was a year ahead and had to attend the Central School in town while he finished his last term at the branch grammar school. We accepted it in numb silence, unable to rebel against the official powers we mistakenly believed to be so much stronger than ourselves. We couldn't even ride the same school bus. We started our days together though, meeting in the early morning for a few games of mumblety-peg or property before riding up to the bus stop a half-mile away.

A surprising number of kids gathered at the stop each morning, all of them younger than us. Some of the smallest we'd never even seen before, standing with their only slightly older brothers or sisters, clutching their lunch bags and watching us with big eyes. They were a pretty sad-looking lot, even by our standards—dirty, dressed in rags, hair stringy and uncombed, ankles black with caked dust. They came on foot, in twos and threes. We'd zip by them on the road, or if we were late (as they never were), we'd skid rakishly to a halt where they waited at the mail-boxes, feeling like big shots as we hid our bikes in the woods. Luckily they all went to the branch school. At Central School they'd have been treated badly.

Later in the year those scruffy kids became a symbol of our separation, not because they forced us apart, but because they came to represent all the things in which each of us was involved without the other's knowledge. I began to notice after a couple of weeks, when the kids, at first so quiet, would smile when Tobey showed up, and even gather around his bike to push the button on his electric horn. Before long we were picking them up on the road, stacking them on the handlebars, the crossbars, and the fenders for the ride out to the highway, sometimes even carrying the smallest on our backs. They were too shy to open up with me (my Northern accent frightened them) but from overhearing bits here and there I learned that Tobey had become the champion of the whole Chula Vista contingent, and on more than one occasion had used his fists in the schoolyard protecting them. I was proud of him, but a bit sad, too, since he never mentioned what was going on, and even changed the subject when I brought it up. There was a trace of envy in my heart, probably because my own position at school was anonymous. But I was more proud of him than anything else.

My bus came first. I hoped for an accident or a flat tire, but it always appeared at the dip in the road down by the dump, yellow and inexorable, engine wheezing as it approached. My secondary fantasy, once the bus came into view, was that it would drive right past without stopping. But that never happened either.

The driver, Mrs. Moon, was short, fat, and hyperthyroid, with kinky red hair and blotched skin. She stared straight ahead every morning, her face set in an unchanging grimace of irritation. She never even looked at me, just pulled the door shut with a beefy arm and threw in the gears. As her short legs jabbed at the pedals her skirt rose under the large white dinner napkin, fresh each morning, that lay on her knees. She drove a steady thirty-five miles an hour over potholes, dead snakes, and fallen vegetation, never veering, never wavering, as if the bus represented an irresistible force separate from the petty realities of life.

I didn't like school. The kids were polite but distant. Well-dressed, healthy, athletic, always with a dollar in their pockets, they were town kids who'd known one another all their lives. I didn't fit. My Northern accent and relatively large vocabulary (from reading) must have seemed suspiciously classy, and yet I dressed like a red neck and lived in red-neck territory. They didn't know what to make of me, and since there was nothing particularly attractive about me they had no great desire to find out. I'd be gone soon anyway, they assumed, back to wherever I'd come from. They were good kids, though, and had circumstances been more favorable, or had I been less shy, I'm sure I would have made friends with some of them. Although as Florida kids they were preoccupied with things physical— swimming, diving, basketball, and baseball went on all year round—they never teased me about being so thin. Instead they emanated a kind of mild concern, as if I were suffering from an illness for which I couldn't be held responsible.

The class hours merged into a day of boredom. The books were dull, mechanical texts from which the teachers rarely strayed. Voices droned at an impossibly slow pace, ideas emerged sluggishly, words and phrases repeated over

and over became incomprehensible—my mind could find
nothing to attach itself to. I was cast adrift, and it frightened me. One could disappear in such a state, simply cease
knowing the difference between up and down, or who one
was, or where one was. So I put myself to sleep and
accepted the mediocre grades I'd done nothing to earn.

I liked the twenty minutes before the first bell. There
was a broad-jump put in one of the athletic fields and the
kids from the buses would line up for turns. I'd take a long
run, kick off, and sail through the air knowing the sand
would be soft at the other end. No one kept records. When
you'd jumped you simply waited for the next man, marked
his leap on the sand, and ran back to the end of the line.
The best jump was marked by a peg or a schoolbook, but
only the older kids were concerned about that. Once or
twice I came within a foot of it.

Lunch hour I often went to the Y.M.C.A. and sat at a
favorite table near the window where I could watch the
other kids or the cars going by outside as I ate my sandwich. If I had a quarter I'd buy a deviled egg on white and
an orange soda—a combination my body craved so strongly
my hands would tremble uncontrollably as I unwrapped the
cellophane. Most often I had a sandwich from home.

(I am intensely hungry, and yet the hunger is held down,
deep in my body, a smothered force that never reaches my
mouth. I've carried the paper bag all day. The top edge is
rolled and crinkled, as soft as cloth under my fingers. The
kids are laughing and yelling at ping-pong or the pinball
machine. Why do I even open the bag? Every step closer
to the sandwich drives the hunger deeper until my mouth
is too dry to eat anything. The wax paper comes off. I already know the sandwich is completely unacceptable. There
is no question. It's an imitation. It isn't real. Eating it
wouldn't nourish me. Look at the paper bag! Look at the
wrapping! The whole thing is a fraud. I separate the bread.
Bacon fat. Lunch meat. I am neither disgusted nor attracted. The sight has no meaning. It isn't food. I look up,
vaguely uneasy. I should get up from the table and go
away. There's no point in staying. I have no money, nor any
way to get some before the hour is out. I should move, yet
something holds me. I can't eat and I can't not eat. I stare
into the paradox with catatonic rapture—a moment more,

a moment more. Hunger is transcended as my mind achieves perfect balance, perfect stillness. The sandwich lies in its waxed paper. My hands lie on the table beside it. I can't move.)

Sometimes after school I'd hitchhike out to the beach and hang around the Olympic-size salt-water pool where all the kids were. I achieved a certain celebrity doing tricks on the yo-yo, and even though no one knew my name they accepted me as part of the scene. When it got dark I'd go over to Lucky's house.

"Frank, don't you want any more than that?" Gertrude asked. "You eat like a bird, child."

"Thank you, ma'm. I'm full."

"His stomach's shrunk," said Uncle Victor, unfolding the *Fort Lauderdale News* over his recently emptied plate. "Coffee. I'm late for the A.A. meeting."

"Leslie, would you clear the table, please?"

Lucky's sister began stacking dishes. I helped her carry them back to the kitchen. Leslie was a tall, good-looking girl, a swimming champion at sixteen. She smiled as I brought in a platter. "Thanks." I always blushed when she smiled at me, and the fact that I desperately wanted not to blush but to look straight in her eyes didn't make any difference.

Back at the table Lucky was talking to his father about Sneezy, his pet squirrel. "But Daddy, he's better since he was fixed. He gets better every day."

"A week more. Then we'll either put him to sleep at the vet's or let him go in the woods, whichever you prefer." Victor had a habit of not looking at his son while talking to him. It was odd—he'd look at everyone else, moving from face to face while addressing Lucky.

"He always minds me," Lucky said, betraying some emotion.

"It's unpleasant, but it has to be done. He bit the mailman and he bit George." (The Negro handyman.) "I could be sued." He pushed back his chair and took a cup of coffee from Gertrude's outstretched hand on his way to the living room. He walked with his head slightly bent, as if he were too tall for the house.

"Damn," Lucky said when we were alone.

"Don't let them gas him. Set him free in the woods in Chula Vista."

"The worst thing is I lose my cover."

"What do you mean?"

"My cover. My excuse if I ever get caught around Schmidt's cottages at night. I'd just say I was looking for Sneezy."

"Of course." I was struck with admiration at his thoroughness. "The girls."

"Damn." He drummed his fingers on the table impatiently. "I'll never think of anything as good."

"Are you going tonight?"

Lucky looked up, hesitating a moment before he answered. "Yes."

"I'll go with you."

"You might not see anything, you know. Sometimes the blinds are down."

"Leslie honey," Gertrude called from the kitchen. "You better hurry. I see your date coming down the drive."

I stood in the darkness doing stages one and two of The Universe. Black Beauty picked up stray fingers of light and sparkled dimly in the air like a dying fireworks wheel. My mind wasn't on the yo-yo. I waited, listening for Lucky on the other side of the hedge. He was due back from reconnaissance.

"Phsst!"

The trick fell apart in my hands.

"Phsst!" he called from the other side.

"Okay. I'm here," I whispered.

"The coast is clear. Come on through."

Bending down to get through the almost invisible break in the hedge I had a moment of panic. The idea of getting caught at something as shameful as peeping through windows was no laughing matter. I'd done bad things, but never anything to earn my parents' scorn. I'd been able to hold my head high and fight them openly. But if I got caught at this I'd be ashamed before my enemies.

Coming up on the other side, inhaling as I rose, the perfume of the flowers rushed into my brain. A lush aroma, thick with sweetness, thick as blood, and spiced with the clean acid of tropical greenery. My heart pounded like a drowning swimmer's as the perfume took me over, pouring into my lungs like ambrosial soup. Slightly dizzy, I took a step and bumped into Lucky.

"Sorry," I whispered, stepping back. His dark shape moved in front of me and I could see Sneezy riding his shoulder. "Chtt-chtt." The squirrel spat in the air.

"Follow me and stay in the shadows," Lucky said calmly, and moved quickly away along the hedge, his arm brushing slightly against the leaves. Sneezy ran over the back of his neck to the other shoulder, still spitting, his small body writhing with excitement.

As we got near the cottage Lucky stopped. "Walk naturally across the lawn. There's a place behind those bushes over there." He moved out over the grass and disappeared into the shadows. I followed an instant later, beads of nervous sweat collecting on my brow. The front of the cottage was dark, but Lucky had told me to expect that. The girls lived in back, in a large room with two windows. As I came up behind him I could see the lights winking through the bushes.

"There," he whispered, pointing to a small hollow in the undergrowth. I moved into position. Sneezy jumped from his shoulder to mine, startling me so severely I almost fell over. His sharp claws dug through my shirt into the skin. Wincing, I listened to Lucky.

"If you pull back this branch you get a clear view of both windows," he said, demonstrating. I looked out, my heart leaping like Ricardo's yo-yo. The blinds were down to within six inches of the sill. Every now and then something moved in the room. "Chtt-chtt," said Sneezy into my ear, his claws scrabbling for better balance on my small shoulder. "You keep him," Lucky said. "I'm going closer."

Alone, with the scent of flowers trickling down my throat like syrup, I watched the windows. Was that a pair of arms moving behind the blinds? Legs perhaps? An immense stone rolled over in my chest. Good God! Was that a thigh? Was that a bare shoulder? Lust exploded inside me, pure, hot lust bathing me like internal sunshine. I hardly noticed Lucky creeping through a bed of greenery to kneel at the corner of the window. "Chtt-chtt!" Sneezy ran up on top of my head and down again, his claws like needles. Lucky leaned forward, his hands touching the wall.

It was Judy! Crossing the room in a bathrobe, her bare thighs exposed with every stride! And there was Redhair in a bra and half-slip! Unable to believe my eyes, shaking from head to foot like an overbred French poodle, I leaned forward and spread the branches farther apart. Sweet Jesus! She was undoing the belt of the bathrobe! She was . . .

"Eeeyow!" I leaped into the air beating at Sneezy, who hung from my earlobe by his teeth, his hot breath roaring in my head. I screamed, crashing blindly through the bushes and out onto the lawn, swatting at him trying to find his jaws and simultaneously trying to hold him up. Lucky arrived out of the darkness at express-train speed, his face mirroring in that one brief instant before he passed all the stunned amazement that must have been in mine. For a moment we became the same person, like facing yourself in the glass with a new suit. Neither of us knew which body was his own. He reached out, plucked Sneezy from my ear, and in a single fluid movement tossed him ten feet through the air into the branches of a pepper tree.

Lights went on behind us. Doors slammed. Voices called. Lucky had disappeared ahead of me, and with fresh blood streaming down my neck I ran after him, trusting his path, hoping I could leap as high, my heart wild with fear.

One late afternoon in the woods everything fell into place. I'd been practicing for an hour, running through the easy tricks abstractedly, the way an expert mechanic might shuffle cards while waiting for his victims to take their seats, when I began to realize something special was happening. Never had I yo-yoed so effortlessly. Never had the tricks clicked with such mathematical precision. The yo-yo seemed to be playing itself as I stood waving my hands like a conductor before an invisible orchestra. The time was ripe for an assault on The Universe, not only the separate parts, but the whole trick as one unit.

Unbelievably, it came on the first try. I was flabbergasted. I'd been trying for weeks—for so long, in fact, I was reconciled to creeping up on it slowly, perhaps over a period of months—and suddenly victory was mine. Breathless, hoping it hadn't been a fluke, I threw again. As I watched the trick unfold, it came to me that a ghost or a spirit was controlling the yo-yo's movements, and that to be really good one had simply to give up one's desire to dominate the yo-yo and instead let the ghost take over. It was as if someone spoke to me through the yo-yo. See how easy, was the implication. Just practice till you get over your clumsiness, practice until you can yo-yo without thinking about it and then let me take over. I threw back my head and laughed. I danced a little dance on the sand and shouted out into the pine trees. I knew that in all of Fort Lauderdale and very probably in all of Florida there was not one other boy who could do what I had just done.

I knew I was best. As for what happened, I was no more than moderately disappointed when my supposedly unobtainable Black Beauty went on sale at the five-and-ten for sixty cents. I'd gone as far as one could go on the yo-yo. I'd learned tricks the demonstrators didn't know. So when the final contest arrived and I learned that after one or two extremely easy tricks the choice of champion would be based on the greatest number of consecutive Loop-the-Loops, when I learned that my skill counted for nothing in the eyes of the non-yo-yoing judges, when I found myself screwed once again as my string broke at seventy-three (eleven less than a muscle-bound idiot from the beach who couldn't do a simple Cannonball)—when, to wrap it up, all this reality was finally absorbed by my brain, the knowledge that I was without question the best yo-yo player around kept me from despair. There was no despair, only a mild confusion at the sloppiness of things, and a faint sickness at my own bewilderment.

I forgot it easily. That same night, hidden in the greenery under the window, I watched a naked girl let down her long red hair.

9
Falling

WE ARRIVED in New York during the last
week of the school term. Over the years I'd put in enough
time at the local grammar school (P.S. 6 of J. D. Salinger
fame) for the authorities to stretch a point and allow me
to graduate along with everyone else, an important detail
since only then would I be eligible for a public high school.
Most of my classmates were signed up for private schools
and I seemed to be the only boy who didn't know where he
was going. In desperation I picked the nearest free school
with entrance requirements—Stuyvesant High School on
the East Side—and went down to take the test.

It was a short exam, a rudimentary intelligence test. I
answered the questions in a small office and was marked
immediately.

"Did I get in?" I asked when the man came back.

He smiled. "Of course. You weren't worried, were you?"

I took his cue and acted as if I hadn't been, but the idea
of four years at some place like the High School of Needle
Trades had weighed heavily on my mind, and I'd resolved
that if Stuyvesant didn't accept me I wasn't going to go to
school at all.

As the result of some stories he'd heard at Stanley's Cafeteria it suddenly became clear to Jean that the fruit vendors
of New York had one of the sweetest deals around. "You
wouldn't think it to look at them," he'd say, "but they're
making a fortune. And the job is simplicity itself. You go
down to Ninth Avenue, buy the stuff wholesale, find yourself a nice corner somewhere, and sell it retail. No boss.
No time clock. Good healthy work out in the open air. It's
a cinch."

We chopped off the back of the old International truck,
built up a set of tiers for the boxes, and went into business.

As always, Jean's enthusiasm was contagious, and I gladly assumed the duties of weigher, fly-shooer, hawker, and charmer of little old ladies. (Jean took care of the young ones himself.) We'd leave early in the morning and not come home till after dark. The first week we moved around, trying different spots, but finally settled on the northwest corner of Sixty-eighth and Lexington just opposite the subway entrance. (My wife, whom I was not to meet for many years, lived in a town house one block away and must have passed us many times. Who knows? Perhaps I palmed off some bad grapes on my mother-in-law. It's not entirely impossible that my father-in-law's mysterious reluctance to receive me into the bosom of his family was related to a buried image of myself with a thumb on the scales, under his bananas.)

I developed a style for dealing with the customers. My usual quietness disappeared and, like an actor onstage, I felt free to let loose a flood of exhortations, aimless commentary, and snappy remarks. (It was probably good for me; in real life I was becoming more and more withdrawn.) Every buyer was someone to win over, and the game fascinated me. My specialty was extreme politeness, which always took them by surprise, and then, if they seemed sufficiently disarmed I'd interject some small bit of myself— a remark about the weather, a subtly couched compliment on the customer's dog, a pun, a big word—anything to get that quick, slightly puzzled glance of recognition. It must have been difficult to ignore me in any case, since I approached even the smallest transaction with all the *élan* of a headwaiter making crepes suzette. Without looking, I'd slip out the appropriate paper bag from a concealed shelf under the scales, lift it high in the air over my head, and snap it down like a whip to open it, at the same time selecting the fruit with my other hand. "One pound of fresh seedless grapes," I'd say with a certain amount of pride, gently lowering a fat bunch onto the hanging scales. My eye was good and when I missed the correct weight it wasn't by much. In a single sweeping movement I'd lift the removable tray, insert the narrow end into the open mouth of the paper bag, and transfer the fruit with exaggerated care. "Some cherries, ma'm? They're very sweet today, very succulent." If they were deaf to my words and blind to my ballet they nevertheless came to the moment when they put money in my hand. At that moment I won the game, or so it seemed to me.

There were quiet times, hot days when the streets were almost empty. I had a spot just behind the cab of the truck where I could sit in the shade and read, or put my chin in my hands and watch the slow, dreamlike movement around us. Jean stood at the end of the truck, one foot on the curb, his elbow on an empty apple box, smoking lazily and watching the girls. He wore sport shirts designed to hang outside the trousers, and huaraches without socks. "Now, there is a nice behind," he'd say, nodding at a girl retreating down the avenue. It wasn't lechery. He'd say it in much the same tone as a man commenting on the pleasing lines of a custom-made car or the gait of a thoroughbred race horse. He knew I was too young to appreciate behinds. Faces moved me, and occasionally a good pair of breasts, but the finer distinctions were beyond me.

One day a policeman stopped in front of us.

"You own this truck?"

"Yes," Jean answered politely. He was terrified of cops.

"It's against the law to stay in one place for more than an hour. You're supposed to keep moving."

"Ahh . . . yes." Jean stalled, not knowing what to say. "I'm sorry, Officer, I didn't realize that law was enforced."

The cop looked at him for a moment, suddenly suspicious of his good diction and bearing. He pointed his stick at me. "Who's that?"

"He's my boy," Jean said. "My son."

I looked at him quickly. He had never before called me his son. It felt slightly odd.

"You got working papers?" the cop asked me.

I shook my head.

Turning back to Jean, he said, "I can see you just started this racket so I'll give you a break this time. You better talk to the guys down at the market. They'll tell you what to do."

Next morning, waiting at a coffee stand until we could load up, we learned the procedure from an old Italian. "You take this," he said, slapping a dollar bill flat on the counter. "Make a small turn like this." He rolled one corner very tightly. "Roll 'em up." His hand slipped forward over the counter. "And she look like this." He held up the dollar bill, now rolled into a thin tube no thicker than a sipping straw and totally unrecognizable. "Stick 'em in corner box, front row. Stick 'em straight up, anh?" He paused, holding the tube at eye level. "Cop snitch it fast." He brought his other hand across and plucked the bill. "Son of a bitch!"

When we got back to our corner I stayed in the cab for a moment and prepared a bill as the Italian had instructed. After two or three tries I made a particularly nice one, very thin, with almost no green showing, and took it out to Jean. "Okay," he said, sticking in the appropriate box. "I guess this is what he meant."

"Really clever," I said, watching it being put in place. "Even if you noticed it you'd never be able to tell what it was."

The cop appeared late that afternoon. No one had noticed the bill, not even an old lady who almost knocked it over reaching for some peaches. I saw him come around the corner, swinging his stick, and alerted Jean.

"Don't watch him," Jean said, and stepped to the back of the truck to sort paper bags.

I couldn't stop myself. He walked toward us slowly, a tall man, his hips bulging with equipment, pistol against his thigh, the long stick twirling in that special way New York police affect, slapping neatly into his palm every few seconds like the piston of an engine. Somehow I couldn't believe he was going to do it. It seemed impossible that a man would compromise himself to that extent for only a dollar. He came to the front of the truck. I was close enough to touch him. He knew I was watching, but he didn't care. Reaching out an arm—a big arm, covered with thick, curly, ginger-colored hair—he calmly plucked the bill and walked away. I drew a deep breath and moved for the first time in sixty seconds.

I felt odd as I watched him go down the avenue, still swinging his stick as if nothing had happened. Approaching, he'd been a policeman, and now, retreating, he was just a man dressed in blue. The transformation stunned me. I couldn't have been more astonished if he'd disappeared in thin air.

It eventually became clear that the fruit-vending business was not as lucrative as we had supposed. We worked long hours every day, seven days a week, we selected the fruit carefully, treated the customers politely, were honest to a fault, but we couldn't seem to make any money. After five or six weeks Jean decided to give it up, explaining to my mother that the best corners were taken by Italians. He started talking about ambulance drivers and how they made a hundred and ten dollars a week and how this terrific character down at Stanley's Cafeteria might be able to introduce him to the right man. . . .

Jean's aristocratic appearance made it hard for him to get an ordinary job. At one point shortly after my father's death, when the estate upon which we relied for support was temporarily in the hands of the court, there was literally not a dollar in the house. Jean applied for a job as counterman in a White Tower hamburger stand and was turned down, the only conceivable reason being that they thought he wasn't serious. We'd have been in trouble if Dan, Jean's brother, hadn't come back from sea. A short, unassuming fellow, Dan got the White Tower job immediately.

When the fruit business ended I didn't know what to do with myself. The one or two kids I'd known from P.S. 6 were gone for the summer, the streets of our rich neighborhood were empty, and even my sister Alison was away on a job looking after some children. I had a pair of roller skates, and with the key dangling around my neck I'd push off in the morning for the Museum of Natural History across the park, or the Metropolitan a few blocks away. (I liked the medieval armor and the Egyptian room. The paintings bored me.) But after being robbed a couple of times I gave up crossing the park. Luckily I wasn't beaten up. I always seemed able to talk my way out of it. In those days the police ignored children and I saw bad beatings administered a stone's throw from the precinct house. The park was dangerous for a kid on his own.

I took to hanging around with the Good Humor man on the corner. He let me sit on the seat of his cart and ring the bells. Very rarely he gave me a free ice stick. I went to the movies whenever I had the money. A lot of the time I'd stay in the house, or more exactly, on the fire escape. After a few weeks, out of boredom, I started to think about jumping. Every child plays with the idea. I played with it more seriously, simply for something to do. As a game it was fascinating. No playmates or special equipment were necessary. Alone in the house, I could go out on the fire escape and have something quite definite happen to me. It never failed, I was exhilarated and purged. Best of all it was a long game. I'd stare down at the squares of sidewalk for hours before making a move. I toyed with the idea of what would happen if I fell, but I never seriously considered going over voluntarily. After a few weeks the pavement five floors below, at first so far away, seemed almost close enough to touch. Every line in the cement, every cracked spot and variation in the surface was memorized. Like an old friend the sidewalk was too familiar to be threatening. It seemed to me that if I fell it would be a painless death. I watched the sidewalk without a thought in my head. I didn't wonder why, it seemed perfectly natural.

At first I just stood outside the rail, hanging on with both hands for a minute or two. Then the trick was to go all the way around the fire escape before climbing back inside. Once or twice I hung by my hands and jumped to the platform below, but gave it up for fear of getting caught.

I discovered the roof of the building with its air-shafts and parapets. Eight stories up, it seemed tremendously high after all the time on the fire escape. I could spend a whole afternoon flat on my belly on the hot tar, my head and arms hanging out into space. After an hour or two of gazing down without moving, a pleasant drowsiness would come over me. As long as I felt the solid roof edge under my chest I knew I was safe. It was like flying. Half asleep, my eyes glazed and my head filled with a familiar buzzing, I'd lose all sense of time and direction. When I moved, or got up to go, I'd do it very carefully, making sure to orient myself correctly, moving each limb a fraction of an inch so I'd know where I was.

Once I walked around the foot-wide ledge of the main air shaft in a kind of slow, sliding shuffle. Eight floors below a cat sat in the exact center of the yard, over a drain, watching me.

The roof became my retreat. I threw little pieces of paper over the side to watch the breeze whisk them away, imagining myself floating down after them to land unharmed on the sidewalk. Pigeons would strut nearby and

10
The Coldness
of Public
Places

EYES CLOSED, head back, I drank directly from the carton of milk, taking long gulps while cold air from the refrigerator spilled out onto my bare feet. Leaving an inch for Jean's coffee, I replaced the carton and pushed the fat door shut. End of breakfast.

In the morning quietness sounds from outside seemed magnified. A bus wheezed across Eighty-sixth Street. Voices from the sidewalk rang out for a moment, trapped in the alley on the other side of the window. The bottom pane was covered with paper from the five-and-ten, a pattern of triangles under a thin glaze of grease. When a train pulled into the subway station two blocks away the window rattled in its frame.

On the table were last night's coffee cups and a few sheets of paper covered with calculations. Bending over, I recognized Jean's almost indecipherable scrawl, and here and there, as if annotating, my mother's larger, firmer hand. No pattern emerged from the jumble of numbers. They'd argued late into the night. I'd heard them as I read in my room, their voices a dull backdrop to the evolving action of the novel in my hands, barely noticing even as my mother began her nightly bout of weeping. Mechanical sobs, regular as clockwork, faintly girlish, expressing exhaustion rather than sorrow. As a plea to Jean, they never worked. "Well if you're going to cry . . . ," he'd say, and throw up his hands.

In my room—a bed, closet, table, and hundreds of paperbacks—I collected my schoolbooks. A mild but quite definite nausea filled me at the sight of them. I hadn't done my homework.

Down the long, dark hall to the front door, my eyes still bleary, my brain numb. In some unthought-out fashion I'd trained myself to get out of the house before becoming fully conscious. On the street corner, waiting for the bus, I'd wake up, my books under my arm, a small crowd around me, like a man on the stage of a theater who finds himself in the midst, as the hypnotist brings him round, of a perfectly normal but somehow inexpressibly mysterious act.

Punching the time clock was a fascinating game. My card seemed to exist on a higher plane of reality than myself. I'd have come to work for no other reason than to hold it in my hands. My name blazed unapologetically. Numbers crowded one another in purple ink. I was reassured, soothed almost, to know that something about me was recordable.

The sleeves of my gray attendant's jacket were starched flat as boards. Putting it on I'd drive my fist through like a wedge to separate the cloth. I paused at the door to check my fly. With my palm flat against the SILENCE sign, I pushed through into the reading room.

A vast space opened over my head. For a moment I felt painfully conspicuous. Row upon row of tables. Dim lamps with green shades. The girls working with bowed heads, their pens scratching like the whispers of a crowd. (How can girls be so good? How can what is so difficult for me be so easy for them?)

As I reached the main desk the woman on duty glanced at me briefly and returned to work, her gray head bending as she searched a file, skinny fingers flipping the cards expertly, her lipless mouth moving in nervous accompaniment. A dolly waited, half full of books. I got behind it and pushed, gliding it slowly away from the desk and out across the cork floor. Far away at the other end of the room, under the tall columns of light from high windows, a girl coughed discreetly.

Safe in a balcony alcove, confident I could hear anyone coming up the spiral stairs in plenty of time to return to work, I settled back in a comfortable armchair with a book on Egyptian tombs. I leafed slowly through illustrations of pyramids, underground chambers, white men in pith helmets, and natives digging trenches. A large color plate of a cat statue caught my eye and I gazed at it for several moments, my mind empty of thought. Without an ego, one simply looks. The image of the cat, entirely whole and entirely static, is a signal to the mind to come to rest. There is no immediate sense of beauty, only the act of seeing. A scanning mechanism in the brain locks in a cycle of cat. Without an ego to break the equipoise one's mind is like an electric motor with the poles perfectly balanced at positive and negative. Flip the switch, the apparatus hums with power, but there is no movement. My eyelids grew heavy. With the book on my lap I let them close and drifted away. When someone started up the stairs I was on my feet instantly, shelving books.

A girl. I could tell from her footsteps. She went directly to the next alcove without seeing me. A chair scraped. Papers rustled. I stood frozen, my nose three inches from an eight-volume set on birds of North America, suddenly paralyzed by the knowledge that only a couple of feet away on the other side of the books, completely unaware of my proximity, a young but physically mature female sat defenseless in her imagined privacy.

I stood as if listening to music, and in something like the way we are told suns are born, that specks of matter in nearly empty space begin to fall, rushing across vast distances toward a hot sphere of turbulence and unimaginable density, in such a way my body, which only a moment ago as I'd watched the cat might best have been described as a vapor, a dimly perceived cloud around my soul, began to coalesce. Warmth flooded my limbs. Fingers and toes, nose and ears, my knees and remote regions of my back defined themselves in space like objects looming up out of a fog. I sank down until my knees touched the ground, and sat on my heels, almost reverently, wishing to disturb nothing in the suddenly harmonious world. With exquisite care I made the necessary adjustments and delved into myself. Hello, old friend. Companion in the wilderness. Gift-giver.

I moved a few books quietly and found her, or rather found a piece of her, neck to breast in white cotton. It was at once frustrating, and for some reason extremely exciting to see only this small part of her. Switching to a lower shelf I cleared the way for a view of her legs, feeling a remote sense of disappointment when I found them primly crossed, although enough thigh showed to hold my interest. My brain raced, dealing with a thousand things—listening for someone on the stairs, wondering if there weren't a better

angle from which to watch her, reminding myself that I
hadn't done my homework—and all the while the warm
steady voice of my old friend speaking to me silently, below my thoughts, sending messages up my spine to the
back of my head, telling me I was indeed alive, I was who
I thought I was, and that nothing else mattered. At moments like this, as all men know, one becomes oblivious to
everything in the outside world not directly related to the
business—and I choose my words carefully—at hand. Entire areas of perception close down and the senses focus on
a small, highly charged target, be it oneself, a few inches
of female thigh, or a mixture of both. In this state one
sees with the clarity of a mystic. A breast, a wrist, a curved
hip become images of pure significance, passing directly
into the tenderest part of the brain. (I go into all this only
to give some idea of what the next moment was like.)

As a glutton standing before a splendid buffet might
suddenly decide to move his poised fingers from the olives
to the lobster cakes, so I chose to return to the higher
level of books for another glimpse of breast, against the
chance that she might have moved to a more revealing
position. Standing straight up on my knees I pressed my
eye into position. There was a moment of confusion. I
saw something, but without a larger frame of reference I
couldn't tell what. Were these fingers? Objects I finally
recognized as hands moved away to reveal, very close, a
face. It was like straining to hear a faraway sound and
having a gun go off in your ear. Her eyes were shut tight,
tear stained, squinting hard as if to avoid some overwhelm-
ing source of light. She wept, her mouth spread wide in a
queer, tight-lipped smile of anguish, her head nodding
slowly. I recoiled from the peephole as if a needle had
pierced my pupil.

In a frenzy of confusion I began sorting books as if
nothing had happened. She had not seen me, I was safe.
Only much later did I wonder what she was crying about,
and if I should have told someone.

The Street

I was already late, having completely missed home-room
period, so there was no great harm in waiting a bit longer.
I bought a hot dog and watched two boys from the morning

session pitching pennies against the wall of Stuyvesant High School. The sun was high, filling half the street, and I moved out from under the vendor's striped umbrella to get its warmth. My heart was calm. Nothing could be done about my lateness and in the meantime there was the street, wonderfully quiet in the steady sunlight, the sharp taste of yellow mustard in my mouth, and the slow rhythms of the game to contemplate. For a few moments I was free, relieved of thought, temporarily released from the faint sickness inside me. Although I refused to admit it, I was getting sick. Delicate changes were going on—the subtle adjustments of a mind that feels itself threatened but cannot localize the threat, the hidden wariness toward all things and all people, a certain suspension of sensibility, like holding one's breath in a moment of crisis and finding when the danger passes there is no need of breath, that one can live without air.

"Get in there, you cocksucker," said one of the boys. Toeing the line, his body bent like a racer waiting for the gun, he launched his coin in a flat arch and smiled as it came to rest a half inch from the wall. "Wins."

"Can I shoot?"

They looked at me quickly. "Okay."

"He has to go first, though," the other boy said.

We threw coins for a while, unhurried, all of us relaxed and easy in the sun. The hot-dog vendor leaned against his cart, half asleep, his chin in his hands. I was about even when the two boys called a halt and set off toward First Avenue. They turned the corner arguing about a disputed play and I started up the steps, my shadow climbing crookedly ahead of me.

The First Floor

I could have sneaked in through one of the side exits, of course, but there wasn't much point since the new attendance taker in home room was above taking bribes and had doubtless included my name in the late list. Approaching the wide table at the head of the main corridor I felt a familiar gathering-of-self at the day's first encounter with the enemy, represented in this instance by the student serving as late monitor. He looked up from his books and gave me a smile. "Again, huh?"

"That's right." I was happy to see him instead of Mr. Schmidt, the teacher who sometimes served, because as fellow students we had a bond that transcended my sins. We shared the stoicism of the helpless, the dreamy *sangfroid* of the abused, playing out our respective roles with tongue in cheek as if to say there's more to me than meets the eye. As a good student he was glad to see me acting out his fantasies of rebellion, while I, the reprobate, was heartened to discover that even the good students were unhappy, that they hated school no less than myself, each in his own way.

"Three times this week and it's only Thursday."

"You have to stick with it to be champ." But my heart sank. I hadn't remembered, and three times in a single week was dangerous. The Dean might feel he should do something.

"Well, I hope you like Seward. That's where they'll send you."

He wasn't being superior, it was a flat statement of fact.

"I don't give a shit what they do."

He shrugged and pulled a pad of forms under his eyes, signed, and ripped off the sheet. "It's first period. You missed home room."

Two teachers came down the marble stairs (Staff Only) from the second floor and passed without a glance. I threw a fuck-you sign behind their backs.

The empty corridor ran the entire length of the building, one city block. The walls were green. Bare bulbs in wire cages glowed in a long line on the ceiling and the smell of disinfectant hung in the air. I walked down the exact center of the passageway, directly under the lights, whispering "fuck you, fuck you, fuck you" to the rhythm of my stride.

Pushing through a door I turned into the upper level of the gym. My chair was lying folded across the banked runway and I picked it up, opened it, and sat down next to the railing. Arms dangling, I watched the scene below. A hundred boys were doing calisthenics, jumping into the air and throwing up their arms in time to the instructor's whistle. Up, down, up, down—chasing the lost beat halfheartedly through the thunder of their heavy feet. The balcony trembled. Almost all of them were too fat, with huge womanly hips and flesh that jiggled under their T-shirts. I laughed aloud. It was too absurd. One knew from the movies what it was supposed to look like—football teams in early workouts, Hitler youth bouncing along smartly like so many machines—and for a moment the grotesque reality before my eyes seemed to reveal the truth so pointedly I wondered how the teacher could let it go on. The truth was, nobody cared. In the back rows they'd already given up, simply faking the gestures, some not even bothering to throw up their arms. Across the gym, on the opposite side of the track, I saw the other door monitor laughing in delight.

The instructor blew his whistle. "Left *face!* Right *face!* Mark *time!* One two, one two, one two. . . ." His voice was drowned in the chaotic roar. As if of one mind the boys made as much noise as possible, stamping their feet like angry infants.

The five-minute warning bell had rung. I sat with my ankles on the railing reading a novel about the Second World War. I should have used the time to do my homework, but the appeal of Nazis, French girls, K rations, and sunlight slanting through the forest while men attempted to kill one another was too great. I read four or five hours every night at home, but it was never quite as sweet as in school, when even a snatch read as I climbed the stairs seemed to protect me from my surroundings with an efficacy that bordered on the magical. And if the story dealt with questions of life and death, so much the better. How could I be seriously worried about having nothing to hand in at Math when I was pinned in a shallow foxhole, under a mortar barrage, a dead man across my back and an hysterical young lieutenant weeping for his mother by my side? I could not resist the *clarity of the world* in books, the incredibly satisfying way in which life became weighty and accessible. Books were reality. I hadn't made up my mind about my own life, a vague, dreamy affair, amorphous and dimly perceived, without beginning or end.

A boy pushed open the door and looked in. My function as monitor was to keep unauthorized people from going in

and out, a responsibility I ignored, and when I turned my
head it was with the pleasant anticipation of the law-
breaker about to flout authority.

"Conroy?"

"Yes." Too bad. I could tell he was licit from his tone.
Shouts drifted up from the gym floor.

He waved a slip of paper. "Two-oh-eight. Right away." I
accepted the pass and began gathering my books.

How strange that when the summons came I always
felt good. The blood would rush through my body, warming me with its cheerful, lively heat. If there was a slight
dryness in my mouth there was also a comfortable tingling
of the nerves, a sharpening of the reflexes, and a sense of
heightened awareness. The call produced a mild euphoria,
not out of any perverse desire to be punished but in anticipation of a meeting with fate, in expectation of plunging
deeper into life. The Dean was less the Dean and more
my dead father than either of us suspected at the time. I
sustained a fantastic belief that the mechanical clichés of
our disciplinary interviews were only the prelude to eventual mutual recognition. His threats seemed of no more
importance than the how-do-you-dos and so-nice-to-meet-
yous one mouthed to any new person, and in my eagerness
to begin a real exchange I hardly heard them. I misread
the boredom and irritation in his face, thinking it came
from frustration at the slow pace of love, investing his dry
soul with juices that had doubtless drained before I was
born. The truth, that among the thousands of students I
was no more than a number to him, that he was so over-
worked he couldn't possibly have remembered me from
one time to the next without his records, that in fact everything between us was totally procedural—that truth was
unthinkable.

The Second Floor

Three boys were on the bench. I sat down with them and
watched the floor for a moment, not, as a naïve observer
might have thought, to dramatize penitence, but simply to
maintain my privacy in an important moment. Drawn close
by their delinquency, the other boys whispered and passed
notes, holding off fear with artificial camaraderie. I kept

quiet, acclimating slowly to the electric air, knowing that where there was danger there might also be salvation.

I never rehearsed a defense. I must have thought the Dean preferred a boy who walked in and took his medicine to one who groveled, however cleverly. And of course when the moment of recognition came, when the barriers fell and we stood revealed, I didn't want to be in the midst of an elaborate lie. To hasten the emergence of love I could only be completely honest. Lies might make it difficult for him to reach me, and vice-versa.

I wanted to be won over by him, but not cheaply. If he won me cheaply he might betray me. The sense in which I knew this is hard to explain. It wasn't a principle I'd deduced from experience, it was knowledge without thought. Had someone asked me at the time what it meant to be betrayed by another person I couldn't have answered. Without being able to conceive betrayal I none the less protected myself against it, unconsciously, in my expectation of a commitment from the other person equal to my own. A perfectly valid stance between individuals but a tragic absurdity between a child and authority.

A side door I'd never noticed before opened and a student came out smiling. I caught a glimpse of a man at a desk, and for no reason at all I became convinced he was a policeman.

"Fischberg," the Dean's secretary called without looking up. The boy next to me left the bench and went through the side door. I heard the man inside tell him to close it.

The smiling student picked up a pass from the secretary and started out. As he passed I touched his arm. "Who's that in there?"

"I don't know. Some jerk asking if I had a happy home life."

"No talking there!"

A soft buzz sounded on the secretary's intercom. "Next," she said.

There was a momentary paralysis on the bench.

"Well, what are you waiting for?" She shuffled some papers on her desk. "Conroy? Is one of you Conroy?"

I walked to the Dean's door and went in.

"All right Conroy, step over here."

I crossed the carpet and stood in front of his desk. He took off his glasses, rubbed the bridge of his nose, and put

them on again. After a moment he pushed against the edge
of the desk and swiveled away to face the wall, leaning
back with a sigh and then letting his chin come down slowly
like a man dozing off.

"Why were you late?" he asked the wall.

"There was no reason, I guess."

"No reason?"

"I mean I don't have an excuse."

"You didn't miss your bus? You didn't forget your tran-
sit pass? The subways didn't break down?"

"No sir."

"I suppose not, since you've been late three times this
week. You can't possibly have an excuse so you don't give
one. Isn't that right?" He stared at the wall.

I didn't answer.

"Isn't that right?" he asked again in exactly the same flat
tone.

"If you say so, sir."

He turned his head to look at me for a moment, his
face expressionless, and then went back to watching the
wall. "I don't have time for trouble-makers, Conroy. I
get rid of them."

"I don't know why I'm late so often. I try to get here on
time but somehow it just happens."

"Don't make a mystery out of it, Conroy. You're late
because you're lazy and inattentive."

I could feel myself beginning to close down inside, as if
my soul were one of those elaborate suitcases street ped-
dlers use to display their wares, the kind that fold up from
all directions at the approach of the law.

He lifted some papers from his desk. "You're nothing
but trouble. Constantly late if you get here at all, inattentive in class, disrespectful to your teachers, twice repri-
manded for gambling . . ."

"It was just pitching pennies, sir."

"I know what it was. Don't interrupt."

"Yes sir."

"At this moment you are failing three subjects."

"We haven't had any tests yet. I'm sure I'll pass the
tests."

He looked up, his eyes narrowing in irritation. "You're
failing three subjects. That leaves the decision up to me.

You stay here or you get transferred to another school. You're in that category now."

I turned away, instinctively hiding the fear that might be on my face. Getting kicked out of Stuyvesant would be a catastrophe surpassing anything in my experience, perhaps because it seemed to eliminate the possibility of turning over a new leaf. I disbelieved in self-betterment. By turning a new leaf I meant no more than avoiding the more obvious forms of trouble.

Secretly, I did hope that things would get better. That I didn't know *how* they'd get better was balanced by my inability to understand why they were bad in the first place. It was a delicate world in which one had to move carefully, dealing with elements one understood vaguely if at all, knowing only that some elements seemed to sustain life and some to threaten it. Getting thrown out of school would disrupt things profoundly. I would no longer be able to experiment with those balanced elements, probing them gingerly here and there, adding some, taking away some, trying, in the least dangerous way, to find out what they were. In a trade school, my bridges burned behind me, I imagined myself in total isolation and darkness, unable to reorganize, unable to make the slightest adjustments in the course of my life, finally and irrevocably in the hands of a disinterested fate.

"What do you think I should do?" he asked.

"I want to stay. I can make it."

"What the hell is the matter with you, Conroy?"

I looked down at the edge of the desk. Something strange was happening. I seemed to be at two removes from reality, crouching behind my own body like a man manipulating a puppet through a curtain. "I don't know." My arms were reaching in through my back to make me talk. "That's the truth."

"If you don't," he said slowly, "you had better find out."

I climbed back into myself and nodded.

He opened the drawer of his desk and took out a small notebook. "Early report for two weeks. Get here fifteen minutes before the first bell and sign in with the hall monitor." He uncapped his pen and made a notation. "Leave plenty of time. Miss once and you're out. Understand?"

"Yes sir."

"That's all." He didn't look up.

I had my hand on the doorknob when he spoke again. "And see the man in the other room before you go back to class."

The bench had refilled and the boys turned as if to read their fates in my expression. I walked past and went up to the secretary. "He says I should see the man in there."

"Go on in, then. There's nobody with him."

I tapped the door lightly and entered.

"Come in. Sit down." He was standing over a desk. "You are . . . ah . . . " He looked down at his papers.

"Conroy."

"Oh yes, Conroy." He smiled nervously, poking one of the papers across the surface of the desk with his fingers. Hunched over, he coughed into his fist as he quickly read it. "Well now, Frank," he began. (It was a slight shock to be so addressed. My official name was Conroy, and neither teachers nor students called me anything else.) "I want to ask you some questions. Understand that I have nothing to do with the school or the Dean. I'm here simply as an observer, and to help if I can. You can answer freely without fear of . . ." he hesitated, searching for the right word.

"Repercussions?"

"Yes. That's right." He sat down. "Now let's see. You're fourteen years old. Any brothers or sisters?"

"An older sister," I said. "And oh yes, the baby. Jessica. She's only a few months old."

"I see. She would be your half-sister, I imagine, since I see here your father passed away some time ago."

'Yes." I began to pick at some lint on my trousers, feeling slightly uncomfortable.

"Do you get along with them all right?"

"What do you mean?" I understood him, but the question irritated me.

"Well, there are always little fights now and then. We all lose our tempers occasionally, I wondered if outside of that you got along with them all right."

"Of course I do."

"Okay." He paused, watching me indirectly. There was no more lint to pick from my leg so I began to brush out the cuff with a finger. "Do you have a job in the morning?"

"Yes. I work in a library."

"How do you like that?"

"It's okay."

"What do you do when you get home from school at night? Do you have any hobbies? Stamp collecting, that sort of thing?"

"No hobbies."

"Well, how do you pass the time?"

"I read a lot. Sometimes I play the piano."

"What kind of books?"

I hesitated, not sure how to answer. "All kinds, I guess."

"I suppose you don't like school very much."

"I don't think about it very much."

The bell rang, all over the building, and was followed instantly by the sound of thousands of students moving through the halls. I listened abstractedly, luxuriating in the knowledge that for the moment I'd escaped the routine. How can I explain the special pleasure of listening to the machine operating all around me while I myself was removed from it? I'd cut class and climb the stairs past the top floor to the deserted landing above. I'd sit with my back against the door to the roof listening to the bells, to the boys shouting on the stairs below, and to the long silences after the halls had emptied. The mood was quietly Olympian.

I hadn't realized how much the Dean had shaken me up, but now, as the bell I didn't have to answer rang again, I felt a tremor of release play over my body. Muscles everywhere began to relax and I threw back my head in an enormous involuntary yawn.

"What does your stepfather do for a living, Frank?"

Instantly I was alert. I knew the man was harmless, but my deepest rule, a rule so deep I maintained it without the slightest conscious effort, was never to reveal anything important about life at home. "He's a cab driver," I said slowly.

"Does your mother work too?"

I stared at the floor. "Sometimes." It occurred to me that my initial relief at getting away from the Dean might have made me careless with the man I now faced. He obviously had some image of me in his mind, some psychological cliché, and by answering carelessly I might unknowingly have supported it. I moved to the edge of my chair and sat up straight.

"Is there trouble at home?" he asked quietly.

My face flushed. A stupid question. An insulting question, as if I were a case to be dealt with by the book, as if he suspected some hidden deprivation or abnormality. "No, of course not. Nothing like that." I knew what he had in his mind. He held images of drunken fathers who beat their kids, slut mothers who roamed the house in old nightgowns, and long, screaming fights with crockery flying through the air. We weren't like that. I knew we were much better than that. I stood up. "Is that all?"

He fiddled with his papers for a moment, looking off into space. "Yes, I guess so," he said reluctantly. "If and when I come back to Stuyvesant I'd like to talk to you again."

I hiked my books high under my arm and went out the door. Standing motionless in the small room, I looked at the secretary and the four boys on the bench. The bell rang.

The Third Floor

Miss Tuts, a tiny red-haired woman, stood at the side of the room screaming at the boy in front of the blackboard. "No, no, no! Didn't you hear what I said? *Soixante-deux! Soixante-deux!* And write it out, don't just put the numbers."

The boy turned slowly to the board and raised the chalk. Hesitantly he began to write.

"Wrong," she yelled. "Sit down. You didn't prepare the lesson." Her figure was black against the big windows as she paced back and forth with quick little steps. "Bernstein! Put the vocabulary for today on the board. And don't forget the verbs."

Bernstein stood up, a perfect pear. "Just the French?"

"Yes," she cried irritably. "Do I have to explain every day?"

Someone laughed in the back.

"Quiet!"

Bernstein finished one column quickly and started on the next, writing the words in exactly the same order in which they'd appeared in the textbook. He could memorize effortlessly, and the pride with which he repeated the same trick day after day had not endeared him to his classmates.

"Bernstein sucks," the boy next to me said quietly.

"Did you say something, Aaronson?"

"No, Miss Tuts."

"Stand up and translate the first column."

"Le shawmbra, the room. Le lee, the bed . . ."

Someone hit Bernstein on the back with a ball of paper as he turned away from the board. Laughter from the rear of the room. Aaronson went on without skipping a beat. "Revay, to dream. Se lavay, to wash . . ."

"Who threw that?" Miss Tuts screamed, running to the front of the room. "Who threw that paper?"

Looking uncomfortable, Bernstein returned to his seat. "Le shapoe, the hat. La . . ."

She slammed her hand on the desk. "Shut up! Sit down! Now, who threw that paper?"

Silence.

Plunk! Someone plucked the short-metal prong under the seat with his thumbnail. Plunk! Answers started coming in from different parts of the room. Plunk! Plunk!

"Stop it! Stop it this instant!"

Plunk! Plunk!

"I'll send you all to the Dean! The entire class!"

We laughed as she stalked out. Her threat was empty. It had been used too often.

The Fourth Floor

Dr. Casey was a big man, well over six feet tall with the build to go with it, but he was getting old. His square face was touched with the gray skin tone of age, and except for rare moments of anger his eyes had lost the flash of life. He stared out over his desk expressionlessly, his hands clasped before him. He talked from the first bell to the last, and no one interrupted him. As long as he talked we didn't have to work. We'd discovered there was no need to listen. We could catch up on homework for other classes, read, or do the crossword puzzle. He didn't care as long as we were quiet and looked busy. Perhaps he even thought we were taking notes.

"I put my sons through Harvard. Both of them. But they're gone now. Things change, that's what you people don't realize. When you're my age it becomes quite clear. Things change, things change constantly and the very things that seem most secure are actually changing very slowly, sometimes so slowly you can't see what's happening even though it's staring you in the face. You must stay alert at all times. Never believe the way things look. The garbage collectors believe everything is simple and that's why they're garbage collectors. You have to look behind the masks, you have to get behind the lies. Most of it is lies, you know. I am aware of that fact." He tapped the surface of the desk with his knuckles. "I can see through the lies because I've lived a full life. I didn't waste my time. In the First World War I was in graves registration. I saw things I can't tell you about. Things so horrible good taste prevents me from mentioning them. You people of course have no idea. That's why I'm here. That's why I'm here. That's why I'm sitting up here at this desk giving my life for your vicarious perusal." He stared out over the lowered heads of the boys and cleared his throat with a tremendous bellow. It was highly overdone, a self-conscious mannerism the boys had learned to ignore. Each day more and more phlegm was rolled more and more lovingly, as if he were testing our unconcern, as if, as the gesture became totally operatic, he were daring us to call his bluff. "My field was etymology. Where words came from. Words, after all, are the tools they use to break us down. I resist them because I know more about words than they do. Every educated man should know about words." He paused to let the thought sink in. "Then when they spew out their poison and their vomit I see it for what it is. Filth! Nothing more or less than that! And we are surrounded by it, gentlemen. The secretions of corrupted minds are the juices that nourish modern society, just as the blood of animals nourishes our bodies. Pus runs free over the body politic. Graft and corruption are everywhere. They've approached me many times, I assure you, whining and wheedling before me, making their filthy offers, trying to break me down. Well they can try for a thousand years and my answer will be the same. They can shove their special arrangements. They can shove their recommendations, gold watches and testimonial dinners. Let them eat their own swill." He spoke softly, as if withdrawn into himself, as if the strength of his feelings had driven him back to a point where he was no more than an observer of his own actions. Leaning far back in his chair, his long legs extended straight out into the aisle, he peered through loosely clasped fingers, his entire body motionless as a corpse. "None of it surprises me. None of it. They show us one man riding another, riding him like a horse, like a beast of burden. That stuff gets through. They call it art. They spit on the nobility of the human body. They lower themselves to the level of animals. Below animals. A man riding a man is going too far. I call them dogs from the bottom of my soul."

The school day is over. A mood of manic hilarity fills every classroom as we wait for the final bell. The aisles are crowded with laughing, shouting boys. The teachers, already on their way home mentally, sit behind their desks with lowered heads and occupy themselves with small unnecessary tasks.

Despite the confusion we're ready to go at the signal. Our books are packed. Our jackets are on. We pour through the door and out into the hall with a collective sigh. We rush for the stairs, dodging in and out among the slower boys. The noise is terrific. On the stairs we really let loose. Screams and yells float up from the lower floors. Fists bang against the metal side panels in continuous thunder. Down, down, down, rushing past the painted numbers, swinging round like crack the whip at the landings, leaping steps when there's room, pushing the boy in front, being pushed from behind, all of us mad with freedom. Down, down. So easily, so effortlessly. The stream carries us safely past the third, the second, the first, and out into the immense throng streaming through the banks of open doors to the street. We flow over the sidewalk and between the parked cars onto the asphalt. In the darkness faces are indistinct. Matches flash for cigarettes. Around the corner the avenue gleams with neon. Most of us have already forgotten the five hours inside school because for most of us school is less than nothing. We spread like a liquid over the neighborhood and disappear into the subways.

11
Blindman's Buff

I REMEMBER coming home the day the baby was born. As I opened the front door Jean strode down the hall, his eyes gleaming. I knew instantly.

"Was it a boy or a girl?" I asked. "A boy? Was it a boy?"

Enjoying the moment, Jean fluttered his hands. "The main thing is it didn't have two heads."

"A girl?" I slammed the door.

"Those things happen, you know. It's all very mysterious about heredity. Of course the doctors have to act as if they know all . . ."

"Jean! For God's sake, what . . ."

"It's a girl. With one head."

So there it was. I stood quite still, conscious of the tremendous importance of the moment. Three of us now. Alison, myself, and the new baby. I stuck out my hand. "Congratulations."

He laughed. "What's to congratulate? You think I did something hard? Any moron can have a baby. It's no accomplishment." But he took my hand.

"What does she look like?"

"Like a baby. They're all the same."

"Is Mother okay?"

He nodded. "They said it was an easy birth."

I started up the hall to the kitchen. "Wow!"

Jessica Fouchet. When she came home her utter helplessness shocked me into loving her. She seemed the quintessence of mortality. It made chills run up and down my spine just to look at her.

And I spent a lot of time looking at her, sitting quietly next to her crib watching her sleep, as if by being there long enough, by imprinting her image on my brain, I would come to understand the mystery (I was a child, remember) of life. But nothing was revealed to me. Jessica simply existed, and no matter how hard I looked, that was all I ever knew. There seemed to be no point to her except the fact that she lived.

I heard my mother crying one afternoon, her long blond hair over her shoulders and the baby at her breast. At first I thought she'd been arguing with Jean, but there was something different about the way she cried. "What's wrong?" I asked from the doorway.

She shook her head, not looking up. I was about to leave when she said, "I can't feed her any more. She has to have a bottle." Tears streaming down her cheeks, she rocked the baby back and forth, leaning down to press her cheek to its brow. I went off to my room, completely bewildered. Why anyone should cry over that was beyond my understanding. With the end of breast feeding my mother's attitude toward Jessica changed considerably. She became much more matter of fact, more practical and nurselike. She didn't hold the baby while it was fed, for example. A plastic sandbag with the bottle strapped in was good enough.

Quite suddenly Jean and I were alone in the house. Mother had taken the baby to Denmark for a long visit and Alison had become a permanent house guest at the home of her best friend. In an attempt to get "ahead of the game" Jean worked long hours in the cab and came home only to sleep.

I ate in Wright's Restaurant by the subway entrance on Lexington and Eighty-sixth street (a habit that was to continue off and on until I left home), occupying the same seat every night. If I had enough money I read a magazine from the stand outside, otherwise I'd borrow a paper from the waitress. The routine pleased me enormously. Eating out seemed luxurious as well as adult. The money came from my job, or if I was broke between jobs, from Jean's taxi earnings. He kept the bills and coins neatly stacked in a tray on the shelf of his closet.

In the mindless, unself-conscious way children go about things I'd become a resourceful sneak thief. If a purse was left unwatched I'd be sure to rifle it. Mother and sister suffered from my new talent, but the real prize was Jean's cash tray. Ah, those neat stacks of gleaming coins!

Those thick, splendid wads of dollar bills! The majesty of the fives and tens!

When my steady pilferage could no longer be ignored a lock was installed on Jean's and Mother's bedroom door. For a while I was stymied, but in the end the presence of the lock worked to my advantage. Alone in the house one afternoon, I found myself attempting to force the tumblers with a bent paper clip. I worked abstractedly, more out of boredom than with any hope of success, the way a prisoner behind two feet of solid rock might begin to pick away at the wall with an old spoon just to keep himself occupied, to give a physical focus to his fantasies of freedom. When an hour had passed without a single encourageing development I gave it up and stepped back from the door. As an afterthought I examined the hinges, ran my fingers around the molding, and then (a beautiful moment) backed up farther and saw the transom. Understanding came in a flash. If I could get through the transom my troubles were over, really over, because then I could steal at will in relative safety. It seemed unlikely that Jean kept close track of the money now that he imagined I couldn't get at it. Stealing small amounts at regular intervals I could very well escape detection completely. A passion ripped through my limbs as I dragged a high-backed chair up against the door.

The transom, its joints heavily sealed with paint, had not been opened in years. I got a single-edged razor blade from the bathroom and went to work. Moments later a few sharp blows with the heel of my hand did the trick. The room lay revealed below me, dim and quiet, full of promise. With shaking hands I grasped the sill and stepped up on the back of the chair.

For once I was glad to be skinny. First my arms, then my head, sideways, and back out again as I realized it wasn't going to work. I took a few deep breaths and put my head in, then wriggled my shoulders through one at a time. I began to laugh as it became clear I could make it —a special kind of body-knowledge, the sudden switch in sensation from pushing the front part of me to pulling the back part of me. Now my arms were free and I hung, bent at the waist, upside down flat against the inside of the door. Outside my legs lifted off the back of the chair. Still laughing, I twisted the rest of the way through and fell on my head. The pain was barely noticeable. (No more than, fifteen years later, a woman's teeth in my arm.) Dancing over to the closet I threw open the door and smiled at the money. I took seventy cents in carefully selected coins, closed the closet and the transom, went out the door, and made it to the movies.

My mother had been gone for some months when Jean made a serious error. His motives were undoubtedly numerous—to alleviate boredom, to establish his independence, to punish Dagmar for leaving him alone, to force her to return (both of these last unconscious), and perhaps to make a conquest. (He was tame, though. Years after their divorce I asked Dagmar if she thought he'd ever been unfaithful. "He wouldn't have dared," she snorted. "He didn't have the guts." An exaggeration, of course, but still . . .) As it turned out, his motives were of no importance whatsoever. Who needs to know, about the man falling down the elevator shaft, that he thought he was stepping into the car, or that his original plan was to get off at the tenth floor?

My first view of her was from the rear, as she bent over to take something out of one of the boxes strewn up and down the long hall. Loose piles of clothing, books, kitchen utensils, magazines, stuffed dolls, blankets, and a thousand other things filled the hall from the front door to the living room. The back of her white housecoat had risen as she leaned over, revealing two thin legs, the hollows behind her knees like white egg cups. Hearing me, she stood up and turned halfway around. A pale bony face, eerily bloodless. Bright, hard eyes. She spoke in a high voice with tremendous speed, slightly breathless, her lips barely moving.

"Hi. This is a mess isn't it? Have you ever seen such a mess?" She touched her hair with the tips of her fingers. "The endless junk one collects. I never *dreamed* there was so much."

I stepped gingerly over an ironing board. "What is it? Where did it all come from?"

"It's mine, sweetie," she said, standing perfectly still. "It belongs to me."

The bell rang and I stepped back to open the door. Jean came in, a load of coats draped over his back, a laundry bag under his arm, and a suitcase banging against his leg. "Move that lamp," he said, and as I obeyed he lowered everything onto the cleared space. Standing up straight, he wiped his brow with the back of his hand. "That's it. One more trip should get it all." As if seeing me for the first time, he said, "You can come along. It'll speed it up."

"Okay."

"I don't know how to thank you, Mr. Fouchet. I mean it's so damn *nice* of you. He's insane, you know. Really utterly off his nut. The things he said to me! The things he called me! I'd die if I had to see him again."

"It's all right."

"Be careful of him. He'll say *anything*."

"Don't worry," Jean said, giving me a wink. "I know the type."

"It's all right."

Going downtown in the cab he explained, talking over his shoulder as I sat in the back, my feet on the jump seat. (In accordance with the law Jean's flag was down. I watched the meter clicking away, filled with a curious sense of luxury at the thought that no one had to pay.) "I picked her up and she didn't have a dime. The son of a bitch landlord was putting her stuff on the sidewalk when we got there. Can you believe that? Right out in the open with nobody watching it. He wouldn't even talk to her and just kept going in and out with the stuff. Then she started to cry and I told her to get in the cab. All the morons were standing around as if the whole thing were a sideshow and what the hell I didn't care about the fare that much."

"No, of course not." A subterranean sense of excitement was beginning to communicate itself to me. Jean's animation seemed to indicate we were embarked on an adventure, some special adventure in which my role might be gratifyingly grown-up. His tone was more affectionate than it had been in months and I was flattered, flattered that he bothered to explain, flattered at my inclusion in the conspiracy. Deep down I knew it was conspiracy, but I was safe. Jean took the chances. I watched.

"She told me the whole story. No place to go, no friends she feels right about, family out in the Midwest someplace." He took one hand off the wheel and gestured, his palm flat in the air. "It's a kind of pride. I understand it. Sometimes it's easier to deal with strangers than people you know."

"What happened?"

"She was living over her head. Spending too much money and getting in a hole, and then when she lost her job she . . ."

"No, I don't mean that. What did you say to her?"

"Oh. Well, I was sitting there watching all that stuff pile up on the sidewalk and I thought it wouldn't hurt to let her leave it at eighty-one. We've got all that room and it'll only be a day or two. She's in a tough spot."

"She sure has a lot of stuff."

"You have to help people once in a while. This city is ruthless. You could die on the street and no one would lift a finger."

At her apartment house—a small brownstone in the East Sixties—Jean opened the front door and we walked down a carpeted hallway toward the back. "Luckily it's on the ground floor," he said softly. It took me a moment to realize we weren't already in her apartment—the public foyer was luxuriously fitted with mirrors, heavy drapes, and antique furniture. The door in back was open and the lights were on.

"You know what she paid for this place?" Jean asked, standing in the middle of the empty room. "Two rooms and a lousy little kitchenette? Almost three hundred dollars."

"Jesus!" This was life on a grand scale, and I felt excitement rising again. "Why so much?"

"Location," Jean said, waving his arm. "Snob appeal."

A short, fat man in a black suit came in from the hall and stood by the door. "You get the stuff out?"

"Almost. There's one more load in the bedroom."

"Okay. Good. I got somebody coming to see the place tonight."

I watched the two men. They both looked at the floor, avoiding each other's eyes. Then Jean turned to me. "Let's go," he said, and moved off into the other room. I followed. "Take that bag and I'll get the rest."

I hoisted a pillow case filled with high-heeled shoes over my shoulder and waited as Jean picked up some boxes and two small wicker chairs.

The man in the black suit was still waiting by the door. He stuck out his hand. "The keys, please."

Jean put everything down and fished in his pocket. "You

shouldn't have put her stuff in the street," he said, holding them out.

Sighing, the man took the keys. "You don't think so? No rent for four months. Screaming her head off at three in the morning. Breaking windows. I had to replace the mirror in the bathroom twice. The place like a pigsty." He shook his head. "She brought the roaches. We never had roaches in here before. Nice people live here. This isn't a crazy house."

"Not out on the street like that without warning."

"Warning! I been telling her nothing else for the past month. You think I wanted to do it? I know she's sick."

"What's the matter with her?" I asked Jean.

"Never mind," he said, picking up the chairs.

The man preceded us down the hall. "You don't know. I tried everything but she wouldn't listen. I don't think she understood the words. I'd say something and she'd go on as if she didn't hear me." He opened the front door and stood aside. As Jean passed he put out his hand and touched him on the shoulder. "Listen, you're okay. You work for a living. Listen to me. Don't get mixed up with that woman. She's crazy. She can't help herself. You understand? Crazy!"

Jean went out the door without answering. As I passed I saw the man shake his head. "All right," he said to himself, "don't listen."

The druggist leaned over the counter and gave me back the prescription. "Tell Miss Smith she'll have to pick this up herself. I can't give it to you."

It flashed through my mind that she might expect me to return the quarter she'd given me to run the errand, a quarter already diminished by the price of two candy bars. "Just this once?" I asked. "You know me."

"I know you, Red, but there are laws. She'll have to come herself."

I folded the paper and put it in my pocket. "What is it, heroin?"

"Not quite." Smiling, he went back to the rear of the store.

I paused for a moment at the book rack by the door to see if anything new had come in. Only a few mysteries, and I didn't read mysteries. Outside it was sunny and warm.

I ran back to the house, making a point to jump over the cracks in the sidewalk. I didn't run for fun, but most often out of nervousness. Sometimes anger. In the elevator I ate one of the candy bars. She came out of her room the instant I opened the front door. "He wouldn't give it to me. He says you have to get it yourself."

She tossed her head and made a hissing sound with her teeth. "Stupid little man." I followed her into the room. "I should have known," she said. "They like to exercise their puny power." With a jerk of her thin arms she pulled a drawer so smartly it almost came out of the bureau. "A glass of water, sweetie."

When I came back she was waiting with a large white tablet. It effervesced as it struck the water.

"What's that?"

"A pill. Just a pill for that old zing." She drained the glass and threw it to me. "Catch!"

Luckily I did. "Hey!"

She laughed and turned away.

She threw off her housecoat without the slightest self-consciousness and stood in front of the closet in her slip. "Ugh!" she said, leafing through the dresses with her long white arms. "Ghastly! Prehistorically old!" She finally selected one and pulled it out, letting the hanger fall to the floor. "This for the druggist. Ho ho."

Her body left me entirely cold. The way the stringy muscles sagged ever so slightly under the skin, the fishy whiteness of her, the quick birdlike nervousness of every move—she was thin soup when one wanted stew. Despite the time she gave to grooming, it was obvious that even to herself her body was beneath notice. She prettied herself with much the same air of dazed inattention as my mother washed dishes, not for pleasure but because it had to be done.

Dressed, she picked through the confusion of jars, tubes, bottles, letters, lipsticks, notes, cigarettes, hair rollers that littered the top of the bureau. "Aha!" she said as she found what she was looking for, a black, dog-eared address book. It was characteristic of her to make small exclamatory noises of accompaniment with even the simplest act. "So!" she would say the instant before touching a lipstick to her mouth, or, as she polished her nails, "This little piggy went to market, this little piggy stayed home." She did it even when she thought herself alone. "Time for a little chat with the outside world." She sat on the edge of the bed, lighted a cigarette, and took the phone on her lap. "Be a dear and see if there's any more coffee, would you?"

In the kitchen I poured a fresh cup. Black, no sugar. Walking back down the hall I heard her on the phone.

"It *has* been ages, sweetie, but it's really the old story. *Zillions* of things to do. Running around like a headless chicken. To top it all off I'm moving. In the midst of everything." She took the coffee without looking at me. "Utter chaos, of course, but the old place was getting me down. It was really too small, altogether too small. And the landlord! He simply *wouldn't* leave me alone. Always lurking around with a wimpy smile and garlic on his breath. An absolute *fiend*." She took a sip of coffee and crushed the half-smoked cigarette. "With friends until I find a new place. It's so impossible to get anything good. I hope this week, though. I have a few leads. Hmm. Would you? That would be marvelous, sweetie, but don't go to any trouble. Oh yes." She glanced down at the dial of the phone. "Atwater nine, eight-five-nine-nine. Now the thing is I have an idea for a piece. I saw the last issue and since you girls are getting so *daring* and *modern* and everything I thought it might be right for you. I thought about two thousand words on career-girl dating. The new mores, you know. The thing about actually being afraid to meet mister right. The independence thing. A short piece. Aimed at the young. That's right." Very quickly, holding the phone against her shoulder with the side of her head, she lighted a cigarette and shook out the match. "Preachy! You know me better than that, sweetie. Of course it won't be preachy. Am I the preachy type?" She stuck out the tip of her tongue, made a pincer of thumb and middle finger, and removed a fleck of tobacco. "If you mean on spec I don't do that." Her eyes closed, the lids trembling almost imperceptibly. "Well, tell them I'm a pro, for God's sake. They must have read my stuff." She listened, her eyes still closed, index finger tapping at the cigarette. Suddenly she sat up very straight and threw her head back, chin in the air, to stare at the ceiling. "No. Forget it. Too complicated. I'll send it someplace else." She grabbed the receiver with her other hand, holding it now with both hands as if anticipating the end of the conversation. "Yes. Maybe so. Thursday lunch? Just a sec, I'll look in my book." She remained motionless. I held my breath, unreasonably afraid that some action of my own might give the lie away. "Thursday's bad, sweetie. I'm tied up with some Hollywood types. Why don't I call you next week. Fine. Bye-bye." She hung up, leaving her hand on the phone.

"What does spec mean?" I asked.

"It means you wait for your money." She lifted the receiver and dialed a number rapidly, her fingers jabbing into the holes almost before they stopped spinning. "Tony? Nell Smith. All right. I'll hold."

I went to the window and looked down into the alley. Two kids were playing handball against the wall. As I watched a point was lost and they exchanged places.

"First of all, where the hell is that check? You said the same thing last week. Call financing, then. Call whoever you have to. I'm sick, don't you understand? I need the money. I . . . need . . . the . . . money," she said, separating each word. "What happened with the screenplay? Did you call Harry?" Another point and the boys in the alley were back where they started. I turned from the window. "He didn't sound that way last week. Tell him I'll go out there if I have to. Expenses of course. I'm *not* counting on it, but for God's sake see if you can't do something. Push it. We've made it before." She paused. "So what? Harry doesn't know that. Why bring it up anyway? You're supposed to be on my side. Yes, yes, I know. I want to see your man—what else do you want? Pompous little Jew telling me I'm too thin. Ridiculous. If you want to help get me some work." Her mouth tightened in annoyance. "I'm typing it up. They'll have it this week. Did you know Greg Peck is in town? What about an interview? Will you try? I'll call him and you get me something in front. Really try now, Tony. I'm not kidding."

I walked past her into the hall to my own room two doors away. Sitting on the edge of my bed I listened to her voice while indulging in a favorite vice, the slow removal, millimeter by millimeter, of fingernails so short there was almost nothing left to bite. Sadness crept over me—a sadness I didn't question, a sadness so profound I understood it could not have come from life, or any source within my conceptual scope, but instead seeped into me from the very air, from the whole extant universe in which I was less than a speck, sadness that was not emotion but the awareness of vast emptinesses. With my head in my hands I looked down at my feet, knowing that at any second my body might fade out, wavering into invisibility like Robert Donat in *The Ghost Goes West*.

Jean parked the car at a hack stand just off Fifth Avenue and we got out. Nell Smith led the way, striding along the sidewalk with her head held high, looking splendidly fresh in spotless white shoes, a suit of blue silk, and white gloves. She smiled as people moved out of her way. The door to the shop opened magically and she entered without breaking her stride. Behind her, Jean and I strove to keep up. The man holding the door nodded as we passed.

A salesman fell in alongside as she moved down the carpeted aisle between the glittering showcases. "I want a portable phonograph for my niece," she said without moving her head. "Something very nice."

"Yes madam. This way."

We moved toward the back of the store. I almost collided with Jean as Nell stopped abruptly, her attention caught by something on one of the counters. "What's that?"

"Ah yes." The salesman raised his arm in the air and snapped his fingers. "Mr. Chambers knows about that."

Mr. Chambers approached quickly on the other side of the counter. "First of all we have an exceptionally fine radio," he said, snapping open the case. "Standard frequencies along this scale," he pointed with a pencil, "long wave ship to shore here, short wave, police band, European, ham operators, and all the rest. The entire spectrum." He opened the back. "Normal antenna plus a directional antenna."

"A fine piece of equipment," said the first salesman at her elbow.

"A map and radio log here m back," Mr. Chambers went on, "and over here a complete weather system." He pointed with the pencil again. "A barometer, delicate enough to be used as an altimeter, and a highly sensitive thermometer."

"There's an instruction book explaining it all in detail," the first salesman said.

Nell extended a gloved finger and twirled one of the dials. "Very nice."

Everyone stood still. I found myself hoping desperately that she'd buy it. It would only be around a day or two, I knew, but what fun it would be. Paris. London. Rome. Police calls.

"Where are the phonographs?" Nell asked, stepping away. "First things first."

"Yes madam. This way."

In another part of the store a selection of portable phonographs was on display, each on its own table. Nell went directly to a machine encased in fine leather. "This looks nice. Frank, pick out a record and we'll hear what it sounds like."

Aware that I'd probably get to keep whatever I chose, I flipped through the musical comedies, vocals, and pop-music albums impatiently, my hands shaking with greed. I was being bought. I could sense it but I didn't care. I deserved a piece of the action. When a boxed, sealed album of Benny Goodman's 1938 jazz concert met my eye I didn't hesitate an instant. It was satisfyingly expensive and heavy in my hands.

After a minute or two of "Sing Sing Sing" Nell nodded. "I'll take it. How much is it?"

"Two hundred dollars plus tax," the salesman answered, flipping the switch.

I couldn't believe my ears. Our old '36 Ford, the inde-structible Ford that had carried us so many miles, cost two hundred dollars. The cabin and three acres in Connecticut hadn't cost very much more. For two hundred dollars I could go to the movies for the rest of my life. It was fan-tastic, and yet Nell seemed almost not to have heard. "Get it ready, will you," she ordered. "This gentleman will take it out to the car."

"Certainly madam," the salesman said, opening his book. "Is that a charge or cash?"

"Charge. The name is Nell Smith." She sat down, crossed her legs and took out a cigarette. Her white foot moved gently in the air as she waited.

The next day Nell and I watched Jean emerge from an Eighth Avenue pawnshop. He leaned over and spoke through the open window of the cab. "Seventy-five dollars. He won't go any higher."

Nell tapped her foot. "God damn thieves." She hesitated, her hand on the window shelf. "We'd better take it. I can always go back for the radio next week. Yes, go ahead. Get the money."

For the first two or three weeks Jean was happy. I remember standing with him at the top of the hall watching Nell walk down to her room. "Quite a gal," he said. He seemed about to break into a little dance. His eyes sparkled. "Look at those legs."

I threw a perfunctory glance. "Oh, I don't know. She's too skinny."

He laughed and winked at me. "Quite a gal, quite a gal." Was he trying to tell me something? Was he so proud of himself he couldn't contain it? It's quite possible, given her hysterical state, that he never slept with her, but the more I think about it, the more it seems he did. Something about that wink, and the twinkle in his eye, something in his irrepressible good humor suggesting a boy with his hand in the cookie jar, something in the movement of his body, the hint of a dandified, cocky jig in his step. . . .

He would sit in the kitchen watching her whip up a *soufflé*. Every now and then she'd make some terribly elaborate meal employing every utensil in the shelves, every bowl and dish there was, only to leave it all at the end for someone else to clean up. Her chatter rarely stopped—a bright, quick stream as she flitted back and forth. He laughed his hoarse, croaking laugh and never took his eyes off her. He told dialect stories by the dozens, keeping them moderately clean while I was around. He even started her on vitamins and wheat germ, ranting by the hour about how it was the only way to fight the poisons in refined foods. He half convinced her the sickness she talked so much about was due to improper diet. They talked and talked in the kitchen, over meals, over coffee, sometimes all day when Jean wasn't working. A Niagara of words, round and round, back and forth in a marathon of gab. Jean emptied his bag of verbal tricks once more. All the techniques grown stale with my mother were fresh again, gambits that she had learned to see through or ignore worked anew. It was delirious! For an oral maniac the chance to pour word-magic into fresh and captive ear satisfies a need as deep as sex. His delight in himself was reborn.

He must have been at his most charming the night they went to Bill Miller's Riviera, an expensive night club on the New Jersey Palisades. He might even have looked around the table at the other members of the party, people Nell knew, successful men and beautiful women—a producer, perhaps, a gossip columnist, a famous actor, a writer—he might have lifted his champagne and believed that at long last he was going to get the break he'd been waiting for. At any moment a word spoken by one of these powerful men might change his life. An invitation that would lead to other invitations. Recognition of his unique talents. The offer of a high-paying job in which his unorthodox ideas would be shown once and for all to be viable, in which he would have a completely free hand.

Why should he have expected these things? Because for all his knocking around his view of the world was incredibly naïve. He believed important jobs were handed out in night clubs by impulsive millionaires and that he was the sort of man they might be given to. Spoiled all his life, supported and fussed over by one woman after another, he deeply believed that the good things in life were given to one. Food, clothing, and the bare necessities had to be earned, but after that, to move on to anything grander than that, it was a question of being in the right place at the right time, or knowing the right people or simply being lucky. It never occurred to Jean to work hard at anything except menial labor. He was always above his work, the secret possessor of an inner wealth untouched by the world —his image of himself.

He believed he was potentially a great man, a visionary on the order of da Vinci or Jules Verne. At the same time he saw himself as a man of simple good sense whose mind was untainted by the prejudices of traditional education. He had no particular discipline, no way to show the world his talent, but far more important was his belief in himself. His fanatical faith in his own potential was the key to his personality and his reluctance to test that faith in the practical world the key to his behavior. "Look at Einstein," he would say. "Failed mathematics in high school!" It was only the world that held Jean back, the petty machinations of a society all men knew to be unjust. He wouldn't bother with the world, and yet, as he sat among men who actually held the power, he must have hoped that one of them would discover him. In the end it was all he could hope for.

Of course no one offered him anything more significant than another glass of champagne. He was an obvious escort—tall, superbly handsome, and an expert dancer—an escort and no more, they must have thought, bought for show like her expensive clothes.

After five or six weeks Jean began to get nervous. The novelty had worn off and she was still in the house, with all her belongings, making no preparations to leave. She'd run out of money and friends and her behavior was becoming stranger with every passing day. She hardly ever left the house, wandering back and forth from kitchen to bathroom to bedroom in a nightgown and pedal pushers, her hair uncombed, her eyes bright from barbiturates. She talked to herself in the hall, sometimes walking past me as if I wasn't there, sometimes buttonholing me for an hour's description of how sick she was. Occasionally a new note crept into her voice—a kind of whine, childlike, as if she were becoming a little girl again. She stopped eating, and even Jean was alarmed in the rapidity with which she lost weight from her already thin frame. She would burst from her room in a manic frenzy and make telephone calls all over the country, shouting into the mouthpiece, her body rigid with hate.

At first Jean simply stayed out of the house, hoping she'd get bored and go away. He worked long hours and went to a lot of movies. He had coffee at Stanley's Cafeteria instead of at home. Eventually he even stayed out for meals, but to no avail. Nell was dug in.

In desperation he got the name of her lawyer and called for advice. He learned to his horror that she was highly suicidal and should be watched every minute of the day. For months people had been at work trying to arrange for her voluntary commitment when she had suddenly disappeared. The doctors believed that if she survived her suicidal compulsion a total nervous collapse was imminent As for immediate advice about getting her out of the house, the lawyer had nothing to say. Can we doubt that Jean's hand shook as he hung up the phone?

Panicked, he did the only thing he could think of. He sat down in front of the typewriter, two packs of Pall Malls and a pot of coffee at his elbow, and wrote a long, detailed letter to Dagmar explaining the entire situation from start to finish, showing clearly and indisputably the innocence and nobility of his motives, the sadness of life in general, and the extreme difficulty of his present situation in particular. Would she come home? Would she come home right away, thus forcing Nell to leave? He needed her help. There was no time to lose. Oh God, I can see him there at the kitchen table, the pages piled up in profusion his eyes squinting down through the cigarette smoke, his hands poised above the keyboard. I know his dizziness, the way he built the verbal edifice into an impenetrable fortress. He knew he was right! The clarity! The honesty! He'd been frightened, yes, badly frightened, but now he'd got things clear. Everything was going to be all right. Dagmar would have to return after reading the letter, she had no choice. As his hands came down to type out the final news, the topper, the supreme fact which by now he felt he didn't even really need to include, that Nell was liable to kill herself at any moment right there in the house, he must have felt a tremendous sense of relief. His brain reeling with ten typewritten pages of nineteenth-century prose, he must have thought, as he divested himself of that ominous intelligence, that at last he could begin to discern the faint rays of a hopeful dawn.

He mailed off his ten pages and waited an inordinately long time for the answer. It finally came. Eight words: "You got yourself into it. Get yourself out." From the moment he read those words he stopped talking.

A gray morning. I stood at the living room window looking down at the street. Behind me the apartment was empty —Alison still away, Nell Smith out to the druggist, and Jean somewhere on the streets of the city in his cab. Had Jean been home it would have made no difference—the most I saw of him since the letter was a brief flash as he came through the front door and crossed the hall to his room, locking the Yale lock quickly to seal himself in. I'd tried talking through the door but he wouldn't answer. I stared at the meaningless stream of cars going by, my brain as empty and silent as the house around me. Within me sadness had given way to hopelessness. And I mean genuine hopelessness, when faith has evaporated and the imagination is dead, when life seems to have come finally and irrevocably to a standstill.

It might have been that—the stillness inside me, the thanatoid silence frightening me into a last-ditch effort to stay alive, or maybe something pettier, the thought of school, the impossible prospect of another day in prison crystallizing my formless mind as the tap of a pencil will crystallize a supersaturated solution. The idea arrived in completed form. In a single breathless moment I became a new person. Run away! To Florida! Right now, this very moment! Blinded by revelation, it didn't occur to me to make plans or preparations. I turned from the window, walked down the hall, and went out the door. It was as simple as that. I put my body into motion and disregarded the pounding of my heart.

As I walked across the George Washington Bridge toward New Jersey the sun broke from behind the clouds. Bright rays caught the highest cables first and slipped down along the long, sweeping curves like molten silver until the whole airy structure shone with radiance. Far below, the water was still dark. A stiff breeze kept whipping my hair over my eyes but I paid no attention. I was seeing a new world. Everything seemed special—a telephone call box, the surface of the walkway, the cables, the cars rushing by—all of it was super-real, each image sharply defined in space and shimmering with vibrancy. The air itself was triple strength and seemed to clean out my lungs as I marched along.

Descending into the architectural chaos on the other side I looked around at the public world—the sidewalks, empty lots, signs, diners, phone booths—conscious that these things were now the furniture of my life, that until I got to Florida they were all I had. I stood for a moment in front of a coin-operated milk machine, paralyzed by its significance. Put a quarter in the slot and the milk would come out. No questions, no ramifications, just the milk. One could live without words and without people.

Route One wasn't far away. I slipped across the traffic and turned south, walking steadily for a couple of miles before I found a long, fairly open stretch of road where cars could stop easily. Then I turned (for some reason I remember this precisely), put my left hand in my pocket and my right thumb in the air. I didn't make the familiar long, sweeping gesture as the cars went by, I just held out my thumb. I was wearing khaki trousers, a light-blue shirt, and a leather jacket.

My first ride was a '49 Dodge. Running down the road to where it waited, I glanced at the license plate, only mildly disappointed to see "New Jersey." (I'd been day-dreaming of a single ride all the way to Florida.) I pulled open the door and jumped in quickly. "Thanks," I said, breathing hard. The driver, a man of about thirty, pulled back into the traffic. A briefcase lay on the seat beside him and in the back I could see what looked like folded cardboard boxes, stacked flat and tied with string. A few loose papers lay beside the briefcase.

"How far you going?" he asked.

"To Florida. Fort Lauderdale, Florida."

"Well, I can take you about twenty miles before I turn off."

"That's fine. Thanks a lot."

We rode in silence for some time. Now that I was on my way I felt almost lighthearted. Inside the comfortable car, mile after mile falling behind me, I felt myself growing expansive. I glanced down at the papers and read a letterhead.

"How's the cardboard box business?" I asked, pleased at my own cleverness.

"Not bad," he said. "It's a living. Gets a little dull sometimes."

"Do you make them?"

"No, I just sell them. Go around to factories and manufacturers and take their orders."

"I had a job working in a drugstore but I got fired for sleeping in the stockroom."

He laughed. "Aren't you a little young to be going off to Florida?"

I watched the road, not turning my head. "No. I don't think so."

"Well, maybe not," he said slowly, "maybe not."

"I'm fifteen."

"You don't look fifteen, I can tell you that."

"I know, but it's the truth."

"Well, I believe you. No reason why you should lie to me." He drove for a while without saying anything. "Florida's a long way. I guess you're going to hitch all the way down?"

"That's right. I'm hoping for long rides, maybe even someone going to Miami."

"You figure on coming back?"

"No."

"Not ever, uh?"

"Nope. Not ever."

"Well there you are," he said, and gazed out through the windshield.

The flat, green Jersey meadows slipped by outside, wiped every few seconds by the dark blur of a telephone pole. "I ran away when I was seventeen," he said suddenly, after miles of silence. "I never went back."

My head whipped around. "You did?" It seemed an incredible coincidence, but I believed him.

"My old man was a bastard." A faint smile appeared on his face. "He beat us up all the time. Best thing I ever did was leave."

"Where'd you go?"

"One morning he came at me in the barn and before I knew it I laid him out with a pitchfork. Wham! Right on the ear." The smile was broader now. "He went down like a tree. I thought sure he was dead but of course he wasn't. Just out cold." He laughed. "I didn't wait for him to come around, though. No sir. I left immediately."

I laughed with him. "Where'd you go?"

"Well, I had a little money. Enough to eat for a while, anyway. I skipped the state on a freight train and moved around the country picking up work here and there. I was a big kid so I didn't have much trouble. Then I got a job on a farm out in Iowa and the people were really nice—best people I'd ever met—so I stayed on there. Every winter I thought about coming East but somehow I'd wind up staying. Finally did leave when their boy came back from the Marines."

I sat silently for a while, absorbing the story. "When you got here you found a job and just . . ." I hesitated, unsure how to phrase it, ". . . just went on?"

"That's right," he said. "This same company, matter of fact. I started in the shop as a cutter."

His words were momentous. I drank them in and stored them away, hoping they could somehow protect me from the dangers ahead. He'd run away, he'd started from nothing as I was starting—and there he was, looking like everyone else in his suit and tie, driving a car, holding down a decent job, living proof that one could bring it off. Perhaps I wouldn't have to live in the woods eating food Tobey stole for me. Maybe I could get a job and begin a new life. I might even learn to laugh at the old days as the man beside me had learned to laugh at the image of his unconscious father. I began to see possibilities I hadn't considered in the heat of my escape. I could even get married in a few years and start a family of my own.

The car was slowing down.

"I have to turn off here," he said. "It's a good spot, though. They'll be able to see you from pretty far back."

I felt a faint twinge at the sight of the deserted intersection. Somehow I'd forgotten that I'd ever have to get out. But I was ready as we came to a stop.

"Now son," he said, turning to me, "if I were you I'd stay away from trains and railroad yards. Just keep hitching and don't get in with anybody who looks funny."

"All right." I nodded. "Why do you say that about trains?"

"Well the bums and the winos. They get rough sometimes."

"Thanks for telling me. I'll be careful." I pulled back the handle and opened the door. As I looked back I could see him hesitate, and then speak.

"Do you know about queers?"

For a moment I thought he meant something specific rather than just whether I knew they existed. "Yes," I finally answered.

"Because they don't always look like queers. That's what I meant about the yards. Some of those bums will do anything. Don't let them catch you."

I nodded and started out of the car.

"If you do get caught tell them you're a very religious boy and you couldn't do anything like that. Tell them Jesus would punish you for the rest of your life. That got me out of a tight spot in Kansas once."

"Okay. I'll remember that." I stepped out into the sunshine. "Goodbye, and thanks a lot."

"So long, kid," he yelled through the window. "Good luck!"

I watched the car pull away and head west, its rear end sinking slightly as the driver accelerated. There was a flash of brake lights as the car approached a curve and then the road was empty. A blast of air struck my ankles and neck as a big semi roared by behind me.

I was in the cab of an old Studebaker truck. The driver, an immensely fat man whose belly cleared the steering wheel by no more than an inch, had told me he was carrying a load of Kotex from a wholesaler in Jersey City to a warehouse south of Camden.

"I've carried everything in my time," he said. He drove with his shoulders, his pudgy hands holding the wheel as if the palms were grafted on. "Pineapples, horseshit, paper clips, bathtubs, you name it. Even a little booze in the old days but my wife made me stop. Yes sir, nothing surprises me any more. I just drive along and work on the old voice." He threw back his head and began to sing. "When that red red robin comes bob bob bobbin' along, a-LONG!" His voice rang out clearly over the whine of the engine. "How about that, kid? Pretty good, eh? Someday I'll go on the Ted Mack Amateur Hour. Oh boy. George Platz the Singing Truck Driver! I'll win in a breeze. Did you see that movie where Mario Lanza is a truck driver and he delivers this piano, you know, and he thinks he's alone and sits down and plays a little and makes with the old voice? Boy, what a terrific movie. It turns out the piano is for some great-looking opera star and she hears him from the other room and he winds up a star too, you know, going around in those monkey suits and drinking champagne all the time. Dee-eep river, my home is O-ver Jordan! That guy can really sing. You gotta give it to him." He beeped the horn as we passed a car.

We rumbled on through town after town. I watched the sun sinking in the sky and realized I should have stolen something from Jean's cash tray. I had a dollar fifty in my pocket and the trip was going to be longer than I'd thought. It was afternoon already and I was still in New Jersey.

The truck slowed down and we pulled up in front of a roadside stand. "Come on kid, let's eat."

I was hungry, but I hesitated.

"Come on," he said, descending from the cab. "It's on me."

"Thank you. I have some money, though." I opened my door and jumped to the ground.

"Don't be silly, kid," he said as we walked through the dust. "Keep it for later. You'll need it." He spoke softly, as if not to embarrass me. At the stand he slapped both hands on the counter. "Hiya gorgeous! How ya been keeping since I saw you last?"

"What'll it be?" the waitress asked, smiling.

"Five hot dogs, coffee, and a big glass of milk for the kid, here."

As she went off to prepare the food he turned and leaned back against the counter, balancing his weight on his elbows. He winked at me, gave his belly a slap and very delicately crossed one leg over the other. I could hear the hot dogs sizzle as they hit the griddle.

"Some enchanted evening," he sang in full voice, "you will see a strange-ahh! You will see a strange-ahh, across a crowded room. . . ."

Night. I walk along the side of a road, my way lighted by the headlights of cars whipping past. I've been walking for a long time, not bothering to hitch since the sun went down. The rhythm of my body takes up my entire attention. I'm faintly drunk with movement. Ahead I see the lights of a town. Suddenly there's a sidewalk under my feet. Houses, most of them dark, are set back behind hedges and lawns. A dog barks a block or two behind me.

Moving through the center of town I am only dimly aware of my surroundings. The shops are closed and the streets nearly empty. I watch for the route signs. The state is Delaware. I don't know the town. I pass under the darkened marquee of a movie theater. The street widens. More houses behind lawns. Tall trees above. My breath makes smoke in the damp air.

On the far side of town I approach the intersection of two gigantic highways. There are lights everywhere—gas stations, restaurants, liquor stores. I stop in front of an all-night diner. A couple necks in a car in the shadows. I go into the diner. Sitting on a stool near the end of the counter, my legs prickling with a thousand minuscule pulse beats, I eat tomato soup and a cheese sandwich. Finished, I push the plates away and order a Coke and a piece of layer cake. On my way out I buy a nickel cigar from a machine near the door.

Outside I regain my sense of direction and continue south. After a few steps the rhythm of walking takes hold of me again and it's as if I'd never stopped. For mile after mile my mind is empty. No, not empty exactly. Imagine a symphony orchestra responding to a suddenly paralyzed conductor by holding a single note on and on, forever, without change.

I look up to see an immense building flooded with light in the near distance. A red neon sign on the roof says State Police. I stop where I am and watch the sign. Then I look around. A path on my left leads away to a dark clapboard house. A shingle on the lawn says Henry Freeman M.D. There are three concrete steps at the foot of the path. I sit down with my back to the house and take out the cigar. The cellophane falls away and I light up. Watching the red neon, I smoke slowly.

The cigar finished, I see a dark shape across the lawn. Moving closer I can make out a small ornamental tree, no more than six feet tall with broad thick branches very low to the ground. Down on my hands and knees I peer underneath. I can feel a bed of fallen needles. I crawl under carefully, the branches closing after me. There's just enough room as I curl myself around the thin trunk. No one will see me in the morning. I fall asleep with the scent of pine heavy in my head, thinking of the woods in Florida.

12
Nights Away from Home

ONCE, as a very young boy, I spent the night in Harlem. Sitting next to Madge on the bus, my pajamas in a paper bag on my lap, I looked out at the crowded streets.

"There aren't any white people at all, Madge."

"I know, honey."

"Why not?"

"Well this is where colored people live. This is Harlem."

When we got off the bus I felt like holding her hand but she carried a bag of clothes and some groceries. I walked close beside her, my shoulder brushing against her wide hip. The world was dark—dark streets, dark houses, and dark people, as if the black sky had descended to a level just above the housetops. I kept looking at Madge, nervous that she might change somehow, that in this dark world she might be different from the way she was at home. A few hours before, when my mother had left, she'd been on her knees scrubbing the bathroom floor.

"Here we are," she said, turning into a building. "We got to climb the stairs."

Inside her small apartment all the lights were off except a single bulb in the kitchen. An old lady with gray hair sat at the table with the *Daily News* spread out in front of her.

"This is Frank," Madge said. "Mrs. Fouchet's little boy. You remember I told you."

I shook hands. "So you gon' spend the night?" she said. "Well, that's nice."

Madge put down her bundles. "I'll show you where you sleep."

We went to a very small room. I sat on the bed and took my shoes off.

"Now you get yourself ready. I'll bring you a glass of milk."

I undressed in the darkness and put on my pajamas. I could hear the women's voices in the kitchen. When Madge came back I was under the covers. I drank the milk slowly, ate half the cookie she'd brought, and slipped the rest under the pillow for later.

"Goodnight, child." She brushed my hair back with her warm brown hand.

"Will you leave the door open?"

"Course I will. You go to sleep now."

In the morning I woke while the house was still quiet. I dressed myself and went into Madge's room. She lay asleep in her bed, lying on her side, motionless under the blankets. I went to the front window and sat on the sill.watching the street below. When she woke up she saw me sitting there and smiled.

"There're some children playing in the street," I said. "Is it all right if I go down?"

"Big children or little children?" she asked.

I looked down. "Both, I guess."

"Well, you better not, honey," she said after a moment. "You better stay up here with me."

Five years later, in Florida, up a tree, I looked down through the branches at my mother standing in our front yard. She was no more than a stone's throw away, across the road, but I was safe in the woods. "Frank!" she called. "Frank!"

In the tree house, I whispered to myself, "Go ahead and yell. Yell your fucking head off. I'm not coming back."

"Frank!"

Her blond hair was faintly iridescent in the twilight. There wasn't a breath of wind. After a while she turned away and went back in the house. The copper mesh of the screen door took on a wavering glow as someone lighted the kerosene lamp in the kitchen. I rolled over on my back and stared at the moon, sick with rage.

Ten miles south of London at four in the morning the fog starts. Long, wispy tendrils float above the road, horizontal ghosts vanishing at the touch of the car's powerful headlight beams. Inside, I'm warm, cozy, and drunk. The instrument panel glows. The heater-fan whirs. The scent of leather wraps me round and a pint of Scotch lies beside me

on the seat. In total communion with the car, I come
down from overdrive to fourth and touch the brakes,
watching the speedometer needle sink from eighty to fifty
with the same detachment I might feel were it recording the
temperature in Bangor, Maine. I am a completely rhythmic
being. I shift down to third as fog mounts the hood. My
arm moves the wheel in constant adjustment, my heart
beats, I breathe in and out, my eyes move in my head—
all of it a subtle counterpoint of rhythms, infinitely synco-
pated, and in my drunkenness, endlessly beautiful.

  I pull over to the side of the road and stop the car. I shut
off the engine and listen to the faint tick of the cooling
manifolds. Suddenly the lights in the car go on, showing me
my own body. I feel something cold against the back of my
left hand. Looking down I realize I've opened the door.
Fog curls around the edges of the doorway. I roll out of
the seat and stand up beside the car, steadying myself by
holding the top of the door. My body burns like an angel's.
I exist in the center of a corona of invisible fire. In one
orchestrated movement I pull the door shut and launch myself out into the fog. When the momentum ends I plant my
feet wide in the ground and open my fly. My urine steams
and splits the air, it flows out of me like flame from a
flame-thrower.

  Going back, the car is barely visible in the thickening
fog. The windows are beaded. I open the door and climb
into the back seat. I arrange my six-foot body across the
four-foot seat and close my eyes. The drunken noise of
my mind suddenly stops as an extraordinary feeling comes
over me. I'm not in the car at all! I'm under the tree in
Delaware! I can even smell the pine needles. Frightened,
I open my eyes and sit up. It's so dark I can barely make
out the windows.

Under the tree on the doctor's lawn, I woke early. Crawling
out carefully, I stood up and brushed the pine needles
from my clothes and hair. Everything was utterly still—
the road, the houses, the damp air itself. I looked around
at the town in the colorless dawn light, seeing it for the first
time. It was smaller than I'd thought in the darkness. Not
even a town, really, just a few houses strung along either
side of the highway. I crossed the road and started south.
As I approached the police station the red neon sign went

out. I went by quickly, without turning my head.

My first ride of the day was a milk truck. The driver, a teenaged boy, seemed to be standing behind the wheel in the tall, open cab. Then I realized there was a very high seat so he could jump in and out with a minimum of effort. I sat down on the corrugated steel floor and lifted my face to the wind. Behind us the bottles rattled in their wire cages.

"Go ahead, kid," he yelled over the wind and the rattling glass. "Take a quart. I'll chalk it up to breakage."

I opened a bottle and drank in long, deep swallows. The milk was ice cold and delicious. Five or six miles up the road the boy had to turn off to begin his rounds. At the corner I jumped out the open door with a wave, absurdly pleased that he didn't have to stop. The sun was out and I took off my jacket, slinging it over my shoulder as I walked.

It was too early for traffic. When a car passed I'd turn around and walk backward, my thumb in the air, whipping my head as it went by to see the license plate. By never losing my forward momentum I felt less dependent on the cars.

Plowed fields stretched away on either side of the road. I measured my progress by sighting something far ahead—a group of mailboxes, a road sign, or a line of telephone poles—and making it my goal. Passing a huge girl drinking Coca-Cola (the sudden awareness of silence as I walked under her immense eyes, one of them bulging slightly where the paper had blistered), I'd already picked my next target, an isolated gas station on the horizon.

I was sweating as I crossed the asphalt driveway and approached the office. Through the wide plate-glass window I could see an old man sitting with his feet up staring out at the pumps. His head came around slowly as he caught sight of me. I pushed open the door. Hillbilly music blasted from a radio on the desk beside his feet.

"Can I use the bathroom?"

"What say?"

"Can I use the bathroom please?"

"Around back." He waved his arm to indicate the direction.

I let the door fall shut and went around the corner of the building. The ground was littered with old oil cans, paper cartons, and fragments of auto bodies. Inside the men's room I looked at myself in the mirror over the washstand, mildly surprised that except for a layer of dirt and messy hair I looked the same as usual. I ran hot water into the basin and pulled my shirt over my head. There wasn't any soap, only a can of Grease-Off, a gray powder that felt like sand between my palms. I scoured myself thoroughly, face, neck, shoulders, and arms, and bent over the small basin to rinse off when the paste began to sting too much.

Back out in front I gathered my courage. I ran my fingers through my hair and went into the office. The old man was cleaning his nails with a penknife.

"Have you got any odd jobs you want done?" I asked, having rehearsed the question in the bathroom mirror. "Cleaning up or washing windows or something?"

He attacked his index finger with exquisite care. "Nope."

"I could clean up that junk around back."

He answered without raising his head. "This ain't my place. I'm just watching it."

"Will the boss be back soon?"

"Nope." He raised the knife to his mouth and blew something off the tip.

I stood by the door, reluctant to leave. "Well, thanks anyway," I said after a minute, and backed out. I knelt down for a drink from the water tap between the gas pumps, wiping my mouth and glancing back at the office as I finished. The old man hadn't moved. I turned away and crossed the black asphalt back to the highway.

Every hour or so I would take a break. I was resting by the side of the road, my back up against a fence post, when a yellow school bus came around the bend and stopped directly in front of me. The folding doors crashed open and the driver stared down his extended arm at me. "Well, come on," he yelled, his hand opening and closing over the handle of the door lever.

I got up and advanced a step. "I'm not . . ." I began, unsure of how to explain.

"What?" he yelled. He squinted his eyes and, peering down at me, raised his upper lip in an expression of annoyance, exposing a quarter-inch of red gums.

"I don't go to your school," I said, stepping back. "I don't ride the bus."

His mouth fell shut and he pulled the lever to close the

doors, his whole body straightening with the effort. "God damn kids."

The children had crowded over to my side to see what was happening. They watched me from behind the glass, their mouths moving silently as they shouted. The bus began to move and they slipped away, pale faces turning into a white blur. I started walking.

As the morning sun rose higher in the sky, traffic picked up, but there were no trucks. It occurred to me that I'd taken a wrong turn somewhere. I was on Route One, but there might have been an alternate, a truck route, that I'd missed. In any event I knew the thing to do was keep heading south. Eventually the roads would rejoin. I wiggled my thumb at a big DeSoto. It went by at a good seventy miles an hour, rocking slightly on the poor road surface. About to turn away, I caught sight of another car in the distance. A flash of sunlight caught something on its roof and I froze in my tracks. A red beacon. The police. It was too late to hide. I turned my back on them and continued walking, my mind spinning in a frantic effort to prepare myself should they stop. Could Jean have notified the police in New York? No, that was out of the question. I realized I should have prepared a story—something from a book I'd read, or a movie. I should have had a false personality and background at my fingertips so they wouldn't be able to trace me back. No matter what happened, I couldn't let them send me back. Forcing myself not to turn around for a quick glance, I kept walking.

At first a faint sighing, like wind in the tops of distant trees. Then the birth of another sound within the sigh, a sharper sound, very faint but growing steadily, a kind of whine, first heard as a pinpoint in the higher registers, building rapidly to a full hum across the spectrum, growing louder and louder, and then (at the very instant a shock wave of air slammed softly across my shoulders) overtaking the sigh, reversing itself, and plunging down the scale to a steady hum. I watched the black car racing away ahead of me. The taillights came on, a bright, burning red. The entire rear end lifted almost imperceptibly.

After a momentary pause the cruiser began to back up. I stood fascinated, rabbit-like, drinking in the image of the approaching car. When it arrived in front of me, so close

I could have touched it, the image was unreal, like something from a dream. The window came down and a pair of blue eyes watched me calmly.

"What you doin' out here, boy?"

"I'm on my way to school. I missed the bus." A certain tranquillity spread like oil over the surface of my mind as I plunged into the lie.

"We saw you hitching. Hitching rides is against the law," he said, his voice neither threatening nor reassuring, leaving me plenty of room to answer. He scratched his nose and watched me.

"Well, I'm sorry," I said, looking down. "I was getting awfully late." He turned and stared out the windshield. A speck of shaving soap had dried just under his ear, very white against the red skin. "Where're your books?"

"In my locker," I said. "We didn't have any homework so I left them."

He turned away and spoke to his partner at the wheel. I couldn't hear the short exchange.

"Okay. Get in," he said, staring straight ahead.

"What?" I felt the beginning of panic, like a giant hand squeezing my heart.

"Get in back. We go by the high school."

"Oh, that's great," I said, talking quickly to conceal my relief. "Thanks a lot. I sure appreciate it." I opened the back door and hesitated with one foot inside. The rear of the car was separated from the front by heavy wire mesh and the handles had been stripped off the inside of the doors. I entered after a split second, dazed, overwhelmed by that particular breathless, lightheaded sensation that comes with the sense of having lost control of events, surrendering myself to fate with the same delirious passivity the awkward diver feels as he springs off the board. My body fell back as the car pulled away and I covered my mouth in a convulsive yawn. Through the black mesh I could see the wide bristled necks of the two cops ramrod stiff above their neat gray shirt collars.

"You drive like an old lady, George."

"Uh-huh. Tell the Governor."

"I might do that."

I slid forward on the seat and reached out to hold the wire mesh. Suddenly I wanted to tell them the truth. I opened my mouth to speak but stopped as I felt tears start-

ing in my eyes. My fingers tightened in the mesh and I
waited for the emotion to pass.

The radio crackled and the driver reached down for
the microphone, pressing it against the side of his mouth.
"Twelve. Twelve," he said. "An assist. We got a kid who
missed the school bus. It's on our way. Twelve out." A
voice responded, talking in numbers. The driver leaned
forward and replaced the microphone.

I ran over his words and decided that despite the mysterious word "assist" they were in fact going to do nothing
more than drop me off at the local high school.

"I sure appreciate it," I said again. The urge to confess
had disappeared. I watched the countryside go by.

That night I came upon a truck depot in Maryland. Hundreds of trucks spaced out in long lines on the hard-
packed earth like the vertebrae of some immense animal.
A quarter-mile down the line I could see the faint neon
haze of the diner. The air was filled with a continuous rumbling as trucks pulled in and out in the distance, air brakes
gasping, headlights flashing against the sky. I walked among
the tall wheels, staring up at the gargantuan trailers, big as
houses, admiring the shiny cabs with their chunky radiator
grilles and fanciful decorations. Most of the rigs were dark,
but every now and then one had been parked with the
running lights left burning—small pinpoints of red, green,
or amber light describing the huge mass of the trailers high
in the air like enlarged examples from a geometry book. I
stopped behind each truck to check the banks of license
plates. I ran through the eastern seaboard states in my
mind, constructing a model of the selection of plates most
likely to indicate a truck going to Florida. I found what
I was looking for at the edge of the parking area—a sixty-
foot semi with plates from Massachusetts to Florida. The
barn-sized rear doors were locked. I went around to the
front and examined the empty cab. Lettered on the red
door were the words "Favario Trucking, North South
Express Shipping, Boston, Mass.," followed by a series of
numbers and specifications. I stepped into the deeper darkness between the cab and trailer, in among the tanks,
hoses, and hydraulic lines, and urinated invisibly.

I waited on the running board for an hour or so, dozing
off and then waking with a jolt as my back began to slip

on the smooth metal of the door. Once I stood up at the approach of voices, but the men passed unseen in the next corridor and continued up the line, their voices dying out after a burst of laughter. I moved away from the truck toward the long grass at the edge of the area. Where the grass began an old cab had been put up on blocks, the wheels removed, umbilical cords dangling on the ground. I climbed up on the running board and pulled open the door. It was dark inside, but as my eyes adjusted I could see the cab was empty. Kneeling on the seat I spread the curtain hanging where the rear window should have been and looked into a small compartment. There were two small round windows at each end and a thin mattress to lie on. I climbed in and closed the curtains.

Suddenly it was morning. The porthole at my feet threw a slanting bar of sunlight across my legs. I heard something moving and opened the curtains in time to see a brown cat leap from the seat to the open window of the door and disappear. Climbing down carefully, I rubbed the sleep from my eyes, kicked the door open, and jumped to the ground. The field was empty. I took a few steps, looking around in astonishment. The flat earth spread before me, almost white under the blazing sun, an empty desert the size of a couple of football fields. On the other side I could see the diner, a small square building at the edge of the road. The cat loped toward it, moving in a straight line over the dusty ground, hindquarters jouncing smoothly and head held high. I followed in its tracks.

And it was as I crossed the empty field that something entirely unexpected happened in my head. A sudden switch, a reversal of polarity, overwhelmingly strong and oddly mechanical, as if my brain were one of those old-fashioned treadle machines that start sewing backward if you catch the cycle wrong. I had to return to New York. The decision to go back was as instantaneous as the decision to start in the first place, but while the latter had exploded like some bright, cleansing, beneficent bomb, the former simply held my soul with irresistible firmness, as if God had reached down out of the sky, grabbed my head, and twisted it north.

I remember quite precisely the single fact I allowed myself to believe was the cause of my change of heart—that I would never see the baby again. Jessica was the only complete and uncomplicated love in my life, and once having conjured her up I knew I hadn't the strength to leave her. I followed the cat through the dust and thought of Jessica, relieved to know it was she, and not the others, pulling me back, that it was love, and not lack of courage, forcing me to capitulate. Thus works the mind of a child, always a bit behind the world, swamped with emotion, and innocent of its own cunning. I crossed the road and started hitching North.

An important rule of hitchhiking is never to let yourself be dropped off in the middle of a city. The reasons are obvious—one can't hitch across and must therefore use public transportation, which takes money and a knowledge of local geography, or walk, which takes time and strength. On the afternoon of my third day on the road I found myself in downtown Wilmington, Delaware, attempting to decide on a course of action. After walking around aimlessly for some time I wound up in front of the railroad station. There would be a waiting room, I suddenly realized, where I could sit down and rest without attracting attention, and perhaps even a newsstand where I could palm a nickel or a dime from the stacks of papers. I moved along the narrow sidewalk to the entrance and slipped inside.

Under the high, vaulted ceiling people walked in all directions, the women's heels clicking against the stone, the men moving with that ghostly, withdrawn air travelers assume everywhere, as if nothing happening were of any importance, as if life itself were in suspension until they reached their destinations. I went to the long benches in the center of the room and sat down. The smell of food from an open lunch counter nearby hung in the air like some exquisite perfume, tickling the underside of my brain and knotting my stomach. I looked around for the newsstand but it was inside a shop, the papers, as I could see through the glass window, well guarded. Next to the shop was a door with the words TRAVELERS AID painted in large letters. My eyes locked on the words. I sat watching for an hour before I made up my mind.

A bell rang somewhere as I entered. It was a small room divided by a wide counter. On my side a small couch with chrome legs, a chair, and a low table covered with magazines, on the other side a couple of desks and a file cabinet. A glass jar filled with white flowers stood on one of the desks catching sunlight from a rear window. A door opened across the room and a middle-aged woman in a blue suit entered to the distant sound of a toilet flushing. She advanced to the counter, a short woman, just beginning to get heavy, her pleasant, slightly chubby face set in a fixed expression of friendly interest like a mask pulled over her skull. "Yes, young man?" she said. "What can I do for you?"

I folded my hands on the countertop and watched them as I talked. "I was on the train going to New York and I got off to get some comic books and then when I turned around it was pulling out. My ticket and everything was inside so now I'm stuck." It flashed through my mind that I should appear to be more upset, but I was too tired to put it on. "I don't have any money."

"Well, that's not so bad," she said, smiling. "I'm sure we can straighten things out. Now tell me, was anyone with you on the train? We can wire ahead, you see. They'll probably be worried."

I shook my head. "No, I was by myself. I've been visiting my grandfather and I was going home."

"You live in New York?"

"Yes."

"I see." She remained motionless behind the counter. I continued to watch my hands through the long silence. Finally she reached down and brought up a pencil and a pad of paper. "Fine. Now if you'll just give me some information we'll see how we can arrange this. Name?"

"Frank Rawlings."

"All right, Frank. Address?"

"Eighty-one East Eighty-first Street."

"Phone?"

"We don't have one."

"Mother's name?"

"Dagmar, but she's not there. She's away on a trip to Europe."

"Father's name?"

"My father's dead. Look, couldn't you just lend me the money? I'll pay it back. I'll sign whatever you want. Or you could just buy the ticket for me and I'll mail you what it costs when I get home."

"We can't do that, I'm afraid," she said. "Now there must be somebody at home. You can't be staying all by yourself."

"That's the way it is most of the time. There's my step-father, but he's a truck driver and he's on the road now. He won't be back for days."

"What's his name?"

"Jean."

"Jean what?"

"Jean Florida."

"Jean Florida? That's an odd name," she said, writing it down.

"I don't see why you can't just put me on the train. I give you my word I'll send back the money."

"I know you would," she said. "But we can't do it that way. Now how about your grandfather. Name and address?"

"That won't help. He's an old man, we have to leave him out of it. He's senile."

She looked up from the pad. "I can't do anything unless you cooperate, Frank. You can trust me."

"Suppose you lend me five dollars," I said quickly. "I could get across town to the highway and hitch back."

"You mean hitchhike all the way to New York?" Her eyebrows went up. "A boy your age? All by himself? I couldn't do that. I'd worry about you."

I turned sideways, my arm lying on the counter. "That's what I'm going to do, even without money."

"Why be so hard on yourself?" she said. "We can arrange something. How long since you've had a decent meal?"

I watched the stack of magazines and listened to my in-sides, to the silent me within me, trying to hear if I should run away before the conversation progressed any further, or stay and tell the truth. I turned the rest of the way, fac-ing the door.

"Now wait a second before you do anything," she said behind me. "Wait just one second and listen to me. When did you eat last?"

I stood quite still, attending myself, but my mind was silent. Very quietly, tentatively, as if the word might de-stroy me, I answered, "Yesterday." I waited for something to happen inside. I seemed to be floating, everything in per-fect balance, all emotion suspended while the logical part of me continued to operate on its own momentum. The sensation was odd, as if I might slowly come apart and go drifting off in all directions.

Her voice was clear. It was pure. "Well, we can fix that right now. You don't have to commit yourself to anything. Sit down and read a magazine and I'll get you some food. You can eat right there at the table."

"No. You'll just get the police."

"I promise I won't do that," she said, and there was something in her voice that made me believe her. "I give you my word. This doesn't have anything to do with the police."

Alone, I sat on the couch, picked up a magazine, and then put it down again. Sunlight was fading through the rear window and I could hear the faint sounds of the station through the closed door. When she came back in with a tray I said, "What happens if I tell you?"

"Unless there's something special," she said as she lowered the tray, "we'll wire home for your fare and you'll be on your way."

The smell of the food made my hands tremble. Franks and beans, thick slices of tomato on a bed of lettuce, bread and butter, two half-pint containers of milk, and a piece of apple pie with a slice of cheese on top. The first mouthful was rapture.

"Don't wolf it down," she said, and sat on the corner of the table. "Try and eat slowly."

I finished one of the hot dogs and most of the beans before I paused. "What does something special mean?"

"If you'd stolen a car, that sort of thing. I can tell you haven't."

I went back to the food. It was amazing how good a simple piece of bread and butter could taste. As the food got into my system the trembling stopped. I could feel a film of sweat on my brow.

"You haven't done anything the police would want to know about, have you?"

I shook my head.

"How long have you been gone?"

"Three days." I wiped up the last of the gravy with the last of the bread. "Excuse my manners." I opened the second container of milk and began on the pie.

"Listen now," she said. "There are some things that are hard to talk about. Things we'd rather forget, or keep to ourselves, but I have to ask, and you have to tell me the truth. It's important. Back home, were you beaten? Were you abused in any way?"

Surprised, I looked up at her, my fork in midair. "Beaten? No. There was never anything like that."

"They fed you and gave you enough clothing?"

"Yes, of course."

She looked me in the eye for a moment and then, apparently satisfied, turned away. "There's no of course about it. We had a boy last year who answered the same as you. It turned out he had scars from his shoulder to the backs of his knees."

"No, really. There wasn't anything like that." I took a sip of milk. "You mean this has happened before? A kid coming in here?"

"Many, many times. Dozens of boys."

I turned the fact over in my mind, examining it from all sides the way a man might study a strange tool to determine its function. She sat silently, watching me while I finished the meal. When the last of the apple pie was gone I leaned back in my chair. "Thank you. You don't know how good that was." We remained motionless, both staring down at the tray. A distant voice was calling out the names of cities over the public address system. "Okay," I said. "Jean Fouchet, Eighty-one East Eighty-sixth Street. Atwater nine, eight-five-nine-nine."

"Why did you run away? Can you tell me?"

I looked away quickly, my face flushing. There was something about the words *run away* that threatened me with loss of control. Hearing them spoken aloud threw my body into a turmoil, as if they were the key phrase in a hypnotic command. I couldn't look at her. "I don't know," I said, shaking my head. "I can't explain it."

She'd been at the desk on the far side of the office for two hours, just out of earshot, picking up the phone every ten minutes. I assumed she was calling New York, and having checked the address and number I'd given her, was trying to get through to Jean. It seemed odd that they were actually going to talk to each other. Suddenly she got up, crossed the office, raised the leaf of the counter, and came and sat beside me on the couch. "I can't get through. He must be out and I'm afraid I can't stay any longer. I have to get home." She looked tired and a bit harassed—thin lines I hadn't noticed before showing around her eyes and at the corners of her mouth. "You'll have to spend the night."

I was on guard instantly. "Where?"

"There's a very nice Y.M.C.A. They even have a pool. You could take a swim and there might be a movie in the auditorium. How does that sound?"

I thought about it for a moment. "All right," I said finally. I'd been wearing the same clothes for three days and the idea of the pool appealed to me. "As long as they don't lock me in."

"I'll give them a call. Harry Brian can come for you. You'll like him. And they won't lock you in if you promise to stay put."

"Okay."

She went behind the counter and picked up the nearest phone. After a few moments of conversation she listened, three fingers against the side of her head, her lower lip between her teeth, and then hung up.

"What's the matter?" I asked.

"They're full up. They don't have any room." She stared across the room at the blank wall. "I tried everything I could think of."

Very alert, moving unconsciously to the edge of my seat, I felt apprehension growing in me, a slow subtle buildup, like a color change, like the start of a long slide through the calm blues and greens toward the eventual terror of red. "Where do I go, then?"

"The Juvenile Home. It isn't as nice, of course, but you'll be perfectly comfortable."

Kangaroo court, my mind screamed in a blast of red. KANGAROO COURT KANGAROO COURT! "What kind of place is that?"

"Now don't worry. It's perfectly all right."

"Do they lock you up?"

"It isn't a prison."

"Do they lock you up?"

"They lock the doors, but they have to do that. I'll explain everything to them. It'll be all right. I promise you."

"Isn't there any place else?"

She turned back to the phone. "No," she said softly. "I'm sorry."

I was up and away so fast I doubt she had time to realize what was happening. Up, running, and through the door before she could turn her head.

A reckless, all-out dash through the station, astonished faces falling behind one by one, frozen by my speed. It was like running through a crowd of cardboard cutouts. I swerved, jumped, and dodged between them to the doors, slipping past the outstretched arms of a guard into the open roar of the street, into the twilight and the high, vaulting sky. Running headlong through the streets I felt my limbs go wild with freedom. My brain raced to keep up, ignoring the present, knowing only what was just ahead—a corner, a vacant lot, an overpass, a man with a dog. Dazed by the sweetness of surrender, I left everything behind me without a thought, all of it forever behind me, falling away, more and more distant with every stride, falling away, falling away, falling away.

Leaning against a high fence, both palms and the side of my head against the wood, I opened my eyes and saw half a boxcar. The rest of the world moved. Only the boxcar and myself were fixed in space. I watched until stillness settled and then moved along the fence. The boxcar stood by itself on a siding, a tall, wooden car without markings. Approaching, I could see weeds growing in the darkness underneath. I went around to the other side. A dilapidated loading shed nearby seemed deserted. The big sliding door of the boxcar was not completely closed and I slipped my hands into the crevice, pulling hard as I fell back along the length of the car. The door rolled open with a thunderous roar. I jumped away from the car and stared into the dark interior, ready to run should anyone emerge.

After a minute or two I moved cautiously to the open doorway and looked inside. The floor was strewn with large, empty paper sacks. I stood listening for a sound from the impenetrably black corners of the car but there was only silence. Holding on with one hand, I bent my knees and leaped like a high jumper rolling over the bar, tumbling in and getting to my feet in a matter of seconds. There was no sound except my own breathing. A vague sweet-sour smell hung in the air, the smell of some chemical. A light haze of white powder covered the floor and walls. Bent over, skittish, ready to bolt at the first sound or the first movement, I went over the entire car and satisfied myself there was no one in it. I picked up one of the bags, white powder trailing from its torn mouth, and read it had contained chemical fertilizer. I shook it out and prepared a place to sleep in the darkest corner of the car.

Sitting in the open doorway, my legs dangling in the air, I watched the approach of night. Over the roof of the loading shed stars began to appear, faint at first, growing brighter as the sky turned from lavender to purple to black. Every now and then I would lean forward and look to the left and the right to make sure no one was coming. When it got so dark I couldn't see more than a car length in each direction I got up and went to the corner. Slipping into the bag I'd cleaned, I pulled three or four more over me for camouflage and went to sleep.

It started to rain just after dawn, a heavy downpour that crashed against the roof of the car and woke me up. I raised my head, saw the slanting white lines through the doorway, and then went back to sleep.

Hours later, when I crawled out of the bag and got to my feet, the rain was still falling. I stood by the door and slapped at my clothes to get the powder out. Clouds of it drifted from my head as I ruffled my hair. I waited for a lull in the rain and jumped to the ground.

It took me some time to find my way back. I was amazed how far I'd run—at least a mile. Wet to the skin, I walked through the station doors, crossed the huge waiting room, and opened the door to Travelers Aid. She was there, standing behind the counter, her head coming up as I closed the door. I avoided her eye.

"I hope you spent a pleasant night," she said.

"I slept in a boxcar."

She went to the end of the counter and raised the leaf. "Well, it's traditional I suppose. Very foolish, though. You could have been locked in." Holding up the leaf with one arm she said, "Come on. You're soaking wet."

"It's all right."

"Please don't argue. You can dry off in the bathroom."

I moved down the counter and slipped under her arm.

"My God, you smell awful. What was in the car?"

"Fertilizer."

"You'd better wash too. There's only a sink but you can't go home like that."

"Did you get him?"

"Yes. Before he left for work."

"What did he say?"

"I explained the situation and he agreed to wire your fare."

"Nothing else?"

She hesitated. "He asked if you were all right and I said you were." I knew she was lying but I remained silent. She opened the door to the bathroom. "Take your things off and hand them to me through the door. I'll see what I can do. I brought my iron." She walked me to the bus station, both of us moving under her umbrella. After a few steps I took the shaft. "Let me hold that," I said, shifting it to give her better protection. We covered the short distance in silence.

At the terminal I stood by the bus while she went inside to get my ticket. I felt a flash of annoyance at Jean. He was too cheap to send the extra couple of dollars for the train, which I would have enjoyed, so I had to take the bus, which I hated.

"Here's your ticket," she said at my shoulder. "And a dollar. Twenty cents is for carfare and eighty for a sandwich and milk at the rest stop."

"Thank you." People elbowed past us. "I guess I'd better go on in."

"Yes, if you go now you might get a window seat."

"I'm sorry I had to run away last night."

"That's all right. Think about what's ahead now." She took a step back.

I climbed into the bus. There was a window seat in the rear, on the far side, and I moved quickly and sat down. Staring through the rain-streaked glass I watched the white puddles on the black asphalt of the empty parking area. After a while the driver climbed in, pulled the door shut, and started the engine. Turning back to the window I saw her standing outside, under her umbrella, watching me. She'd come around the back of the bus and stood about twenty feet away. Neither of us moved. Then, very slowly, the bus rolled forward and she was gone.

13
Death by
Itself

             I DON'T remember how old I was, but the small steps and low banister of the up staircase in P.S. 6 didn't seem small and low. Fourth grade, perhaps fifth grade—it doesn't matter. Climbing the stairs with my pal Pete Stein, climbing through the gray light, I swung my heavy wooden pass and listened to his high child's voice. When the subject of fathers came up I suspected nothing.

"Your father has cancer," Pete said. "He's going to die pretty soon."

I stopped where I was, not really understanding, but aware that something important had been said. How was I to respond? What did the world consider a proper response at such a moment? "What did you say?"

"You don't have to put on an act." Several steps above, he turned back to look at me. "I listened in on the extension when your mother was talking to my mother. She said you don't even know him. She said you've hardly ever seen him in your whole life so you don't have to put on an act."

I climbed a couple of steps and stopped again. Something in Pete's tone made me realize he was telling the truth— a certain distance, a touch of haughtiness, faintly patronizing, that was entirely out of character. I realized he had been thinking about it for days. In some mysterious way he had appropriated it, absorbing the power into himself and filling me in on the facts as if I was only superficially connected to them. And because he in fact *had* a father, because he possessed a real father, I accepted his attitude. I knew Pete would cry, for instance, if his father died. I knew I wouldn't.

Walking home after school I resolved to force my mother to tell me. I would hide the fact that I already knew since it seemed reprehensible to have learned in such a casual, roundabout fashion. I wondered why she'd told

Pete's mother, whom she had never met, their entire relationship consisting of short phone calls when I stayed at
the Steins' for dinner. My mind stopped there—at wondering. I hadn't the courage to think about it, sensing that
more might be revealed about my mother than I wanted
to know.

I opened the door at home in a very odd mood—nervous,
expectant, a little scared, but filled with a kind of righteous
determination I had never before experienced, knowing
with certainty that no one, *no one*, not even my mother,
could deny me this moment. In claiming what seemed to
me to be my birthright I felt I could not be ignored. My
mother was in her room reading *Life* magazine.

"Somebody in school asked me why Father doesn't live
here, with us."

"Hmmmn."

"I said because he was in the hospital."

She turned a page. "That's right."

"And that half his face was paralyzed because of an
operation."

She glanced up at me, looked away, and put down the
magazine. "Is that the door? I thought I heard a key in the
lock." She got up and moved past me into the hall.

"But that operation was a long time ago and he's still in
the hospital." I followed her up the hall and stood at the
open door while she went into the bathroom.

"He's been in and out of hospitals for a long time. Almost your whole life." She lifted the lid of the toilet, hiked
up her skirts, and sat down.

"But this is a real hospital, not like those places in the
country, those rest homes." I felt very odd asking these
questions. I knew what I said was true, but somehow it felt
like I was making it up.

"He's still very sick. He has to stay in the hospital because they have all the things he needs." A faint hissing
sound as she made water.

"What's wrong with him? What does he have?"

She didn't say anything for several moments, sitting
quite still staring at the bathroom wall as if I wasn't there.
Watching her profile I could see something happen to her
face, a subtle change coming over it as she decided to tell
me. "I guess it's time you knew. I told Alison already because she's older. Your father has been away so long I

knew she wouldn't be upset. These things happen and we just have to accept them." She reached out and unrolled some toilet paper. "Your father has cancer," she said, and reached between her legs to wipe herself. "Luckily it's not the painful kind, but they don't expect him to get well." She stood up.

"Is he going to die?"

She looked at me in a very special way, a way she seldom used, letting me know she was about to tell me something important, something larger than herself. It was a tone of concern, and yet of abandonment. "Yes. That's what the doctors said."

"Do they know when?"

"They're not too sure. Six months or a year." She flushed the toilet.

I went to my room.

I had returned from Delaware, my mother and the baby from Europe. Jean, who hadn't come out of his room when I came home (he slipped a letter into my room while I was in school saying he couldn't understand why I'd run away, or what I was running from, and that I must have done it simply to hurt him; I slipped a letter into his room while he was out driving the cab saying it never occurred to me he would be hurt, that I'd run away for my own reasons, and that I felt better for it), emerged for Dagmar, and after a couple of tense weeks even convinced her to move back into their bedroom instead of the room Nell Smith had occupied. Mother had taken care of Miss Smith pronto. She put everything on the landing outside—clothes, suitcases, furniture, files—and told Nell over the phone that the Salvation Army had been instructed to pick it up in twenty-four hours. Nell charmed another cab driver and took it all away. When people called for her on the telephone mother would say, "She doesn't live here any more and I don't know where she's gone" in one breath and hang up. But if Jean shared Dagmar's bed it was all he shared. She never forgave his peccadillo and as a result finally completed the retreat into female strength and self-sufficiency with which she'd always threatened him. As the months passed Jean's behavior became odder and odder.

I remember sitting in the kitchen one evening watching my mother chop celery when Jean came home. We heard him striding up the hall and then he was at the kitchen door. He leaned against the counter and took the coin-changer off his belt.

"What would you say if I told you I saw Kurt on the street today?" he asked me.

"Who's Kurt?"

"Nancy's husband."

"You mean the woman who painted Mother's portrait?"

"Yes." Tremendously attentive, his eyes never left me, as if a great deal depended on my answer.

"I don't know. What am I supposed to say?"

"What would you say?" he asked Dagmar.

"I'd say you saw somebody who looked like him."

"Yes," he said. "You would."

"Isn't he dead?" I asked Mother. "Didn't he die a while ago?"

"Last winter," she said, and went to the sink to wash the vegetables.

"That's what we were told," Jean said. "We were *told* he died."

Working at the sink, my mother kept silent.

"You mean he didn't?" I asked.

"I didn't say that. I said what would you say if I said I saw him on the street."

"Did you?"

"I'm not going to tell you. Let's assume I did."

"Well, he can't be dead and walking around at the same time," I said. "You'll agree to that."

"I'm not agreeing or disagreeing. I'm just asking." He sat down at the kitchen table.

"He's either dead or he isn't."

"How do you know?"

"How do I know? Its obvious!" My voice rose a little.

"You know so much. What happens to people after they die?"

"They rot. They disintegrate."

"So in your opinion it couldn't have been him?"

I nodded.

"But it was."

"It was somebody that looked like him."

"No, that's out. I got a very close look."

"You mean you really saw him?"

"Assume I did."

"Then he didn't die. If you saw him he's still alive." I had a flash of insight. "Maybe he just wanted to get away from everybody."

Jean lighted a Pall Mall and leaned back. "But everybody says he's dead. There's the death certificate and all the rest."

I turned to my mother. "What do you think?"

"It was somebody that looked like him."

"But he says it wasn't."

She lifted the colander and poured the vegetables into a pot. "I don't know then."

I turned back to Jean. "He must be alive."

"No." Jean's face was expressionless. "He's dead but I saw him in the street."

"Is he a ghost?"

"Nonsense."

"I don't understand, then."

"It's very simple. He's dead but I saw him walking down Fifth Avenue."

"That's impossible," I said. "You're fooling. You're talking about something else."

"No. I'm completely serious."

"Oh, Jean," my mother said.

His back straightened. "What do you mean 'Oh, Jean'? I'm telling you I saw him on Fifth Avenue." He spit a fleck of tobacco off the tip of his tongue. "I'm telling you!"

My mother went back to the sink without looking at him. I kept quiet, feeling spooky, knowing there was more going on than I understood. They both seemed to be waiting for something. Then Jean got up and started out of the room. At the door he paused and looked back at me.

"You see," he said. "That's why I'm not going to tell you if I really did see him. Because you've made up your minds in advance. I'd be talking into thin air."

One evening after a bad morning at school and a long afternoon at work I emerged from the Eighty-sixth Street station of the Lexington Avenue subway feeling reluctant to go home. Reading a magazine I ate dinner at my special seat in Wright's Restaurant and then crossed the street for the double feature at the R.K.O. The movies were good, full of violence and color, lifting my mind to the level of life and death, pure good and pure evil, friendship, love,

and honor. When the lights came on I sat in my seat for a
long time watching the blank screen while the theater
emptied around me. I left when the usher started folding
up the seats.

On the street, out of nowhere, desire swept me away. I
wanted to live. I wanted to see something beautiful. Or to
die. Anything definite, anything clear, visible and tangible,
like dying, or saving someone's life, or being kissed by
Jean Simmons. Tears of frustration started in my eyes.
Something strange started to happen. My body felt it first
—warmth, a sense of something gathering, a feeling of
being possessed by magical powers, as if I could make the
parked cars rise in the air by simply willing it. Suddenly a
tremendous force carried me away, some really immense,
earth-shaking power igniting like the unexpected second
stage of a rocket already in flight. I screamed in the street
and started running, flat out, crossing the intersections
without looking. At home, in the elevator, I bent over and
ran my head into the wall again and again, stunning myself
but feeling no pain, hearing the hollow boom echo down the
shaft each time, hitting harder to increase the sound. At the
fifth floor I got out and stood in the hall for a minute,
trembling, my fists and jaw clenched, feeling the power
race around inside me, burning out my nerves. I opened
the door to the apartment. Jean and Mother were talking
in the kitchen. I went to my room, closed the door, and
sat down on the bed in the darkness.

After a while the door opened and my mother stood silhouetted. "Where have you been?" she asked angrily. "It's
almost one o'clock and you have school tomorrow."

I didn't answer, listening to my own breathing.

"Well, where were you?"

"In Brooklyn," I said. "At a funeral."

"What?"

"One of my friends from school was run over by a car
and his parents asked me to be a pall-bearer. It was way
out in Brooklyn so that's why I'm late."

"What?" Incredulous, she almost laughed.

"Leave me alone."

She stood silently in the doorway for several moments
and then went away.

14
License to Drive

I went back to Florida during a summer vacation when I was sixteen, with my mother's blessing. It had been a hard winter for everyone, Jean and Dagmar fighting constantly, Alison tense about college, and myself either completely withdrawn or raging when Mother interfered with my life. At school I'd failed four subjects.

I got on the train with thirty dollars, a suitcase, and my four-string guitar. Florida shone like a vision of paradise in my mind's eye. At night I sat on the steel floor between the cars and sang, feeling the wind, watching the darkness, my heart bursting.

"Lauderdale!" the conductor called. "Fort Lauderdale!" The hydraulic door closed with a hiss and he was with me in the rear of the car, moving past me to swing open the big side door and fold down the steps. I looked out at the scrub woods rushing past, momentarily perplexed. Then I realized we weren't stopping in town, but at the inland station, seven miles from Fort Lauderdale and only a mile or two from Chula Vista. The brake shoes screamed against the wheels and the train slowed smoothly, winding down to the magic instant when it stopped completely. I followed the conductor down the steps into the sun.

I walked a little way along the platform and stopped. The station was empty, desolate in the white glare. In the distance, where the long silver wall of the train began to curve out of sight, someone else was getting off. An old lady in black. A gust of wind blew across the platform and I smelled the woods. The train began to pull out. I sat down on my suitcase. Something was wrong. I listened to the sound of the train fading away. The old lady in black was met by a man with a small child and taken away in a car. The journey was over and something was wrong. The woods smelled the way they should, the stillness was as it had been years ago, the sun was hot—yet there was some indefinable lack, a peculiar hollowness to everything. I looked out at the woods, and then at the sky. Loneliness swept over me. I got up and moved toward the station house.

There was a single taxicab behind the station. I put my stuff in the back seat and got in. The driver started the engine and turned to me. I stared at him.

"Town?" he asked, breaking the silence.

"Wait a second. I'm not sure."

"Didn't you just get off the train?"

"Yes. Just give me a second." I wanted to go to Chula Vista, but for some reason I was afraid. "You know the drive-in out on Flagler Street?"

"Yes."

"Okay. The place I want is just across from it."

The old trailer stood in the middle of a sandy lot ten yards back from the edge of the road. I went up and knocked on the door. "Flaviano!" He was an Italian house-painter who'd once parked his trailer on a corner of our Chula Vista lot. He hadn't paid for the privilege, so when I'd written from New York asking if I could stay for a week or two he could hardly refuse. "Flaviano!" I tried the door but it was locked. I found the key under the concrete block which served as a doorstep and entered. Flaviano's tiny bedroom was in the front, and the rest served as kitchen and living room. Across the rear wall was where I'd sleep, a built-in seat running the width of the trailer. I put my suitcase and guitar in a corner and sat down. It was very quiet. The light was filtered tawny yellow through the drawn shades. After a few moments I got up and went outside, locking the door behind me. At the corner I hitched a ride into town.

My first job was ushering at the Dumont Theater for sixty-five cents an hour. They gave me a uniform (too big) and a flashlight and told me never to sit down, even if the theater was empty. After the first few days the images on the screen, repeated into meaninglessness, brought on a mild nausea, a faint, continuous sense of seasickness. When the bill changed I'd stay after closing and do the marquee. High in the air atop a swaying ladder I arranged the gigantic letters one by one, holding them with both hands as I fitted them into place. Every ten minutes the manager would come out, walk a few yards down the sidewalk, and turn and look up to advise me on the spacing. From my vantage point the huge message was meaningless. The marquee filled my vision. Constructing the end of a word whose beginning was lost in the distance, holding a letter larger than my head, I felt I was disappearing, drifting away through the hole of an O, shrinking into the intersection of an immense X.

At night, after supper in a cafeteria and the long bus ride home, I'd lie under the window in the rear of Flaviano's trailer listening to the sound track from the drive-in theater. While the ceiling flickered above me words echoed from hundreds of speaker stands, every sound sandwiched in the air, receding like the image of a man between two mirrors. Mysterious murmured words, with long silences in between, doors closing, violins, footsteps, silences.

I went out to Chula Vista in Uncle Victor's '38 Chevy one-seater, very proud of my brand-new driver's license, excited because I was occasionally to be allowed the use of the car. My mind raced ahead to Tobey. As boys we'd always dreamed of the things we could do if we had a car.

The Rawlings' house looked the same. Old Popeye sprawled in the sand at the edge of the yard. A line of wash billowed in the breeze and the tin roof of the outhouse gleamed dully under the sun. I got out of the car and started toward the house. Tobey pushed open the screen door and stepped into the yard. I hadn't thought about how he would look. The image I'd carried through the years was too bright, too strong to have changed. But Tobey was not the same. His slender body had thickened and his face was swollen with acne. A black motorcycle cap was jammed onto the back of his head.

"Well Jesus Christ if it ain't Frank," he said in a new deep voice.

I looked down at the ground. Deep inside me gates were closing, one by one, locking up a vital area I couldn't afford to lose all at once, sealing my love in private darkness. When it was done I lifted my head and faced him. "Well," I said, waving toward the house, "it looks the same." I tried to keep my tone as casual as his.

"Well, I guess it is."

"How's your momma? And Sean and Pat?"

"Sean's still in jail and Pat's working in Miami." He started walking toward the car and I fell in beside him. "Momma's fine. She's in town today. Where'd you get the car?"

"It's my uncle's. You remember, out at the beach."

"You come down from New York City?"

I nodded.

He slapped the fender of the car. "Thirty-eight. Has it got a rumble seat?"

I went to the back and pulled it open. "It's pretty torn up, though."

"Why don't we go over to my girl's house and give her a ride?" he said suddenly.

"Okay. Hop in."

He gave me directions and we drove in silence for a couple of blocks.

"I guess you go to Central now," I said.

He didn't answer right away and I glanced over. He was looking out the window. "Naw. I quit school a while back."

"Oh." I shifted down, showing off a little, and turned the corner. "I'm about to get thrown out myself," I said. "I failed practically everything last year."

"Is that a fact? I figured you'd be good in school. All them big words you used to know."

"I played hooky all the time."

He laughed. "Me too."

"It's funny," I said. "It hasn't changed much around here but it looks different. It's the same but it isn't the same."

"You see the new gas station out on Brady Street?"

"I went past it. We used to hide our bikes there, remember?"

"Sure. Waiting for the school bus."

"I mean the part that hasn't changed looks different for some reason. It *feels* different."

"Well, hell," he said. "You got to expect that. You're a lot older now."

"I guess so."

"Remember how we used to run around in the woods all the time? We weren't any more'n a couple of bare-ass little kids back then."

"Yeah. It was a long time ago, I guess."

"You used to go on about how the niggers was as good as anybody else, and I believed it." He slapped his leg. "Daddy threw you out of the house once. He was drunk. Remember that?"

"Yes." (Tobey had caught up with me on the dark road, both of us having wiped our eyes, hiding our tears from each other. He walked me home, risking his father's violence.) "I remember it all."

"We had a lot of fun, raising hell and all." He laughed. "It wasn't the same after you left."

I held on tight to the wheel and kept my voice casual. "All I ever wanted was to come back down."

"That's the house up there," he said. "Yeah, we sure had some times."

I stopped the car in front of a small stucco house and turned off the ignition. Construction material littered the sandy yard—sawhorses, a trough for mixing cement, old paint cans, and odds and ends of two-by-fours and planks. A small black dog stood stiff-legged by the screen door, yapping.

"A new house," I said.

"That's how I met her." He opened his door. "My daddy and me painted it. I'll go get her."

I watched him through the windshield. He trotted the first few steps across the yard and then, as if suddenly remembering himself, slowed down to a walk. Approaching the house he reached up and scratched the back of his neck, knocking the motorcycle cap a bit higher on his head. He called through the screen door and went inside.

In the car I folded one leg against my chest and rested my chin on my knee. The black dog lay down in the sand and began to nip ticks on its back. After a while Tobey and the girl came out. She was about fifteen, wearing blue jeans cut off at the thigh and a white blouse that was too small for her. Her breasts lifted the material so that every now and then a thin line of belly showed at her waist. She kept her head down and stayed close to Tobey. As they came up to the car he tried, very gently, to push her forward a bit, but she stayed behind him.

"Mavis, this here is Frank from New York City," Tobey said. "Him and me were the first kids in Chula Vista."

"Hello," she said without looking up.

"Hi."

"Mavis don't want a ride. Come on inside."

As I got out of the car she was already halfway back to the house.

"She's feeling bad," Tobey said as we followed.

"What's the matter?"

"I don't know. She gets that way."

The black dog lifted his head, looked me over, and went back to nipping himself. His teeth chattered like barbers' scissors. Inside, the air was full of the smell of paint and plaster. The small living room was almost empty —a couple of kitchen chairs, an old love seat, and a table. I caught sight of a steel guitar leaning against the wall. Tobey dropped onto the love seat and put his feet on the table. Mavis stood in the doorway to the kitchen. "Y'all want a Coke?"

"Okay, honey," Tobey answered.

"Thanks," I said, and moved to the guitar. "Is it all right to look at this?"

She nodded and disappeared. I picked up the guitar and laid it flat on the table, hefting the heavy steel bar in my left hand. I ran my index finger over the strings. The tuning was unfamiliar.

"Can you play it?" Tobey asked.

"No. I've never seen one before."

"It's my favorite instrument," he said. "Someday I'm gonna learn it."

I ran the steel bar up and down the strings, experimenting until Mavis came in with the Cokes.

"Don't you want one, honey?" Tobey asked.

She shook her head. Suddenly tears started running down her cheeks and she turned and ran into the bedroom. Through the open door I saw her throw herself on the bed and curl up like a little child. In the heat, beads of moisture had formed on my Coke bottle. I began to be aware of an atmosphere around me—a kind of steamy, sex-charged heaviness in the air, a faint girl scent, lush and sullen like the smell of bed. I stared at the smooth curve of her hip. She rolled over and I could see the swell of her breasts. I looked away, my body quickening.

"Maybe I'd better go," I said.

"Wait a while," he said, getting up. "I'll be right back."

I watched him sit down next to her on the bed. She turned her face away and he put his hand on her back, bending his head down to talk softly. I got up and moved to the window at the other side of the room. A small sticker had been left on one of the panes of glass and I scraped it away with my fingernail. I could hear Tobey murmuring to her.

After a while he came out of the bedroom and, together, we went out into the yard. He picked up a stick and swished it through the air. "Well, I don't know," he said, and threw the stick away. "I better stay around, though."

I saw her breasts again in my mind's eye. I took her clothes off.

"Maybe she has the rag on," Tobey said.

I nodded, not sure what he meant but unwilling to reveal my ignorance. "Yeah, maybe that's it. I have to get the car back anyway."

We walked to the road. I got in the car, started the engine, and pushed the gear shift into reverse. Holding the clutch down with my foot, I leaned out the window. "Say hello to your momma for me, okay?"

"I'll do that." He started back toward the house. "You come on out when you can."

I back into the road, straightened the wheels, and drove away.

Sitting on the smooth board with my legs dangling down into the hole, I drummed my heels against the padded sides. The other alleys were dark, the catwalk deserted on a slow afternoon. I was lucky to be working. The long thunder started, gathered power, and exploded underneath me as I lifted my legs. Pins flew in all directions and the ball hit the rear padding with a heavy thump. I dropped into the hole, my hands and feet going into the light as if into a pool of water. I heaved the ball up onto the track and watched it roll down the slope to start the long journey back to the front. After clearing the gutter with my foot I jumped up on the board.

It was nice work, simple, with an easy rhythm. I liked the way the pins fell into place in the rack like bottles of wine. Watching the other boys I'd discovered you didn't have to place each pin, you simply grabbed them by their necks four at a time and threw them into the rack, aiming them toward the particular part of the pyramid you wanted to fill. They slithered and clattered across the metal and fell into their holes like live animals going to ground. When the rack was filled you reached into the darkness for the bar and pulled. The whole apparatus descended and bounced off the floor, leaving the pins trembling on their spots, each one perfectly placed. From that moment on you were exposed—the bowler could throw at any time and it was up to you to get on your board and out of the way.

Once, at the county fair, Tobey and I had been paid twenty-five cents an hour to sit, fully clothed, on a trick seat six feet above a huge tank of water. It was a delirious afternoon. Our instructions were to be as insulting as possible to the customers—an activity at which, once warmed up, we excelled. They lined up three deep to throw baseballs at a red bull's-eye. A solid hit would trip a switch and open the seat underneath us, sending us, arms and legs flailing, into the water with a tremendous splash. We came up shouting insults, climbing back to the seat without a moment's pause in the torrent of abuse, two evil monkeys.

A dark shape came moving down the catwalk and dropped into the hole two alleys away. It was Sam, the oldest pinboy, a middle-aged Negro who worked in a bathing suit. He placed his pins and got up on the far side of the hole, facing me.

"You doing all right?"

"It must be fifty frames by now."

"Good. Make some money today. Tonight's league night."

The pins exploded underneath us almost simultaneously and we dropped into our holes. He was back up before me, of course. He was fast.

"You gonna get hurt one of these days, you keep on like that."

"What?"

"Those games you play. Hanging your legs, jumping in when the pins are still flying around. I seen you."

I laughed. "I've got it timed."

"I'm telling you, boy. You're gonna miss the jump to the board one time and get your legs broken."

"You think a pin could break your leg?"

He shook his head and hissed at my ignorance, not even bothering to answer. The ball thumped underneath him. He pushed against the board with the heels of his hands, slid his rump forward, and dropped out of sight.

My man got a couple of spares and signaled that he was through with a wave of his hand. He threw two dimes down the alley and I had to climb out under the rack to get the second one. I switched off the lights and went over to Sam's alley. His black body gleamed with sweat as he worked.

"Sounded like two dimes," he said.

"It was." I stretched out beside his hole, leaning on my elbow, my head on my fist.

"Be careful."

"I'm okay." I watched him racking the pins. "He looks pretty good."

"He's getting a spare every damn time," he said, pulling the bar. "But he bowls fast."

"Did you ever try it? Bowling, I mean?"

"We ain't got no alley."

It took me a second to understand. "We'll do it here some afternoon. I'll set up for you."

The pins exploded. A strike.

"You ought to try it," I said.

"Maybe I will, sometime." He threw four pins into the rack. It was a pleasure to watch him work—absolutely no waste motion or fumbling, and he could hit the holes in the rack without looking. He seemed to be taking his time, but he was the fastest boy in the place, capable of handling two alleys of League bowlers simultaneously without the faintest strain. More than once I'd seen him work three.

The ball came rolling toward us, louder and louder, and closing my eyes, I lowered my arm into the hole and left it there. I felt some wind on the back of my hand as the pins flew. My body was completely relaxed, the muscles in my back aching comfortably. I pulled my hand back up but kept my eyes closed listening to the sounds of Sam racking, the ball rolling, the pins exploding—the long, slow rhythms of the game.

"Look out!"

I opened my eyes to see a pin coming toward me. Sam had launched himself off the board and, like a magician or a juggler, he caught the pin in midair. The wood slapped against his palm with a snap. "Was you sleeping?" he asked. "Sleeping back here?" He threw the pin into the rack. "You're crazy, white boy," he said sharply. "Get on out of here."

The girl had been standing outside the Youth Center, waiting for the rain to stop, and I'd offered her a ride. She'd accepted, and when I parked in the darkness on the beach road she didn't protest. Her mouth was oddly formless, but warm. Shaking, I felt her breasts and tried to get my hand between her legs.

"No," she said.

I went back to her breasts, slipping my fingers under her sweater. Her skin was warm and smooth. After a long time she let me force my way under her brassière and find her nipple. I tried to open the snap in back.

"No." she said, twisting away. "You can do what you were doing, but no more."

We wrestled for an hour and she started to get scared. "I have to go home," she said. "It's late and my father will kill me."

I agreed to go if she'd show me her legs. After a moment's hesitation she raised her skirt to her hips. In the darkness the whiteness of her panties was eerily luminous. I kissed her and grabbed her sex—squeezing, feeling. She turned her head and pulled at my arm, her fingernails piercing my skin. "You promised!"

She wouldn't let me drive her to her house. I let her off at a corner and never saw her again.

Toward the end of the summer I ran out of money and couldn't find a job. I had my return ticket, so I sold my guitar and went back to New York.

15
Hanging On

I PAUSED briefly at the bottom of the stairs, looked both ways, and walked quickly across the hall to the side exit. The heavy door had a horizontal brass bar instead of a knob. I lifted my leg and kicked, catching it right in the center where the Board of Education seal was worked into the metal. The door opened with a crash. Standing outside on the iron deck in the sunlight, I lit a cigarette. Fifteenth Street was still empty. The final bell for the morning session wouldn't ring for ten minutes. I shifted my books, climbed down the stairs, and crossed the street to the Hero Shop.

"A bologna hero and an orange soda," I said at the counter. "Not too much mustard."

The old Greek made the sandwich without looking up, his stubby fingers picking out the ingredients with tremendous speed. The crusty rim of the mustard pot was lined with black flies. They didn't move as he reached for the spoon. Behind him in the shadows four or five men were cutting bread at a rear counter. I ate slowly, conscious of the luxury of having the place to myself, watching the high, gleaming windows of Stuyvesant, listening for the bell. When it rang, very faint but audible, I bent my head and drank the last of the soda. The old Greek started to yell at the men cutting bread. They put down their knives and began sprinkling oil over the open loaves. I picked up my books and moved away.

Walking west on Fifteenth Street I heard the students pouring out of the building behind me, their voices joining in a long, continuous roar up and down the narrow cavern, building steadily as hundreds of them streamed from the exits to stand in the street. I had no friends among them. I knew some of them, and one or two interested me, but that was all. Most of them lived in other boroughs.

A few minutes' walk from school there was a building on the south side of the street I always looked up at. A brownstone, four stories high, with a stoop and garbage out in front. I never knew I was going to look at it. Something would trip me off—perhaps the act of stepping up on the curb and turning to avoid the mailbox, or the quality of the surface of the sidewalk, or the sound of children's voices from the small park nearby. My head would turn automatically, before I had time to think, and I would find myself staring up at that particular building. Because I'd been told, I knew I'd lived there for many years as a child. Passing it my mind became still. All the noises of the world stopped abruptly, like a movie running on without a sound track. I had lived in the building until I was eight years old and yet I lacked memories of it. No image of the apartment, no image of having lived there, no image of myself. It was spooky. Walking by, I watched the entrance as if expecting someone to emerge.

At Third Avenue I took a left along the sidewalk under the El. When a train rumbled overhead I'd look up at the buildings to watch the shadow streaking by. At Eleventh Street a cigar-maker was rolling stogies in the window of his shop. I stopped for a minute to watch him work, resting my books on my knee. At Ninth Street the smell of wine and urine began. A little farther on were the bums.

I walk with my head locked straight ahead, trying not to look, trying not to see. I walk close to the curb to stay as far away from them as possible. They stand against the walls of the buildings, crouch in doorways, or sprawl on the sidewalk. From the corner of my eye I see a man push himself off the wall near the end of the block. He means to intercept me before I reach the corner. I step off the sidewalk out into the street and make a wide semicircle around him. He stands quite still, watching me, the skin of his hands and face dead white under a mottled black crust, his eyes wet and gleaming like inner organs unnaturally exposed. He fakes a move at me, very slow, like a zombie, and I control my impulse to shy away.

One more block. They sit against the wall, their white, swollen ankles covered with sores, their limbs akimbo on the pavement, lifeless as bleached driftwood, as if some giant had thrown them one by one against the wall to lie

powerless where they fell. Their clothing is all of a particular neutral brown. Their tanned necks and wrists are criss-
crossed with black hairlines like ancient porcelain.

I turn the corner at Fourth Street and stop in midstride.
Ten yards away in the middle of the sidewalk an enormous
female bum is holding one end of a pair of black trousers
trying to pull them away from a small, weeping man. With
an audible grunt the woman jerks back with both arms.
The man is lifted off the sidewalk like a feather and swung
around in the air until he loses his grip. He hits the ground
without a sound. Across the street two men laugh, applaud,
and walk away. The fat woman rolls up the trousers and
advances on the motionless man, her lips going in and out
very quickly in a kind of silent kissing movement. Still
weeping, the man starts to get up on his hands and knees.
A gargantuan little girl, she skips once and kicks him in the
stomach. The air goes out of him at both ends—a hollow
whoosh from his gaping mouth and a fart from his anus as
he falls on his side. She kicks him again, rolling him over
onto his back. I am frozen in my tracks, unable to move or
make a sound. Standing beside him, she raises both arms
for balance, lifts her huge leg and stamps down on his
crotch. As he screams his legs fold up and she stumbles
over him, falling awkwardly on her hip. She gets up, spits
in his face, and moves down the block with the black
trousers under her arm.

Tony the elevator man didn't speak English, but he smiled
and nodded as we rode up. He had a scar over his right eye
where a young Negro had struck him with a revolver during a payroll robbery the previous year. Whenever a Negro
shared the elevator with us he'd let the man off, hold me
back by the arm and whisper into my face with tremendous
intensity, "Goddam blacks no good!" I always smiled and
nodded, touching the place on my brow where he'd been
hit. "Yes yes," he'd say, delighted. "Fie day doctor. No
pay. No good."

I got off at the fourth floor and went into the office. Mr.
Malinos, the boss, to whom I'd spoken only once, when I
was hired, was at his desk in the rear with Shad, his im-
peccably dressed West Indian secretary and clerk. They
twittered and murmured through the day like old pigeons,
rustling papers and cooing into the phones without pause,

oblivious to the rest of us. A year earlier I'd stood in the Student Employment Office at school listening to a description of the job I now held. "Lab assistant," the man had read from a white card. "Electro Research, a service company for electroplaters. Knowledge of chemistry and math desired but not necessary. Chance for advancement." Immediately there had risen in my head visions of white-clad workers moving softly through a world of ethereal cleanliness and purity. My ears seemed to catch the murmur of hushed voices as chemists huddled over elaborate projects of glass, flame, and fluid constructed on immaculate marble counters. I took the job on the spot before anyone else could snap it up. It was too late to back out when I discovered the place was situated in a dilapidated building in one of the worst slums in New York, and that the laboratory for which I'd held such high hopes was in fact a large, dark, filthy room filled with a twenty-year collection of industrial-scientific refuse.

I presented myself to Willie, my own boss, who ran the lab by remote control from behind his desk.

"All right, Conroy. Today you get off your butt and do some work for a change." A fat man, Willie was quick-witted and nervous. He shifted his Life Saver from one cheek to the other (click! over his teeth) and smiled. "There's a limit, you know. I don't know why we keep you."

"I add tone to the place. My English is good."

"Three boys from Stuyvesant. They all stayed till college. You are the first fuck-up."

"Everybody likes me. I'm a sort of mascot."

Rocky the bookkeeper looked up from the next desk. "What a wiseguy," he said evenly.

"You see?" Willie said. "Better shape up, pal. Your days are numbered."

"Don't joke about it. Please. This job is one of the few decent things in my life." I paused. "You can imagine what the rest of it is like."

He snorted, shifting his huge, almost liquid bulk in the chair. "Conroy, I like you. I like your sick sense of humor, but you must stop being such a *fuck-up*."

"Can I run the nickel solutions? You said you'd let me."

"We have Bernie for that. Anyway, you're too slow and your math stinks."

"I can titrate as fast as Jimmy."

He sighed. "Forget it, Conroy. Now get in there and wash the flasks. After that you can make a load of Plate-Rite. Ten-pound cans."

"Right." I turned away.

"And for Christ sake get a little zip into it!"

"Right," I called from the hall.

The lab resembled nothing so much as the homes of eccentric recluses one reads about in the newspapers, an immense, junk-filled rabbit warren shot through with a network of narrow paths along which one scurried with tucked-in elbows. The long work counters, most of them unused for years, were buried under piles of rags, tubes, clamps, stoppers, newspapers, bottles and jars, broken gauges, beakers, flasks, and ancient scientific machines like props from a Jules Verne movie. High, overloaded shelves leaned this way and that in the air above and every surface was coated with grime. I went over to Jimmy's bench by the window. "Hey."

"Hey slugger," he answered, looking up from his computations. He was a small man, not much heavier at twenty-five than I was at a skinny sixteen, but in perfect shape, his chest and arms well muscled and hard as oak. There was an air of mystery about him, a hint of strangeness in his almost painful gentleness, his oddly impersonal style of dress, and the ritualistic neatness with which he performed even the smallest tasks. After months of working together he told me he'd been in prison for ten years. More than once, since then, I'd walked him to the State building for his visits with the parole officer. "How was school?"

I shrugged. "Same old shit."

"You're making a mistake," he said. I avoided his hypnotically clear blue eyes. "You want to get those grades. Go to college. Get the jump on the other guy."

"I know. I know." I picked up one of his Erlenmeyer flasks and swirled the solution around. "Finished already?"

He nodded and looked down at his clipboard. I envied him. While I spent most of my time cleaning up, running errands, and labeling bottles, he was working with pipettes, flasks, reagents, and solutions, analyzing samples from electroplating baths for metallic content. It was respectable work, and moreover it could be done sitting down. He gave his figures a last, quick glance and moved away. "If he finds a mistake I'll drink the samples."

Eight at a time, I carried the dirty flasks from his bench to the sink. I washed them under the open tap, my hands tingling at the slight sting of the chemicals. From the old radio on a shelf above me Les Paul and Mary Ford played "How High the Moon."

Sid, our man in the field, arrived at about the same time every afternoon with the day's load of sample solutions from the electroplaters of New York. He was six and a half feet tall. His short black hair merged with the afternoon stubble on his round face, leading me to believe that, like those trick drawings one used to see in the puzzle section of the Sunday comic strips, his head would look exactly the same upside down. The floor trembled as he walked in, an enormous hairy bear, his arms bulging out from his body as he held a dozen ammunition boxes filled with samples against the sides of his chest. "Yo!" he bellowed. "Yo!"

"Hey," Jimmy answered.

As Sid approached I slipped around the counter to get between him and the door. He stacked the boxes on Jimmy's counter and caught sight of me leaning against the sink. Pausing, he made a kind of growling sound in his throat.

"They gave him raw meat again," I said.

"Suicidal," he said to Jimmy, as if I wasn't there. "He wants to die."

"You have to catch me first, big man."

He waved an immense paw in the air. "Go away."

"Is it true you once did the hundred-yard dash in twenty minutes?" I asked. "Is that true?" He unloaded the bottles without answering. "Is it true it takes so long for the signals to get from your brain to your extremities that you have to make up your mind about everything a few seconds ahead of time?"

"Where does he get the nerve? I ask you?" He shook his head. "I could kill him with one arm tied behind my back."

The suspense was delicious. I felt light and fast and went up on my toes. "Is it true . . ." I started, but he lunged down the counter. Two strides ahead of him, I turned the corner and ran down the side of the lab to the door. I could hear him slowing down as he saw I was going to make it. I even had time to pause at the door and look back, laughing, before I slipped outside.

Going into the office I composed myself. "Tea break!" I called out. "Orders please!"

"What's going on in there, Conroy?" Willie asked.

"In where?"

"You know where. In the lab."

"Nothing at all. Sid just brought the samples."

"Fun and games?"

"No."

"Playing chemistry set? You couldn't have been working."

"I was helping Jimmy set up the next run."

He pursed his lips and gave me a wry look.

"Now, you want black coffee and a prune Danish I presume?" I asked, taking a pencil from his desk.

"Yes, and give that pencil back when you're through."

"Tea break! Orders please!"

We were sitting in the small packing room just off the lab —Sid at an old desk, Jimmy on a mailing crate, and myself, feeling vaguely like a host since it was my workroom, on the window sill.

"My God, what a crud heap in here," Sid said with a mouthful of Drake's Raisin Pound Cake. He looked up at the junk piled high against the walls. "How do you ever find anything?"

"I manage," I said. "It's no worse than the lab."

Jimmy finished his coffee and forced the empty container into the overflowing trash barrel. "Got to start the next run," he said, standing up. "I want to leave on time tonight."

"Got a date, uh?" Sid asked.

I ignored my automatic twinge of jealousy. The only girls I knew were the ones I picked up in the balconies of Loew's Orpheum and the R.K.O. Eighty-sixth Street, girls I never saw, and would probably not have recognized, in the light of day.

As we entered the lab Sid said, "You know why I don't fool around? Because I'm scared of catching something and giving it to my wife." Even the thought seemed to upset him. "I'd never forgive myself."

I walked away to go set up the cyanides and he gave me a quick blast from a plastic squeeze bottle of distilled water. I wiped my neck with the side of my hand and said nothing. Water fights were a traditional part of the late afternoon scene in the lab. At the counter I took down clean flasks four at a time and lined them up in front of the sample bottles.

"Shall I pipette the samples?" I called to Jimmy in the next aisle.

"Better not. Willie'll give me hell."

"That old fart."

"A little respect for your superiors there, Conroy," Sid said. I could see him through the bottles stacked on the shelf dividing us. Unaware that he was being watched, he leaned against the counter beside Smitty, cleaning his nails with a toothpick. I raised a plastic squeeze bottle, aimed with care, and hit him square in the eye. I had to move fast. I could hear him running on the opposite side, his huge feet pounding the wooden floor. As I turned the corner his outstretched hand plucked at my clothes but, laughing, I broke away. Running for the door with Sid in close pursuit, I heard ominous noises in the hall. A huge crate was being rolled out of the elevator, sealing me in. For one mad instant I thought of leaping over it, but momentum carried me past before I could make up my mind. I ran directly to the farthest corner and jumped behind an empty cardboard barrel—the only protection I could find.

"Aha!" said Sid, slowing down. *"Ahaa!"*

"Wait a second, now. You started it, remember. You got me first."

"This is it, Conroy."

I laughed nervously. "Sidney. Act your age. You're too old for this sort of thing."

He advanced slowly, the fingers of his immense hands flexing rhythmically. Grabbing at straws, I looked out over his shoulder. "Mister Malinos! It's not my fault, sir. He's always chasing me." He was so close I had to begin dodging behind the barrel. "Jimmy! Help!"

"Four buttons down from the top, kid," Jimmy called back. "One good punch. The bigger they are the harder they fall."

Sid reached out with one hand, grasped the lip of the barrel, and tossed it across the room as effortlessly as a bear brushing away cobwebs.

"Oh God," I said.

"Slow, uh?" He began jabbing me with fingers the size of hammer handles, short, quick jabs in the ribs and stomach, making me fold up like a surprised nude. "Raw meat, uh?" He caught me in the ass with a stiff thumb.

"You big ape!" I yelled, fighting back. I struck out at him, or rather at what I could see of him, a vast wall-to-wall chest looming over me. My fists bounced off without effect except for the pain in my hands. I felt myself rising mysteriously into the air, lifted up and away with incredible smoothness by an irresistible force. My arms pinned to my sides, my legs dangling helplessly, I hung squirming in space while Sid laughed.

Half an hour later I lighted a Bunsen burner, adjusted the mixture of gas and air, and held a glass tube over the apex of the flame. When the glass softened I bent it to a right angle. At the sink I filled a large, narrow-mouthed flask with water and plugged it firmly with a two-hole stopper. I pushed a short piece of tubing into one of the holes and slipped a rubber squeeze bulb onto the exposed end. By then the other glass tube was cool. I pushed it through the stopper and stepped back with my hands in the air. Unsuspecting, Jimmy whistled "Alexander's Ragtime Band" on the other side of the lab. Bernie, the nickel man, was talking to Sid while cleaning up his counter after the last run of the day.

The effective range of the plastic squeeze bottles was roughly one aisle—that is, a man in aisle A could reach aisle B, but not aisle C. This limitation had been the mother of my invention. Well-hidden behind a wall of cardboard boxes, I pointed my apparatus at the sink and squeezed the bulb. Instantly a fine, steady stream of water shot through the air as flat as a tracer bullet, striking the back of the sink exactly where I'd aimed. It was beautiful. I tried a few more shots to get the feel of it and noticed with satisfaction that the water level fell very slowly. Hunched over so they wouldn't see me, I slipped across the lab to the aisle behind Jimmy. They were already at it in a desultory sort of way, trading shots through the

shelves every now and then, Jimmy directly in front of me
alone against Sid and Bernie in the aisle ahead of him.

I removed a couple of bottles from the shelf in front of
me and waited. Jimmy's back was to me. I could see Sid
and Bernie moving on the other side of the next row of
shelves. Sid went to the window and I threw off a quick shot
that missed, but struck the glass right in front of his nose
and sent him scurrying back to shelter. He retaliated immediately, getting Jimmy on the arm. Jimmy stalked back
and forth with his squeeze bottle looking for an opening.
He found one and got Bernie.

Biding my time, I waited till Sid's head appeared between a box of cadmium powder and an old pH meter. I
squeezed off a short, quick shot in his ear. Bernie tried to
edge around the corner for a try at Jimmy and was met by
a blinding deluge. I shifted my position and got off another
shot through both shelves with rifle-like accuracy. Confused, the enemy became cagey, shooting blind to avoid
the risk of exposure. When I started arching long, curving
streams that almost struck the ceiling before raining down
on the far aisle, everyone caught on. Jimmy turned, expecting an ally, but filled with a sense of reckless power I let
him have it. They advanced en masse, trying to get close
enough for a shot with their inadequate squeeze bottles. I
retreated slowly. They marched forward with their arms in
front of their faces. As I passed the door I put my back
against the wall and squeezed faster, forcing them to duck
behind a counter. "Intelligence wins again," I shouted.

Willie came through the door, right into the line of fire.
He flinched as the water struck his chest—not with his
huge body, a body he had long ago stopped trying to move
quickly, but with his head. It jerked back a fraction of an
inch, turtle-like, his mouth slightly open.

"Willie, I'm sorry," I said. "I didn't mean it. I didn't hear
you coming."

He tucked in his chin and looked down at the dark stain
across his chest.

"Really. I swear to God."

He pinched the material between thumb and index finger
and pulled it away from his skin as if he could somehow
get rid of the wetness without taking the whole shirt off.
His mouth closed slowly and he looked up at me.

"Willie," I gave a sick little laugh that died in my throat. "Willie . . ."

He reached out, took the water gun from my limp hand, and held it in the air, turning it around several times. Then he put it down. "Okay, Conroy," he said evenly. "You're fired."

My hands came up involuntarily, palms outward, as if I could somehow catch his words in the air and push them away. "Wait a minute," I said quickly. "You can't mean it."

"You were warned," he said, turning away. "You get paid off on Friday and that's it. Period." He went out the door.

Stunned, I walked past the end of the counter and looked down at Sid, Bernie, and Jimmy, all sitting on the floor, hiding. Only Jimmy met my eye.

"What am I going to do?" I asked him. In the silence I felt a gulf opening between us—a kind of slipping away, a telescoping away, as if he were a visitor at my bedside when the doctor told me I was going to die. They got up from the floor, still holding their plastic bottles, and moved back to work. Jimmy clapped me on the shoulder.

"It's a cruddy job anyway," he said gently. "You can do better than this."

His solicitude scared me. "Jimmy, they can't fire me. They can't just *fire* me after all the time I've been here."

"Sure they can."

"I'll stop horsing around. I'll really work."

He looked down at the floor.

"I'll clean up the packing room! I'll fix it up!"

"You can't do that in two days."

"Yes, I can. I bet I can." I started to move away and he caught me by the arm.

"Don't count on anything," he said. "Willie's a nice guy, but like a lot of fat men he's stubborn. You'll probably be breaking your back for nothing."

I nodded. "I know. Okay." I went to the packing room and closed the door behind me, amazed at the tears starting in my eyes. "Jesus," I said as I bent down and started cleaning out junk from under the work table, "they can't just *fire* me."

For the next two days I avoided everyone. I'd come up in the elevator and go directly to the packing room, walking quickly with my head low. If Willie had expected me to continue coming into the office for my daily orders he was tactful enough to let it go. Jimmy brought tea and remarked on my progress, but I was so quiet he could tell I wanted to be alone.

First I washed the window, removing years of grime and doubling the available light. I moved the large work table to a new position and drew up a map for the rearrangement of the entire room. (The packing room was used primarily for the bottling, sealing, labeling, and packing of Plate-Rite, an electroplating additive. I made the stuff myself most of the time, working from a simple recipe, pouring the various solid and liquid chemicals into a huge crock and stirring till clear. It looked like cherry soda and smelled like wet leaves.) I installed a bank of metal shelves over the table, put fresh paper and tape in the dispensers, nailed three balls of string overhead, and cleaned out the drawers. I made a special water-tight tray for the white sealing strips and the solution that kept them flexible. Squatting on the floor, I sorted thousands of bottle caps according to size. I repaired the faulty latch on the door, washed the woodwork, and scrubbed the floor. Toward the end of Friday it was done. The transformation was astonishing. From a dark, crowded, junk-filled cave to a bright, open workroom with a place for everything and everything in its place. Jimmy whistled when I called him in. "Beautiful," he said, sincerely impressed. "I hope it works."

For a moment I didn't know what he meant. I'd gotten so involved in the job I'd forgotten why I'd started it. "Yes," I said. "So do I."

I waited until almost everyone had left for the night. I paused in the hall to get control of myself—my pulse was racing and my throat was tight. As I entered, Willie looked up from his desk, his quick eyes betraying nervousness. He spoke gently, as if reassuring me that he held nothing against me. "Ah yes Conroy," he said, and reached into his drawer for the check. He held it gingerly, flicking a corner of the blue paper with his nail. "I'm sorry about this, but there it is. Work is work."

I kept my hands at my sides. "Have you got a second?" Despite my plans to surprise him, I rushed on. "I fixed up the packing room. I reorganized the whole place."

"The packing room?" He was surprised, as if he'd for-gotten there was one. "Okay," he said, and got up and followed me through the hall into the lab.

At the door I said, "I used the principle of the assembly line and organized the room accordingly." Then I opened the door and turned on the lights.

He stepped into the center of the room and looked around slowly. "It's big," he said. "I didn't realize it was this big."

"It was all that junk."

He went to the work table and walked slowly along its length, trailing his fingers across the surface. He stopped at the watertight tray. "What's this?"

"A tray for the sealers. Before you had to fish them out of the jar with a pencil."

He nodded and moved on. He noticed the cartons of bottle caps. "These were all mixed up, weren't they?" He examined the entire room carefully, not saying anything more, and we went back to the office. He sat down, rubbed his eyes behind his glasses, paused, and then lowered his hands. "That's a beautiful job. It shows intelligence and hard work. I only wish you'd done one-quarter as much before."

Carefully controlling my voice, I said my piece. "Couldn't you give me another chance? I'll stop screwing around, I really will."

"I don't believe in personality changes. It doesn't hap-pen."

I stood silently, unable to think of anything to say, be-cause I agreed with him.

"Anyway," he went on, "it's not just me now. Rocky is seeing another kid from Stuyvesant tomorrow."

"He is?" I was hurt in a new way. The loss of the job was bad enough, but the thought of someone else in my place was especially painful.

"Look Conroy, I'll tell you what. First, I'll give you a week's pay. I'll get the bookkeeper to make out another check and you can pick it up tomorrow. I don't have to do that. Second, I'll write the recommendation for your next job myself. No mention of all the screwing around. I'll make it good. That's all I can do."

I lowered my head and he held out the check. "There's no reason to feel bad about it, you know. Everybody here likes you. The boys in the lab all put in a word for you. It's nothing personal, Conroy, it's just one of those things."

Saturday morning I stationed myself at the window of a small grocery store across the street and watched every-one arrive for work. While the proprietor and his wife yelled Italian at each other through the curtain separating the store from the apartment in back, the man gesturing as if she could see him, I sipped a container of hot tea and ate a doughnut. One by one they arrived—Jimmy and Bernie on foot from the subways, Willie, Rocky the book-keeper, and Sid in their cars, and finally Malinos himself in a taxi. I watched and waited, the hot tea warming my belly and the spicy odor of hanging salamis sharp in the air.

After half an hour Bernie came down for coffee. He went into the neighboring candy store, emerged with both hands holding a cardboard tray full of coffee containers and Danish pastry, and went back upstairs. I finished my tea and pushed through the door.

The street was quiet. Up toward the Bowery a few bums drifted at the corners, moving slowly back and forth like underwater plants. In the other direction a jungle of fire escapes stretched away, long, curving lines of motionless wash threading them together. A few kids played stickball in the distance, moving silently through the haze. I crossed the street and went into the building. Tony got up from his chair and started toward the elevator, but I waved him back. I sat down next to him on the floor.

"No up?" he asked.

"No up," I said. "Later."

He nodded and leaned back in his chair. We stared out at the brightness of the street.

The kid showed up at about ten-thirty, hesitating on the sidewalk, looking up at the number and then down at a slip of paper in his hand, peering into the dark hall, backing up and shading his eyes to look at the higher floors. I knew what was going on in his mind. Like me on my first day, he couldn't believe there was a lab inside. I sat in the dark-ness watching him decide to come in. He was about my own age, well turned out in jacket and tie, with a clean, chubby, intelligent face and feminine hips. He entered and began searching for a directory on the filthy walls. Finally he caught sight of us and came over.

"Electro Research?" he asked. "I think I'm in the wrong building. Is there an Electro Research here?"

"Fourth floor," I said. "Did you come about the job?"

"Yes. Why?"

"It's gone. Filled."

"What?"

"Some kid was here at nine in the morning and got it."

He fingered his tie nervously. "But they told me to come at ten-thirty. I had an appointment."

"Yeah, well I had one at ten and they didn't even see me. Told me it was filled already."

"But I came all the way from the Bronx. They can't do that!"

I took out my cigarettes, offered him one, which he refused, and lighted up. "I know," I said. "I came from Brooklyn, but to tell you the truth, after seeing the place I'm just as glad. A really crummy outfit. Dirty and dark with stuff lying all over. They call it a lab! What a laugh. Are you from Stuyvesant?" He nodded. "Me too. They ought to check these places out before they send us."

"I thought they did," he said.

"They couldn't have."

He stood quite still. I got up, took a couple of steps toward the entrance, and then came back. "I thought it was my father," I said. "He's picking me up."

Tony sat watching us, picking his nose with a gnarled finger. The kid looked down at him, not really paying attention, but with a faint, automatic expression of distaste on his face.

"If you go up watch out for the fat guy. I think he's a queer."

"What?" His head snapped around.

For a moment I thought I might have gone too far. "Well I don't know, but he kept giving me these little pats on the ass on the way out. Hardly touched me. Just these soft little pats."

He laughed, incredulous. "You're kidding!"

"Well, I'm not sure."

The kid turned away. "The hell with it. I can tell I wouldn't want the job anyway."

"You ought to go up and complain," I said.

"It isn't worth it," he said, and walked out.

I sat down next to Tony and took a deep breath. My hands were shaking. After a few minutes I got up and went into the elevator. "Now up."

"Hokay, boy!" he said, sliding the gate shut with a crash. "Four floor!"

It worked. Saturday I hung around and left without picking up my check. Monday Willie asked me if I thought the place was an orphanage. Tuesday there was no one else to make a quick load of Plate-Rite. By Wednesday I knew I was safe.

16
Losing
My Cherry

ALISON and I were fond of each other, but we lived in different worlds. To defend ourselves we had been forced to extremes—Alison's of disengagement and calmness, mine of rebellion and anger. We sent heartfelt but necessarily simple messages to each other, like mountaineers from peak to peak. "How are you over there? I love you, but I can hardly hear you. I don't pretend to understand you, but I wish you well." By a monumental effort Alison had created a life for herself quite separate from the chaos of the family. As a child she'd shown remarkable self-sufficiency, reliability, and good sense, and had therefore won the right to be left alone. Or so she thought. Actually it was not so much a right she had won as it was Jean's and Dagmar's lack of interest. They were preoccupied with their own problems. As a teen-ager she did nothing to endanger that privilege. She was a model student and eventually became president of the student government at Washington Irving High School. She never argued with her mother, or allowed herself to be sucked into Jean's harangues. In many ways it was as if she were a guest in the house, or a boarder who had her own family somewhere else. When she won a scholarship to Barnard College no one was surprised. She'd been a good, industrious girl for so long everyone took it for granted. "I never have to worry about Alison," my mother would say. "Alison is a sensible girl." What we didn't know was the terrible price she was paying to keep up the front.

In her senior year at college Alison acquired a steady boy friend, Jack, a tall, good-looking fellow she'd met in the dramatic group. Because of an anomaly in his earlier education he was a freshman, although only a year younger than herself. I liked him immediately. In classic little-brother style I made something of a pest of myself, but he never seemed to mind. Coming home, I often went straight up to Alison's room, eager to talk and enjoy some reflected warmth. Her room, separated from the others by a long hall, was always tidy and managed, in a cold house, to convey a bit of cosiness. There was a fake leopard-skin bedspread, brown corduroy drapes, books, a throw rug, and a few tasteful knickknacks. It was like the rooms one sees in magazines. I'd knock on the door, give them a couple of seconds, and walk in. They were usually on the couch on the far side of the room, in mild disarray, but fully clothed. Unlike young people these days, it took Jack and Alison quite a while to achieve the ultimate union. She had, I later learned, a hymen as tough as the plastic window on a convertible.

"Hi. Can I come in?"

"You are in," Alison said, taking her arms from his shoulders.

"Well, I can come back later if . . ."

"You're here now. It wears off after a while."

"What wears off?"

"Never mind." She laughed, sitting up.

"How's the boy?" Jack asked.

"Pretty good. There's a great movie on the late show tonight. Mickey Rooney."

"Oh yeah?"

"We have to go over your history paper," Alison reminded him.

"Oh, it's okay," he said. "It's good enough the way it is."

"No. We'll rewrite it together." She reached forward and smoothed down the hair on the back of his neck. "We'll make something of you yet, young man."

"Anybody want a glass of milk?" I asked.

When I came back they were kissing. I sat down and drank my milk, watching abstractedly.

"Hmm," she said. "Delicious."

"You sound like you want to eat him."

"Maybe I do."

"Disgusting," I said. "Cannibalism. That's very unhealthy sexually."

She laughed, and sticking her finger in his ear, said coyly, "I'm a very sexually unhealthy person, in a certain healthy kind of way." She jumped up from the couch. "Oh, isn't he beautiful?" she cried. "Isn't he the most beautiful thing you've ever *seen?*"

"All right," I said. "Cut it out."

"My sexy freshman. My wild black Irishman."

"Alison, for Christ sake."

"Well, let me preen a little!" she said, suddenly annoyed. "Let me enjoy it."

"I don't know how you put up with all that goo," I said to Jack.

He winked. "It's not so bad when you get used to it."

"He loves it," Alison said. "He loves every minute of it."

"Yeah," I said. "Okay."

"You'll find out about it," she said. "It'll happen to you."

"In a pig's ass."

"Don't be vulgar."

"How about Mickey Rooney?" I asked Jack. "I'll go down and get some oatmeal cookies."

"Is it a western?"

"Jack, you *can't,*" Alison said quickly. "You got a C minus on the last quiz." She came down on his lap and put her arms around him. "How am I going to make you into a beautiful silver-haired professor with a beautiful pipe in a beautiful book-lined library if you don't cooperate?" She kissed him on the ear. "I'm your mentor, remember. You've put yourself in my capable hands."

They started kissing some more, their jaws working, and after a while I got up and left, closing the door behind me.

It was the winter of my seventeenth birthday, presumably my last year of high school. I made a half-hearted attempt to pass my courses, knowing that in any event I'd have to go to summer school to make up for previous failures. I wanted the diploma that year. I wanted to get it over with so I could leave the country, go to Denmark and meet my grandparents, see Paris, but mostly just get away from home. I withdrew into myself and let the long months go by, spending my time reading, playing the piano, and watching television. Jean too had retreated into himself. He'd watch the screen silently for hours on end, wrapped up in a blanket Indian fashion, never moving his head. Night after night I'd lie in bed, with a glass of milk and a package of oatmeal cookies beside me, and read one paperback after another until two or three in the morning. I read everything, without selection, buying all the fiction on the racks of the local drugstore—D. H. Lawrence, Moravia, Stuart Engstrand, Aldous Huxley, Frank Yerby, Mailer, Twain, Gide, Dickens, Philip Wylie, Tolstoi, Hemingway, Zola, Dreiser, Vardis Fisher, Dostoievsky, G. B. Shaw, Thomas Wolfe, Theodore Pratt, Scott Fitzgerald, Joyce, Frederick Wakeman, Orwell, McCullers, Remarque, James T. Farrell, Steinbeck, de Maupassant, James Jones, John O'Hara, Kipling, Mann, Saki, Sinclair Lewis, Maugham, Dumas, and dozens more. I borrowed from the public library ten blocks away and from the rental library at Womrath's on Madison Avenue. I read very fast, uncritically, and without retention, seeking only to escape from my own life through the imaginative plunge into another. Safe in my room with milk and cookies I disappeared into inner space. The real world dissolved and I was free to drift in fantasy, living a thousand lives, each one more powerful, more accessible, and more real than my own. It was around this time that I first thought of becoming a writer. In a cheap novel the hero was asked his profession at a cocktail party. "I'm a novelist," he said, and I remember putting the book down and thinking, my God what a beautiful thing to be able to say.

The piano kept me occupied when I didn't feel like books. Music had always affected me strongly. As a small boy I'd stand on the coffee table in the living room and conduct scratchy records of Grieg, Rachmaninoff, and Tchaikovsky with a pencil, watching myself in the mirror all the while. I memorized pieces well enough to anticipate tempo changes with exactitude. My baton technique was flamboyant and I moved around as much as the limited area of the coffee table allowed. More than once, carried away by the sweep and grandeur of it all, I fell off. But I always climbed back up.

There were violent scenes with my mother. I was beginning to realize I could outsmart her in arguments, and equally important, that I was too big for her to attempt the use of force. I adopted an attitude of haughty independence, as if I didn't care what she said or how she felt, and loosed a storm of sarcasm and invective whenever she threatened to overpower me emotionally and destroy my pose. I remember actually laughing once when, speechless and spluttering, she threw a shoe at me. "You missed," I said with tremendous outward calm, "why don't you try again?" We groped through life in mutual misunderstanding, unable to help each other, unable to think of anything more intelligent to do than endure the war, hoping that somehow, mysteriously, it would end.

Summer school was ridiculously easy. I cut classes with impunity and showed up for the tests with no more preparation than a vague memory of what I'd learned at Stuyvesant. It was enough to get me through.

The school library had twenty or thirty back issues of the London *Illustrated News* as well as a few copies of *Punch*. I spent hours looking through them, soaking up their strangeness, projecting myself across the sea. I wasn't going to England, but it didn't matter. The magazines were proof that another world existed, that many other worlds existed into which I might escape. I counted the days until my departure, frustrated by the slowness of time. Life around me was meaningless—my grades, the struggle at home, the fact that I probably wasn't going to college, everything was eclipsed by the fact that soon, soon, in a matter of weeks, I would leave it behind. Finally, at last, I was going to *get out*.

A few students crossed the hall in the distance but no one was coming my way. I pulled open the door and entered the stairwell. A wire-mesh door closed off the up staircase. There was a foot and a half of space at the top. I climbed the door carefully, shoving the pointed toes of my shoes into the wire and pulling myself up with hooked fingers. On top, I slipped through sideways and fell to the steps on the other side. Instantly lightheaded and alert, as if waking from sleep, I climbed the stairs.

Three stories above the floors in which school was in session I wandered through deserted corridors, whistling, peering into empty classrooms, stopping every now and then to throw a few blackboard erasers into the ventilation cowls up near the ceiling. In the music room sunlight streamed through the huge windows. I sat on the sill and smoked a cigarette, watching the tenement rooftops far below. Flocks of pigeons circled in the air over the Lower

East Side. Striding down the aisle to the grand piano I
clapped my hands in imitation of an audience applauding
the featured soloist. I opened the piano, took a short bow,
and sat down at the keyboard. I played the blues in the
key of C.

I paused in the aisle, unsure which of my two favorite techniques to use. I could sit in the row in front of her, drape
my arm over the back of the seat next to me and attempt
to contact her knee with my hand, or I could sit next to
her, with one empty seat between us, and play footsie. The
small balcony was almost empty. I entered her row and
sat down. From the corner of my eye I could see her
white raincoat going on and off in the reflected light from
the screen below. I watched the movie for half an hour
before making my move. Shifting around in my seat, I
extended my legs in the darkness until my foot almost
touched hers. After a while I raised my toe and applied a
gentle pressure to the side of her foot. To my astonishment
she answered immediately, giving me three firm, unmistak-
able taps. I moved into the seat next to her and she turned
her head for the first time.

"It's you!" I said. I'd picked her up in another theater
a few weeks before.

"Didn't you know?" Her accent was heavy. She was
Belgian, nineteen, and she had a job looking after two
children.

"No. Of course not."

"I hoped I should see you again."

I put my arm around her. "Me too." Congratulating
myself on my luck, I kissed her cheek. She turned and I
kissed her mouth. She wasn't very pretty, and there was an
odd bloodless quality to her, almost as if she was under-
nourished, but she was a girl, the most cooperative girl I'd
ever met. I slipped my free hand over her breast.

"The movie is bad," she said.

Fifteen minutes later, my leg up on the seat in front to
screen us off, I had my hand between her legs, slipping my
finger in and out of her wet sex.

"There," she whispered. "No, there. Yes. That's right."

She reached out and grabbed me through my trousers.
Her fingers touched and pressed. She unzipped my fly. She
pulled me out into the cool air and squeezed. I couldn't

believe what was happening. She struggled to get her hand all the way inside. "That's what I want," she said as her hand closed over me.

"Let's go somewhere," I said after a while.

"Where?"

"We'll find someplace." My mind was racing. If I could get her alone she would let me fuck her. Under the stairs in the service entrance to my house. In the alley. In the park. Anyplace dark. "Let's go."

"We better not."

"Why?"

"You know why."

"No, I don't. It isn't wrong." I stared at her profile. Her mouth was set in a faint smile, barely perceptible. I pulled her shoulder gently. "Come on. It's all right."

She leaned forward, sitting on the edge of her seat, and stared out over my shoulder into the darkness. For a moment I thought she was going to leave me—simply walk out on her own and go home—but then she looked at me, nodded, and stood up. I followed her down the aisle, my eyes locked on her back.

As we emerged from the theater I turned toward the park. "This way." The marquee lights threw our shadows on the sidewalk in front of us, long, thin shadows stretching away up the block, growing longer and fainter as we walked.

"You're going too fast," she said.

"I'm sorry." As we passed my house I gave up the idea of the alley or the service stairs. We continued toward the park in silence. I was conscious only of movement, of the girl beside me, and of the blood roaring in my head.

At the corner of Madison Avenue she said, "I'm scared."

"Why?"

She didn't answer.

"What is there to be scared of?" I helped her over the curb. She shook her head, watching the sidewalk moving under us. Suddenly I understood. "You mean you're scared of having a baby."

"Yes."

"Don't worry. We'll take care of that." It flashed through my mind that I could buy a prophylactic at the drugstore on the corner. Then I remembered I'd spent the last of my money for the theater ticket.

We went into the park through the same entrance I had used as a child. After a few steps I led her off the path into the darkness. There was a place I remembered from years ago—a little hollow between the footpath and the sunken roadway to the West Side. Leading her by the hand, I found it quickly.

"Let's put your coat on the ground," I said.

She took it off slowly and gave it to me. I spread it over the rough grass and went down on my knees. We remained motionless as someone walked along the path on the other side of the bushes. Light from a distant lamp post filtered through the trees and played over her shoulders and neck. When the footsteps died away she came down into the darkness and lay beside me.

She lifted her hips as I raised her skirt, and again as I pulled her panties to her ankles. Opening my clothes I looked down at her white belly glowing in the shadows.

"Do it," she said. "Before someone comes."

I got on top of her and, after a moment of blind fumbling, drove myself into her. She cried out in pain and threw her head to one side.

"What's the matter?" I asked, pausing, but she didn't answer and I began to move again. I found myself thrusting hard once more, and when she didn't flinch I got up on my elbows and quickened the pace. She lay motionless, her head averted.

As I fucked her, a certain moment arrived when I realized her body had changed. Her sex was no longer simply the entrance way one penetrated in search of deeper, more intangible mysteries. It had become, all at once, *slippery*—a lush blossom beyond which there was no need to go.

Afterward, I lay still, dazzled. Coming out of her was a shock. I seemed to be floating weightless in space. On my hands and knees I paused to feel the earth and orient myself. A noisy bus went past in the sunken roadway. I looked up and she was on her feet, waiting.

"Hurry," she said. "I am so late."

We walked to the subway without talking. At the top of the stairs she turned to me. "Goodbye."

"I'll look for you," I said, aware of how feeble it sounded, knowing we would never meet again. "We'll see each other."

She started down.

"Goodbye," I said.

She turned, holding the rail. "What is your name?"

"Frank." I said quickly. "Frank Conroy."

She turned again and went down the stairs into the roar of an arriving train.

17
Going to Sea

THE SHIP began to move, slipping away from the pier without warning. I lifted my arm from the wide rail and waved. Down below, shielding their eyes from the sun, my mother and Jessica waved back. The air shivered from a tremendous blast of the ship's horn. Across the widening water their figures shrank. The deck trembled under my feet and a faint breeze sprang up. I looked forward for an instant, into the wind, and when I turned back I couldn't find them in the crowd. I waved anyway. The pier, suddenly very small—a knot of people gathered under a black roof—slipped smoothly around the back of the ship and out of sight. I stared down at the brown water for a moment, watching the wavelets, hearing the excited voices of people moving behind me. When I turned from the rail it seemed to me that every move I made was significant, as if I had never walked before, or paused in a doorway to let a lady go first, or met another person's eye. I stood in the elevator and descended to C deck, conscious of the newness of my clothes. Everything I wore, from shoes to necktie, was brand new. I lighted a cigarette and stepped out into the corridor.

My cabin, built to accommodate four, was occupied by only two, myself and an old man whom no one had come to see off. There was some champagne left from a bottle my mother had brought and I poured two glasses and held one out to him. He paused in his unpacking and accepted it.

"Danke."

"Skol." I raised my glass and we drank. *"Nicht sprechen Deutsch,"* I said.

"Was?"

"Nicht sprechen Deutsch. I'm sorry."

He waved his hand in the air. "I speak no English."

We turned away from each other. I knew from the card

on the door that his name was Drevitch. I took the upper bunk on my side of the cabin, unpacked a few clothes and some books, and lay down to read the leaflet explaining how the ship was run. There were, I discovered, movies every night, a library, several bars, dancing after dinner, a swimming pool, a gym, a ship's newspaper, live music in the cocktail lounge, ping-pong, chess, bridge and mah-jong contests, and a dozen other diversions. One had only to push the buzzer by the light switch—I looked up—to summon a steward who would bring food or whatever else one wanted. I placed the leaflet next to my books and left the cabin for a tour of the ship.

I'd asked for the second seating at dinner. At the door, I studied the plan—a large placard on an easel-like affair—and found my name and table. I crossed the dining room through the soft clatter of silverware and crockery and spotted my empty chair. Five young women were already seated at the table eating their soup. I sat down quickly and hid behind the menu. When I looked up, the girl on my left was smiling at me. She had black hair and very large blue eyes. "You must be Frank Conroy," she said.

"Yes. Hello."

"Well Frank, I'm Paula, and this is Judy, and Didi, and Carol and Betsy." I nodded to each in turn. "And we're certainly glad you're here because with all these women and no man it would have been a very dull trip." The girls laughed and I blushed.

"Are you all together?" I asked.

"We're Army wives. Our husbands are stationed in Germany."

"Oh. I see."

"Where are you going?" Judy asked. She was a plump blonde.

"To Denmark. I'm going to school there. A sort of school, that is."

"Here comes the waiter," Paula said, touching my elbow. "You know you can have as much as you want of everything. Unlimited seconds."

"Really?" I was surprised. "I don't eat much, though."

Judy buttered a roll. "Wish I could say that."

I ordered a ground beefsteak and a chocolate parfait for dessert. When I handed the waiter the menu, Paula winked at me. Next to her, Didi lowered her spoon. "My goodness," she said. "Will you look at that boy blush!"

I laughed, looked down at the table, and then, suddenly reckless, raised my head. "Well, what can I say? I'm a young, innocent boy on his own for the first time and you can tease me if you want. But if you do I'll just be flustered all the time and won't be able to tell all my jokes. I know about a thousand and I'm sure you'll like them, but you have to promise not to take advantage of me." Paula laughed and started a round of applause. After a moment the others joined in. "Thank you," I said, blushing again.

"Whoops!" Didi said, but she looked away.

After dinner I went to the movies with Paula and Judy, sitting between them in a back row of the small theater. Every now and then I'd make a wisecrack and they giggled appreciatively.

"You see that dimple on Kirk Douglas' chin? They say he can stick his finger in there, open his mouth, and wave hello from the inside."

"Now stop that," Paula said, shocked.

"Well, that's what they say."

When the movie ended and the lights came on we went to the lounge for a drink. In the hall I noticed, for the first time, a gentle roll to the ship.

"Oh-oh," Judy said.

"Don't pay any attention to it," Paula said.

Judy reached for the rail, unnecessarily. "You don't *know* the way I get seasick."

"It's all psychological," I said. "Entirely in the mind."

"That's right." Paula pushed open the glass doors to the lounge and we went inside. A steward came over immediately.

"I'll have a rum and Coke," I said quickly, nervous that he might refuse to serve me. "Ladies?"

"A whisky sour," Paula said.

"Make it two." Judy sank back into the couch as the steward left. Outside, through the heavy windows, it was completely dark—a special kind of blackness, as if the world ended there. Some children ran across the room, weaving in and out among the armchairs.

"I should have flown," Judy said. "But then I'm scared of planes."

Paula smoothed her skirt and crossed her legs. "You'll be all right."

"Have you ever crossed before?" I asked Paula.

"No."

"Me neither. I almost went to sea once as a cabin boy. My uncle is in the merchant marine."

The steward brought our drinks and I attempted to pay for all three.

"No," Paula said very firmly. "This is Dutch." She held out some money to the steward. "For the whisky sours."

I sipped my drink while the girls talked. Then I got up and went to the piano and began to play very softly. "Tenderly," my best ballad, "Honeysuckle Rose," and a reduced version of "The Man I Love." A boy about ten years old came and stood at my elbow, watching. I slipped in some extra flourishes while he was there.

"Boy, that's neat," he said.

I looked back at the girls but they were still talking. After a few minutes of boogiewoogie I stood up. The boy ran to join the other children. I went back and got my drink. Paula looked up. "That was nice. Why don't you play some more?"

"Oh, I just fool around," I said.

Judy sat forward suddenly. "I'd better go below, as they say. I ought to lie down."

"I'll come with you," Paula said, getting up. "It's been a long day."

I finished my drink. "Goodnight," I said as they started away. "See you tomorrow." Disappointed, I watched them leave. I'd expected them to stay for an hour or so and now, without warning, they were going. They pushed through the door and I cursed myself for being so young. I went to the bar, took a stool, and ordered another drink.

"Mix it?" the bartender asked.

"What?"

"Shall I mix it?"

"Oh yes. Sure."

He made the drink and moved away. At the other end of the bar a few couples were laughing and drinking. The room was beginning to empty out as people went off to bed. I watched a blind man in a red beret cross the lounge unassisted, his white cane moving delicately in the air ahead of him. The ship rolled gently and the ice cubes in my drink clinked softly against the glass.

The nature of time had changed. Sitting at the bar I slipped effortlessly from one moment to the next, each perception dying gradually like a slow movie fade-out while the next built up underneath it. I got up from the stool and crossed the empty room, surprised to find myself in motion. Outside, on deck in the darkness, a cool wind made my jacket billow around my body. I went to the rail and stared down at the water. I imagined jumping. The ship would keep going, eventually disappear, and there would be only the sea, me, and the sky—nothing else. For a moment the purity of it overwhelmed me. I felt I had to jump, not just to die, but to experience the moments of total solitude as I waited. From another deck I could hear the music of a small orchestra. Someone passed behind me. I turned and walked along the deck, my fingers trailing along the surface of the rail.

The next day I made arrangements with the steward and got a deck chair. All morning I lay wrapped in a plaid blanket, dozing and reading. The sea was calm but the sky was overcast, with only brief moments of sunshine warming the chilly air. I watched the sea and hardly noticed the people going by on deck. When the steward bent over me he brought me out of a trance.

"Bouillon, sir?"

"Yes. Thank you." It was still a shock to be addressed as sir. The stewards were almost all German, studiously formal. I pulled myself up in the chair as he reached back for a cup from a rolling cart. "Do you know what time it is?"

"Eleven o'clock," he said, handing me the soup.

"Thank you." I took a sip and decided I'd make it a point to be in my chair every morning at eleven o'clock for the luxury of the experience. Two chairs away a young man sitting on the edge of the footrest had just accepted a cup of broth. Our eyes met.

"This is the life, eh?" he said.

"You bet."

"First trip?" He was about twenty-five, dressed in a

rather loud sport jacket, black trousers, argyle socks, and brown loafers.

I nodded. "You too?"

"No. I work on the ship. This is my fifth trip."

"What do you do?"

"I'm the pianist up in first class. In the orchestra."

"Really?" I leaned forward. "I play too. Blues and boogie and stuff."

"You ought to come up and hear us, then."

"I'm cabin class, though."

"Shit, man," he said scornfully, "just step over the chain and keep going. Nobody's going to stop you."

"Can I do that?"

"Sure. Follow the signs to the ballroom."

"Then I'll come tonight. What time do you start?"

"Nine." His head turned as he watched two girls walk by, arm in arm. "No good," he said when they'd passed. "Slim pickings this trip."

I laughed. "I've got five girls sitting at my table."

"You're kidding," he said. "Bring a couple along. A kid like you doesn't need all that for himself."

"They're all married, unfortunately."

He gave me a long look. "This is a *ship*, man," he said finally. "You heard about ships." A girl glanced at us as she went by and he stood up immediately. "That's the whole reason I took this gig, baby. Even with my delicate stomach and all." He gave me a nod and moved off after the girl. I rewrapped myself in the plaid blanket, read the day's issue of the ship's newspaper, and went to sleep.

At dinner I told the girls of my plan to crash first class.

"Have you got a dark suit?" Paula asked. "It's dressy up there."

"If you get caught just keep talking," Didi said. "You could get out of anything the way you talk."

I laughed. "Yes. I'll tell them I'm an impoverished artist on his way to study in Paris with special permission to practice on the Steinway in the first-class lounge."

"That's just what I mean," Didi said. "That kind of thing."

"Or that I'm the captain of the cabin-class volleyball team on his way to arrange a play-off match."

"Hey, that's *good!*" Judy said. "That'd really work, I bet."

"Well you better eat something," Betsy said. "Look at that. You haven't even touched your roast beef."

Embarrassed, I bent over my plate and moved the food around with knife and fork, making the motions of eating.

"I don't know what keeps you going."

"Oh, come on," Paula said. "Stop mothering him."

"Yeah, stop mothering me," I said. "Why do you think I left home?"

They all laughed.

At nine o'clock I climbed the stairs to B deck and walked toward the front of the ship. Eventually I reached a gate with the words First Class Only Beyond This Point lettered across the narrow, saloon-type doors. I checked my tie, made sure my fly was zipped, rubbed the toes of my shoes against the backs of my legs and, after making sure there was no one on either side to see me, pushed through quickly, breaking the message in half.

There was a different color scheme. Blues and purples in the fabrics, with gleaming white woodwork and walnut handrails. The corridors were wider than those in cabin class and there were fewer doors along the walls. I rounded a corner into an open space where an old man in a wheelchair sat staring at his knees, his white head bent forward. Behind him a huge Negro held the rubber grips of the chair, absolutely motionless as they waited for the elevator. I walked past them and started up the curved staircase, glancing back as the elevator doors rolled open. The Negro pushed the chair, the old man's head jerked back a fraction of an inch, and they disappeared. I climbed to the main deck and followed the signs to the ballroom.

People moved unhurriedly through the wide halls toward the center of the ship, smoking and chatting as they walked. Most of the men were in dinner jackets, although a few wore dark suits like my own. Jewelry flashed on the necks and wrists of the women. As I walked through the crowd I seemed to grow older and more confident, as if I'd gained a year or two by simply pushing through the gate. I paused at the entrance to the ballroom, looking down at the placard beside the door. Ernest Millborn and His Orchestra in the Grand Ballroom. There was no mention of my friend, but as I stepped inside I could see him at the piano, slightly hunched over the keyboard as the band played "Once in Love with Amy."

It was an immense high-ceilinged room with a vast black marble dance floor. The spaciousness was almost dizzying. Recovering from my surprise, I moved forward. Row after row of white tables stretched away from the edge of the dance floor, each table with a lighted candle in glass at its center. The polished floor picked up the constant flickering, and as the few dancing couples moved smoothly back and forth over the wide expanse they seemed to be gliding on a sea of lights. I went to a corner near the band and sat down at an empty table. The other passengers in the room were sitting on the other side of the dance floor, gathered around fifteen or twenty tables as if for warmth. I supposed it was too early for a crowd. After a while a waiter spotted me and came over to take my order.

"A rum and Coke," I said. "And mix it, please."

"Yes sir." He moved away.

I turned in my chair and watched the band—three saxes, three brass, four strings, and rhythm. The leader was on his feet at center stage, dipping his violin over a standing microphone, his wrist pumping a slow vibrato, his pink brow gleaming with sweat. As my drink arrived the trumpets broke into an up-tempo version of "Sweet Georgia Brown." I tapped my foot and sang the words in my mind.

At the end of the set the pianist, my friend, came down from the stand wiping his face with a folded handkerchief. I stood up and caught his attention. He stuffed the handkerchief into his pocket and joined me. "I see you made it," he said.

Nodding, I offered him a chair.

"Naw, man," he said. "Let's go get some air."

"Okay. I have to pay for my drink, though."

"That's all right. Come on."

I followed him down the aisle between the tables. As we passed a group of waiters he said, "He's coming back. Leave his drink," and then pushed through a door. We stepped out onto the deck. There was a fresh breeze blowing. "Ahh, yes," he said, taking a deep breath.

I walked along beside him. He kept up a good pace, his thin head held high. "The music was fine," I said.

"It's all right. That kraut is a pain in the ass, though. His time is terrible. Did you hear the way he dragged 'Spell-bound'?"

"Millborn? Is he German?"

"His real name is Grubel. It's a bitch. He can't hear any-thing."

I laughed. "Well, the horns sounded good."

"Yeah. They're okay." He leaned his head toward me. "You see those people over there by the rail? That guy is a vice-president of General Motors."

"Really?"

"Yeah. I wish I was the telegrapher around here. Think what he sends to his broker every day. You could make a fortune."

"They probably use a code," I said.

He turned, surprised. "I bet they do. I never thought of that."

"They always do in books."

"You read a lot, huh?"

"I guess so. Yes."

"I used to when I was a kid. Not so much any more, though." He paused and pulled open a door. "Come on, there's a piano in here."

We entered a small empty lounge—a sun room during the day—with a miniature piano set against the wall.

"Go on," he said. "Let's hear what you can do."

I sat down and played "Blue Moon." When I was through he shook his head. "Naw, man. You're just playing shells. You have to fill in those chords." He reached down over my shoulder and played a chorus very quickly, his hands and fingers close together in a series of black chords. "You have to get those ninths and thirteenths in there. Get the harmony going." Fascinated, I watched his hands and tried to pick up one or two of the chords. "Get a book," he said. "Learn harmony."

"I can't read music," I said.

"Well, you have to read, man. You can't work if you can't read."

"Yes, I know." When he lifted his hands from the key-board I started to play some boogie. He laughed.

After I'd finished he nodded his head. "Not bad at all. But don't play too much of that stuff. You'll ruin your left hand. The muscles get all tight."

"Play with me once," I said, and moved over on the bench.

He laughed again, but sat down, and we played till it was time for him to go back on the stand.

Back at the corner table in the ballroom, my fingers around a fresh drink, I watched the dancers. A woman in an orange dress emerged from the crowd, alone, crossing the wide floor like a nervous animal over an open field. She flashed a quick smile and shied away as a foxtrotting couple almost ran into her. Through at last, she straightened up, throwing back her shoulders like an actress in the wings getting into character. To my amazement she came directly to my table. "Hello, young man." I started to rise, but she sat before I could get out of my chair. "You must excuse my barging over here like this, but we saw you sitting all by yourself and we didn't think you'd mind."

"Not at all," I said. She was forty-five or fifty, plump, and nervously cheerful.

"We *are* on a ship after all." She touched her throat with her fingertips. "My niece and I saw you. We're sitting over there." She nodded across the floor. Turning my head, I caught a brief glimpse of a girl in white leaning forward to sip from a champagne glass. "Since you seem to be alone and there aren't too many young people I thought I'd ask you to join us."

I stared at her blankly. For a moment I seemed to be totally paralyzed.

"My niece just loves to dance," she said, standing up. "Shall we go?"

"I can't," I said suddenly.

"What?"

"I can't. I'm not really first class. I just snuck up to hear the piano player."

She stood motionless over me, her mouth slightly open. Then we spoke simultaneously. "But that doesn't . . ." she started.

"I'm sorry," I said at the same moment. Flushing, I looked down at the table. "It was nice of you to ask. I'm sorry."

She didn't seem to know what to do. For several moments she seemed to be about to speak, but then she smiled

—an odd, polite smile, absolutely automatic—and moved away.

I opened the door to the cabin and tiptoed inside. Drevitch was in bed, turned to the wall, his white wispy hair catching the light from behind me. A small pile of orange peelings overflowed the ashtray on his dresser. I closed the door and moved to my bunk. Undressing in the dark, I became aware of Drevitch snoring softly. I got into my pajamas and, slightly drunk, climbed the ladder into bed. As I pulled back the covers I saw something lying on the pillow. An envelope. I picked it up and switched on the small reading light. It was a telegram, addressed to me. I turned it over, unable to think who could have sent it, and as an afterthought pulled out the small curtain so Drevitch wouldn't be bothered by the light. Tearing open the envelope, I took out the message, which said *Thinking of You,* and was signed *Mom.* I stared at it for several moments, disappointed that it wasn't something more exciting, and surprised that my mother had allowed herself such sentimentality. The signature was particularly out of character. All my life I'd called her Mother, never Mom, and yet Mom was how she signed it. It seemed spurious somehow, and I crumpled it up, threw it away, and thought no more about it.

In the morning I awoke to a new world. Lying in my bunk, staring at the ceiling, I felt the ship plunge forward, lean to the right, pause, and then rear backward, lean to the left, pause, and begin the cycle again. Nothing moved in the cabin except the curtain over the door to the bathroom. It went back and forth slowly, its movements corresponding to the forces tugging gently at my flesh. A creaking sound filled the cabin, as if the room itself were twisting imperceptibly out of shape with each dip of the ship. I climbed down from my bunk and stood in front of the large mirror over the dresser. Drevitch had made his bed and gone. I glanced at the porthole and saw a circle of light gray, the sky, a brief glimpse of the horizon rushing upwards, and then the black sea. The black remained behind the porthole for what seemed like much too long a time. I felt a flash of fear as I realized how far the ship was heeling. Automatically, I tried to relate what was happening inside the cabin to what I saw through the round glass, and immediately felt a wave of nausea rising in my stomach. I sat down in a chair, waiting to see what would happen. Moments later I rushed to the bathroom and threw up in the sink. I drank some water and returned, trembling, to bed. I pulled the curtain shut, put the pillow over my head, and tried to go to sleep, my knees coming up to my chest of their own accord.

I remained in bed all day, only getting up every few hours to retch bile. In the evening I rang for the steward and asked for some soup. He brought a cup of bouillon and a few small, crustless sandwiches, saying that if I didn't eat I'd be sick all the way to Germany. His advice was only half heard. He seemed to be talking to me across tremendous distances, but I managed to keep the food down.

After two days the sea calmed a bit. I emerged from the cabin and made my laborious way to the open deck and the chair I'd reserved in a previous lifetime. I lay comatose until nightfall, weak, sweating, wrapped in a plaid blanket, my stomach shrunk to the size of a crabapple. Back in the cabin the steward, unasked, brought an entire dinner on a tray. I ate most of it and fell asleep reassured that the next day we would make a landfall.

On deck, in the bright sunshine, I looked over the water to the green hump of land they said was Ireland. Miles away, it shone in the faint haze like a fresh brush stroke between sea and sky. I regretted that we would go no closer. My great-grandfather (whose name I didn't know) must have stood at the rail of another ship, going the other way, watching what I was watching. I stayed on deck and looked at Ireland until it disappeared.

Now the ship was on an even keel. As we approached our first port, on the coast of France, the atmosphere on board quickened. People rushed here and there, seeing to their luggage, queuing up for passport control, making special arrangements with the harried officers and crew. As the ship docked it seemed almost not to be a ship any more, but a large, crowded hotel with every man elbowing his neighbor aside in the struggle to leave. Night fell and I watched the disembarking passengers walk down the long gangway under the white brilliance of a hundred spotlights.

Below me the stevedores moved back and forth with platforms of freight, their blue shirts stained with sweat. Testing the reality of the scene, I called down to one of them.

"Bonjour," I said, my heart beating wildly. A man looked up, and unable to think of anything more intelligent to say, I cupped my hands around my mouth and shouted, *"C'est un grand bateau, n'est-ce pas?"*

He lowered his head and after a moment turned to another man working a few yards away. I caught the end of what he said ". . . *S'quil a dit? Que c'est un grand bateau!"* They laughed and didn't look up again. I moved away, filled with mysterious shame. But I'd found out what I wanted to know. French, which I'd failed three times in high school, was in fact a real language, spoken by real people. Europe existed.

At dinner the girls were nervous, talking fast and laughing too much. I bought a bottle of wine to celebrate our last evening together and Paula had a picture taken of the table, all of us with glasses raised, myself with eyes carefully crossed. When I said my goodbyes she kissed me on the cheek. I left the dining room with my head full of perfume and my cheek tingling where her lips had brushed against me.

The next day we docked at Bremerhaven. Making my way along the crowded deck I reviewed the morning, making sure I'd done everything I was supposed to. I'd tipped everyone mentioned in the chapter on tipping in my Traveler's Handbook, I had all my luggage (a suitcase and an Army-surplus duffel bag), I'd cleared customs and passport control, and my embarkation pass was sticking up out of my breast pocket. By getting an early start I was ahead of everyone else, ready to go. Two screaming children almost knocked the duffel bag from my shoulder as they ran by. I hitched it up and continued forward saying, "excuse me, sorry, excuse me," as I struggled through. A brass band was playing somewhere forward, trumpet runs clearly audible above the shouting and confusion. As someone moved away from the rail I stepped into his place to rest for a moment. On the pier down below a crowd of soldiers stood with upturned faces, some of them waving and calling up to the people looking down. As I started to turn away I caught sight of Paula and two or three of the girls on the rail a few yards away. I could see Paula quite clearly through the crowd, and was about to call out when she turned in my direction. She was crying, her mouth twisted up as if reacting to some terrible pain. Her eyes passed over me without a trace of recognition. She looked down at the pier, raising her arm to wave, her head going forward, her whole body strained with longing. Behind her one of the other girls, also crying, seemed not to be able to look any longer and collapsed against Paula's back, holding on to her shoulders and lowering her forehead against her friend. Stunned, I turned away instantly and re-entered the crowd.

Near the gangplank I came upon the brass band standing with their backs to the wall, playing hard. My friend the pianist was at the end of the line, a glockenspiel resting on his hip, his eyes narrowed to read the music clipped to the top of the instrument, his fingers holding, with almost visible distaste, the little mallet with which every now and then he struck the silver bars. It was so ludicrous I felt embarrased for him, and moved past without attempting to catch his eye. At the gangplank my heart began to race. I got on line and moved slowly past the officials. My pass was checked and my luggage marked on a list.

"Okay?" I asked an officer.

He nodded and I stepped off the ship. The music fading behind me, I moved down the long, covered gangway toward the square of light in the distance.

18

Elsinore, 1953

DOCTOR BLOCK took my knight with his bishop. Surprised, I stared down at the board. He would lose a bishop to gain a knight, with the rest of the exchange, as far as I could see, coming out even. Was it a trap? Perhaps he was simply determined to break up my developing offense earlier than usual. After playing the man two games a day every afternoon for the past two months I had developed the knack of responding to his response, of building my attack along the lines suggested by his defense without actually being able to see (as he could) how it was supposed to turn out. I invariably lost, but I was becoming a good player. Doctor Block's straightforward defensive play (he was not tricky, and always defended himself at what was, empirically, his weakest point) elicited increasingly complex attacks from myself, showing me the way, as it were. Without a common language, we played in silence. He was German.

I took his bishop, he took my other knight. I took his knight with a pawn, but instead of taking my pawn as I'd expected he brought out his second bishop and put my rook *en prise*.

"Shit," I said softly.

He sucked his pipe. "Hmmmm."

I studied the board, trying to find a way to save my rook. In a flash, I saw something. Not bothering to think it out past a couple of moves I surrendered to a delicious impulse and brought out my queen. "Check." If I had to go down, I'd go down fighting. He blocked my queen with a pawn. "Check," I said, developing my bishop. He nodded calmly and moved his king behind a line of pawns. My queen was threatened. I sacrificed a knight. "Check." He took the piece and I moved my freed queen. "Check." He retreated farther behind the pawns, but now, at least, I could exchange bishops and save my rook. I was down a piece, but I had a rook for the end game.

He looked down at the board, up at me, held two fingers in the air, and said "Mate."

"What?" I looked at the board, trying to see how he could finish me off in two moves. It took me several moments. Nodding, I stood up. *"Tak,"* I said in my awkward Danish. *"I morn."* We shook hands and he began to put away the pieces. There was no one else in the common room, so I left, passing through the cold hall, up the stairs, and into my room.

The youngest student and the only American at the International Folk High School of Elsinore, I'd been given a room of my own. My grandfather (a small, gentle man with whom I could not converse but who nevertheless managed to convey his interest in me—he'd met me at the Copenhagen railroad station the night I arrived, alert, grey-haired, almost apologetic as he struggled with me over my suitcase which, despite his age, he insisted on carrying) had given me an old radio, a rug, and some colorful maps to animate the room. I'd bought a small table lamp with a red shade. My typewriter stood on the desk, surrounded by the pages of a short story I was writing. I liked the room. At night I lay in my bed listening to the bitter wind outside, congratulating myself on its cosiness.

I walked to the window and stared through the double panes at the girls' dormitory across the way. It was already dark at four in the afternoon. Light from my window spilled out over the snow and mixed with light from the Frog's window directly opposite. The Frog was a big, hulking farmgirl from Aarhus, so named by the French boys because of her acne. As I stood watching she appeared at her window (her long shadow wavering across the snow), saw me, and darted away like a frightened animal. I rubbed my nose. The mixture of ugliness and extreme shyness was interesting, but I couldn't help wishing that someone pretty, someone like Christina, lived there instead.

There was a knock at the door, and as I turned, Henri entered. He was by tacit agreement the leader of the French group, six boys and one girl, to whom I had attached myself. They were kind about my French, ignoring my grammar and praising my vocabulary.

"Come on," he said, "we're playing Hysteria."

"Immediately. I'll change the shoes." I sat down on my bed and reached underneath for a pair of sneakers.

Henri went to my desk and looked down at the pages of my story. "Does it march?"

"Yes. But slowly."

"Good."

"Is everybody there?"

"They've started already."

I tied my laces and jumped up. "Let's go."

We went down the hall toward the far staircase. A few of the German boys were practicing a dance in the open area by the stairwell, big, clumsy oafs in lederhosen, slapping themselves and shaking the building as they jumped around, their red faces glowing. They didn't look up as we passed.

"What a bunch of cows," Henri said as we jogged down the stairs. "Have you observed how they never talk to anyone but themselves?"

"They wouldn't last five minutes in the game," I said. He laughed. *"Tu parles!"*

The gym, a large room perhaps sixty feet long, had gone unused until the afternoon we invented the game. There was a small stage at one end, and the other three walls were banked with horizontal wooden bars, six inches apart, covering the whole surface from floor to ceiling. Assuming that the stage was "safe," it was possible to make a complete circuit of the room without touching the floor. In a storeroom we'd found ropes and gym equipment which, when placed intelligently around the floor, added another dimension. The ropes hung from the ceiling, gym mats and jumping horses were strategically lined up, chairs stacked here and there, and it became possible to leap from a wall, swing to a safety zone, have a rope thrown by a confederate, and wing again to another wall. The game was tag, with only two rules—you couldn't touch the floor, and in the event that you were tagged and made "it," you had to count to twenty-five to give the person who'd tagged you time to get away. Hysteria was the most exhausting game I've ever encountered. We could hear the screams of the players echoing off the high ceiling even before we entered. Pushing open the door, we jumped up on the stage.

"Who's It?" we yelled together.

"Midou!"

Midou the Algerian, a bony, slope-shouldered boy of nineteen, was the youngest student after myself. He glanced at us from his perch high on the wall and began climbing down, angling toward us. We trotted across the stage and clambered up onto the bars on the opposite wall. In the center of the room Albert sat on the jumping horse combing his hair, patting the high wave over his forehead between strokes like a sculptor working with clay. We scuttled across the wall to a place opposite him.

"Albert!" I called as Midou landed on the stage with a thump.

"One second." He stood up on the horse and motioned for Georges, spread-eagled on the far wall, to send a rope. When it arrived he held it with his right hand and threw us ours with his left. Henri leaned out from the wall and caught it in the air. Midou quickened his pace and I could feel the bar under my hands vibrating as he approached. Henri swung through the air to the horse as Albert swung to the·far wall. I climbed up a few rungs and looked back over my shoulder for the rope. "Hurry."

Henri stood on the horse, smiling. "Softly," he said as he threw, "grace is everything."

It was a perfect toss, allowing me to jump into the air to meet the rope. Henri reached out and caught me around the waist as I arrived. Laughing, I turned to taunt Midou, but he kept on moving across the wall, having shifted his attention to Marcel, who was resting on the stacked chairs in the corner.

"He's wasting his strength," I said. Marcel was the fastest of us all.

"Bien sur," Henri said. He took the rope, jumped, swung back to the wall we'd just left, leaving the end entwined in the bars.

Midou and Marcel, ten feet apart, were moving fast across the wall. "Pig!" Midou shouted. "Son of a dog!" Marcel began to laugh. "Maggot!" Midou yelled, sensing an advantage. (In the game of Hysteria, laughter was dangerous. Once you started, it was often hard to stop. The tension of the chase and the inherent ridiculousness of the game itself brought on fits of uncontrollable laughter, and more than once I'd found myself at the brink of safety, with a rope in my hands and nothing more to do than jump, unable to move because I was laughing so hard, my will utterly sapped.) Still laughing, Marcel slipped. He hung by his hands, flat against the wall. With an eerie scream Midou pounced, slapped his arm, and moved away gibbering like an ape. Marcel rested for a moment and then turned around. I was the first person he saw. "Prepare yourself, my friend," he said. I called for a rope the moment he began to move.

I'd been "It" for ten minutes. Swinging off the wall, I let go of the rope, flew through the air and landed on a gym mat at the precise instant Russe left on another rope, climbing hand over hand up to the ceiling, across a rafter to the safety of the wall. Too tired to follow, I collapsed on the mat and folded my arms over my head. Instantly a chorus of jeers, catcalls, and shrill whistling sounds filled the air.
    "Sleepy-head!"
    "The poor child is tired!"
    "Too many cigarettes!"
    I struggled to my feet, my chest heaving, and surveyed the situation. I had the strength for one more attempt. They were all in the corner—Henri, Midou, and Albert on the stacked chairs, Marcel and Georges on the wall, with Russe climbing down to join them. Albert played with a rope, faking clumsiness, gasping theatrically as he almost dropped it. I studied the placement of the gym mats. My single advantage was long legs. Except for Midou, not one of the French boys was over five and a half feet tall, and I knew from experience that I could jump farther than any of them. In the course of the game one of the gym mats had crept a bit closer to the wall than was usual. With sudden decisiveness I began to run, leaping easily across two mats, and then, as I got to the third and last, I put on a burst of speed. There was a sudden panic in the corner.
    "Attention! He's going to jump!"
    My timing was right. I pushed off from the last mat with every bit of strength I could muster, sailed through the air, my arms outstretched, and hit the wall. My foot was on the lowest rung and hadn't touched the floor.
    "Hola!" someone called. "Bien fait!"
    As I began to climb they converged on Albert, screaming like girls, everyone trying to get a hand on the rope. They came away from the wall as I arrived, a tangled knot of humanity, laughing and cursing as Midou's foot caught

in the bars and stopped their movement. I could have tagged Midou easily, but I didn't. I watched as he extricated himself. Without momentum, and with all that weight, the rope simply hung over the open floor. Gradually the entire group began slipping down a few inches at a time, the few hands with a firm grip on the rope unable to keep hold. They fell to the floor with a tremendous crash, those from the top of the rope landing on those from the bottom. I climbed down from the wall as they separated themselves and lay on the floor catching their breaths.

"It must be time for supper," Midou said after a while.

Someone loosed a long, splintering fart and we all laughed.

Meals at the school were simple and, for me at least, almost entirely inedible. Breakfast consisted of porridge, bread, and coffee. Lunch and dinner were boiled potatoes, a boiled vegetable, and meat every other day. No one seemed to mind. The French boys complained occasionally in private, but in the dining room they remained cheerful and stoked it down without a word. (I do remember a raised eyebrow from Henri one night when, instead of the usual fatty meat, each table was served a huge boiled fish-head, eyes and all.) All I ever ate was potatoes with salt, pepper, and margarine. Since room, board, and tuition cost the students less than a dollar a day, I suppose no one expected much in the way of food.

The school was part of a Scandinavian movement called Folk High Schools. The idea had originally been to provide some sort of informal education for the agrarian poor. The Elsinore school had survived the death of the movement because it took students from all over the world, thus enjoying the continued support of an internationally minded government. Most of the students were there to learn Danish. When spring came they would go to work on Danish farms, learn Danish agricultural methods, and return to their own farms the following winter. Others were at the school simply because it was cheap. Like myself, they had wanted to leave their own countries but could not afford tourism. Some of the girls were there to catch a husband, some of the men to find wives, and a few naïve souls perhaps expected to learn something from the curriculum. Toward the end of my stay I learned that there was a con-

tinuous flow of students from one of the larger mental in-
stitutions in Copenhagen, that the school was also being
used as a sort of way-station between the hospital and
society. It was not so much a school as a hostel for all
ages. The oldest student was a woman of sixty-seven who,
were she not at the school, would have been in a rest
home.

On the way to the dining hall I saw Christina coming
down the steps of the girls' dormitory. She was alone. On
an impulse I stopped in front of the dining room door, as
the French boys went ahead, and went through the motions of tying my shoe. Christina approached and I straightened up. She walked with her head down and would have
passed me by if I hadn't reached forward to open the door.
She glanced up quickly. "Thank you," she said, with the
faintest trace of a Swedish accent.

"Do you speak French?" I asked.

"A little. Why?"

"Why don't you sit with us?"

I followed her through the short passageway and the
second bank of doors. Once inside, we stopped. It was
warm, the air filled with voices and the sound of chairs
being pulled from the tables. She turned, her thin face
slightly puzzled, as if she'd forgotten something. She wore
square rimless glasses and her blonde hair had been pulled
into a tight bun on the back of her head. "I usually sit with
Karen and Hanna. But I will change tonight."

"Good."

We crossed the room to the French table. Feeling slightly
self-conscious, I held her chair. She sat straight, her back
not touching the wood. A faint, lemony scent rose from
her head. "This is nice," she said, smiling as I sat down.

At the faculty table Dr. Maniche, the headmaster, stood
up and tapped his glass with a spoon. The room fell silent.
He spoke first in Danish and then in English.

"Tomorrow afternoon we will have some visitors from
the Esperanto Society. For those of you who don't know,
Esperanto is an international language made up of phonetic
elements from the major languages of the western world.
The delegation will be in the common room at three o'clock
to answer any questions you might have."

At the faculty table my friend Roger Finlie-Pursel, a
young Englishman, glanced at me, rolling his eyes into his

head to signify his desperate boredom. When I laughed, Christina asked, "What is funny?"

"Roger," I said. "He's always fooling around."

"I don't like him."

"Really?" I was surprised. "He can be terribly funny."

"He is horrible to his wife."

"Yes. I guess he is." Roger had gotten a Danish girl pregnant and married her, so he'd told me, solely to give the child a name. "His lectures on Coleridge are certainly a farce."

"You will be pleased to hear," Dr. Maniche went on, "that despite the cold weather the work on the west field has been going well. I want to thank all of you who've been out with pick and shovel, and to urge the rest of you to come and join us. Manual labor is good for the soul as well as the body. I will now say grace." He bent his head and said a few words in Danish. As he sat down the room filled with sound—chairs scraping, plates crashing, and the aural potpourri of seventy-five people speaking five languages, each group shouting louder than the next. It quieted down a bit as people began to eat.

Beside me, Christina put food on her plate. There was an air of calmness and deliberation in the way she moved, as if she were sitting at a formal dinner. She wore a gray flannel suit, cut simply, with a buttonless jacket over a white blouse. The glasses were perched on a straight nose. My eye followed the steel wire to a small, perfectly shaped ear. Her skin was white as milk, with a touch of pink from the cold in the slight hollows under her cheekbones. Watching her, I became momentarily disoriented, as one does after staring too long in a mirror.

"François! The potatoes!"

I turned and Russe winked at me, holding out his hand for the bowl, which I immediately passed along.

"Tonight," Henri said, leaning across the table to Marie, "our dreams will come true. Yours and mine." He stroked his short black beard.

Marie, a plump girl glowing with health, giggled and looked down at her plate. "I thought you were going to the Casino."

"Tomorrow," Midou corrected, and raised his arms to hold an imaginary girl.

"You are wicked boys," Marie said. "Imagine the disgrace if you got caught in the girls' building."

"Disgrace?" Henri looked around unbelievingly. "Disgrace?"

Albert laughed. "Well, for her maybe."

On my left Marcel leaned forward and asked, "I'd like to hear Radio Moscow tonight. Can I come by?" The only Communist in the group, Marcel stood, by choice, somewhat apart from the others. He affected an attitude of tremendous earnestness, and took a lot of teasing. He thought of himself as an intellectual.

"Of course," I said. "I'd like to hear it myself."

There was a scream of laughter from Marie at something Midou had whispered in her ear and some of the boys at the German table turned to look. Flashing her splendid white teeth, Marie waved and then collapsed with the giggles.

Christina laughed—a soft, tentative laugh, as if she were trying it out—and looked down at her plate.

After supper Dr. Maniche stood up with the day's mail. When he called my name I felt, as always, a faint anticipatory excitement. The letter was from my mother. The only other person it could have been from was a spoiled, pouty, but incredibly sexy sixteen-year-old girl in Copenhagen, vaguely related to my family, whom I'd attempted, unsuccessfully, to make. She'd written me twice, short, perfunctory notes in bad English with nothing in them to suggest that I'd be any luckier the next time I saw her. Returning to the table, I said to Christina, "Nothing for you tonight."

"My parents write once a month," she said, pushing back her chair. "I didn't expect anything."

People began leaving the dining hall, streaming out through the double doors, letting in the cold air. As Christina got up from the table I stood motionless, watching her. "Where are you going?"

She paused for the briefest possible instant, her head slightly averted, and then said, "It's my turn to help in the kitchen."

The French boys were leaving behind me. "Okay. I'll come too."

We crossed the room and went into the kitchen. Some of the other students were already at work sorting out dirty dishes and stacking them next to the sink. The Frog stood over the steaming water, her big arms glistening, stringy hair hanging down.

"I'll rinse and you dry," I said to Christina. We moved to the sink and took up our positions.

On my left, the Frog looked up with an expression of surprise. *"Naa du!"* she said, and rattled off some quick Danish.

"What did she say?"

"That she's surprised to see you here and she assures you it won't hurt."

I laughed, rolling up my sleeves. "Tell her it should hurt, otherwise it isn't good for the soul."

Christina translated and then said, "She doesn't understand. Don't tease her."

"I didn't mean to." I rinsed some dishes in the clear hot water and handed them to Christina, her hands hidden under a huge dishtowel. She smiled.

"They're all surprised to see you here."

"Why?"

"Your group seems to spend time having fun. You're the first to help in the kitchen, for instance."

"Do people resent it?"

"Oh, no. It's as if you're having fun for all of us."

"Well, that isn't right. I mean people shouldn't think that way," I said quickly. "They're great guys though. You should see them at the Casino in town." I laughed at the memory.

"Do you dance there?"

"Me? Oh, once in a while. I go for the music more than anything else."

"I've heard you play. You're very good."

"Thank you."

Even though she knew no English, the Frog was listening to us, pretending not to, as she worked.

"Music is the most important thing for me," Christina said without embarrassment. "I am a student of Bach."

"Really? I didn't know that." I paused for a moment, my hands in the hot water. "But you never play. Why don't you play?"

"I play the organ. Last summer I took a tour of Germany, playing all the organs Bach played. It was . . ."

she hesitated, searching for words, "it was a very important trip. I decided things."

"I'd love to hear you."

She held out her arms for some dishes. "Well, perhaps you will someday. But I like the jazz you play. The freedom of it. It must be a wonderful feeling."

"Yes. It's fun. But I'd like to play Bach."

"Do you like him?"

Rinsing dishes, I began to sing the little fugue in G minor, very slowly. At the first entrance I looked at Christina, but she didn't join in. "That's where you come in," I said.

"I know, but I can't sing."

"Well, good Lord, neither can I!"

"You keep the pitch, though." She moved a pile of silverware. "How old are you?"

"Seventeen. I'll be eighteen next month."

"I am twenty-two," she said. "I come from a very small town in north Sweden. Only five hundred people. You're from New York City. I know from the book."

I laughed. "That's right."

"Why do you laugh?"

"I don't know." After a moment I said, "My mother is Danish, though. I have relatives in Copenhagen."

"You don't look at all Danish."

"Don't I?"

"No. You are the perfect picture of an American boy. Like the films."

I busied myself in the sink. "That's the freckles, I guess."

When the work was finished we stood drying our hands on different ends of the same towel. The Frog was taking off her apron and everyone else had left.

"Well, I must go," Christina said.

"Aren't you coming over to the common room?" I didn't try to hide my disappointment.

"No. I have some things to do upstairs." She folded the towel and hung it on the rack. Then she looked at me, smiling. "Thank you."

I didn't know what to say. She took a few steps and opened a small door into a circular stairwell.

"What's that? I didn't know about that. Does it go upstairs?"

"Yes. It lets out right across from my room." She stood posed at the bottom, holding the curved banister. "Good night, Frank."

My body suddenly flushed with heat. I stood paralyzed, watching her slender figure turn quickly and disappear up the stairs. I took a step forward and then remembered the Frog. She stood by the sink, watching me, her big, brown, cowlike eyes staring sadly. As I passed I heard her catch her breath.

"Good nat, Frank," she said, echoing Christina.

"Good nat."

Outside the wind had risen, sweeping across the Sound from Sweden. As I walked along the cleared path to the boys' dormitory the hollow whining made a sudden lunge up the scale and for a moment I was immersed in a bright cloud of swirling snow. I kicked my boots against the wall in the hot entrance way and went into the common room. Henri was standing by the door with a copy of *Paris Match*. He lowered it and gave me a nod.

"It begins, eh?" he said. "With *la belle Suedoise*."

I sat down and pulled my boots off, wriggling my toes under the heavy socks. "Oh no," I said, covering my embarrassment, "she's five years older than me."

"That means nothing," Henri said, handing me the magazine. "You're lucky, my friend. She's an angel. What bones! Magnificent!"

"Enough, enough."

He shrugged.

"Here's a man that refers to his father with the formal *vous*," I said, tapping the page. "Is that usual?"

He looked over my shoulder. "No. It's very old-fashioned."

"What is?" Marcel asked, joining us.

"To use *vous* with your father," Henri said.

"What do you mean? I know families that do."

"Nonsense. Hey, everyone! François has a question. Does anyone use *vous* to his father? I say it's a ridiculous, old-fashioned affection."

Very rapidly every Frenchman in the room was shouting, cursing, waving his hands in the air, and trying to be heard over the noise. The Danes and Germans watched us with quiet amusement, as if we were putting on a play.

I read my mother's letter in my room. She asked me not to tell her parents that she'd gotten Jean out of the house and was divorcing him. ("It's the second time and they might not understand.") In speech she could easily pass for a native-born American, but in writing she made small mistakes, reductions of the same mistakes I heard every day from Scandinavian students. Thousands of miles away from her I discovered she unconsciously accepted her limitations, confining her written statements to a level of almost childish simplicity. She stated facts, nothing more. Her letters were peculiarly dead—dead with all the outward signs of life, like stillborn infants. I later learned that she wrote them at top speed, without reflection, and could not remember what she'd written from one letter to the next.

I folded the letter, put it away, and surveyed my desk. There was the short story, destined never to be finished, my correspondence with the College Entrance Exam people, and partially completed application forms to Harvard and Haverford colleges, neither of which I had ever seen. I was applying out of reflex. My abysmal high school record precluded, I'd been told, acceptance anywhere.

I looked up and the Frog darted away from her window, the curtain moving slightly as she pulled away. A gust of wind made the building creak and forced a cold draft through the wall. The Sound was frozen all the way to Sweden. They said it was the coldest winter in years.

I began going to classes (which were optional) in order to see Christina. Sometimes I'd sit near her, and sometimes next to her. One afternoon just before vacation we stayed behind, sitting at the huge table, and talked.

"Are you going home for Christmas?" I asked.

"Yes. I don't really want to, though. I'd rather stay here."

"Henri and Albert are staying. I have to see my family in Copenhagen. And take the tests for college."

She folded her notebook and clasped her hands over it. "Where will you go in the summer when school is over?"

"Paris. If I have enough money. My sister will be there."

"That's good. There'll be someone to look after you."

I laughed. "Well, I don't know that I want to be looked after."

"Still, it's nice to have someone you know in a strange city," she said.

"I guess so."

"You're getting a cold."

"I know."

That evening after supper she came to the common room, as had become her habit. Midou had repaired the old Victrola in the corner (applause as the ghostly voice of Bing Crosby seeped out of the horn) and Henri was dancing with Marie. In a corner, giggling, the Frog danced with Hanna, her roommate.

"Shall we dance?" I asked Christina.

"I don't know how," she said, and sat down on the couch.

"Oh, come on. Everybody knows how to dance."

"I've only danced with a man once in my life. It was my uncle and I fell down."

I sat beside her. "That's impossible."

She laughed.

"Well, it is," I insisted.

She turned and looked at me. "In America, perhaps. My village is very small, and my father is a minister. People live an old way, a way you've never seen. That's part of the reason I'm here."

"I thought Sweden was supposed to be so modern."

"Oh yes, in the cities. The country is something else."

I looked away, watching Henri and Marie. As in the Casino, Henri danced with his hand very low on his partner's back, flat against the cleft in her buttocks.

"I'll teach you," I said suddenly.

"What?"

"How to dance. It's easy."

She didn't answer. I got up. "Come on."

"You mean now?"

"Sure. Why not?"

"But everyone will watch and . . ."

"Don't be silly. They won't pay any attention to us. Come on."

I went to a clear corner of the room. She followed hesitantly.

"Now you do a square, is what you do. Like this. One two, one two, one two, one." I put my arms up as if I was holding someone and danced in time to the music. She stood a few yards away, watching my feet, her head at a slight angle.

"Is that all?"

"That's the basic move. You can get tricky and do variations and everything, but that's the fundamental step. Stand next to me and try it."

She came and stood by my side, glancing at me quickly and then bending down her head. I started slowly and she mirrored my moves.

"One two, one two, one two, one. That's it! Try it alone now."

She went through the pattern rather stiffly, but on the beat, watching her own feet through the square glasses.

"That's it. Now do it without looking down."

She raised her head and smiled. "Like this?"

"Perfect. Exactly right. Now we just do it together."

She stood motionless as I approached her, the smile gone and her eyes on my chest. She raised her arms into the air and bit her lower lip. As I got close she seemed very small. Her left hand landed lightly on my shoulder as I touched her waist. Her other hand was cool, clasping mine gently. We stood at least a foot apart, waiting for the beat.

"Okay. Here we go now." I went backwards, pulling her into the pattern. "One two, one two—that's right—one two." She moved awkwardly at first, but got the idea very quickly and began to follow my lead. My hand was just above her hip and I could feel the warmth of her body through the flannel. "Now back, that's it, turn, that's it. Here we go." We danced back and forth in the corner of the room until the record ended. I released her immediately. "Well, you see?"

"You're very good. It's quite easy with you."

"Of course it's easy. I told you."

"Are they going to turn the record over?"

I glanced up to see Henri doing exactly that. When the music started I put my hand on Christina's waist again. "Now, one thing is if we dance a bit closer together it's easier for you to tell what I'm going to do. You'll be able to anticipate my . . ."

"All right," she interrupted. "That's all right."

We both came forward a little. My hand slipped around her waist to the narrow part of her back. The faint scent of lemon soap rose from her body. As we danced her small breasts brushed lightly against my chest and her hair touched the corner of my mouth.

"I can see why people like to do this," she said after a while, completely serious. "It's very nice."

Night. I'd been laid up a day and a half with a bad cold that had moved to my lungs. The entire school was in the gym watching the various Christmas skits put on by each nationality group. I'd directed the French in theirs, a satirical piece I was sure would win the prize. My fever was high —at its apex—and I could no longer concentrate enough to read. I lay in bed dozing, half-hearing the music from the radio, drifting through time, dreaming, my body drenched with sweat. At intervals I would open my eyes, surprised each time to find the same reality around me. The fever heightened perception—every color in the room sensationally vivid, every texture magnified. When some soft jazz came out of the radio the bass notes seemed to vibrate at the base of my skull, note after note blooming inside me like black flowers. I closed my eyes and drifted away, slowly peeling off from the jazz, as if the music and myself were two airplanes splitting high in the air.

When I awoke the music was different and Christina had entered the room. She closed the door behind her and came to the bed. I could not believe it was she, until she spoke. "They told me you were sick."

"How did you . . ."

"It's all right. Everyone is in the gym. No one saw me."

I started to rise up on my elbows but she put her hand on the blankets over my chest. "No," she said, "stay."

I took her hand, a cool, smooth hand, and she sat down on the edge of the bed. "You'll catch whatever I have," I said.

"I don't care. I leave for Sweden early in the morning and I wanted to say goodbye." She looked down at our clasped hands and then withdrew hers. I reached up, took her glasses off, and tried them on.

"They make you look far away," I said, putting them on the night table. "Can you see without them?"

"Yes. Do I look different?"

"A little bit." I reached out and touched the high cheekbone next to her eyes. She turned her head and kissed my palm. Then she raised her hands behind her head and pulled out the pins holding up her hair. It fell to her waist, long, softly waving blond hair gleaming in the light. It was an astonishing transformation.

"Do I look different now?"

"Yes." I reached up and guided her down to me, holding her face in both hands. When my head touched the pillow her lips touched mine, a warm, sweet mouth pressing gently, motionless except for a single tremor at the end of the kiss.

She lowered her forehead to my shoulder and said something in Swedish.

"What's wrong? What's the matter?"

"Nothing," she said slowly. "Nothing is wrong."

"Lie down next to me."

She lifted her legs onto the bed without raising her head. I turned her face up and kissed her again, tasting, moving kisses all over her mouth. Her arm came around my neck. I slipped my hand under her shoulder and kissed her harder. She turned away. "I'm frightened."

"Don't be frightened." I kissed her neck.

"Wait. Please wait." She rubbed her cheek against me. "Please."

Why did I heed her? I stopped, poised above her, listening to the world within and the world without, waiting for a sign, my soul suspended like an orator caught in a photograph at the top of his breath, his hands in the air, forever about to speak. I was afraid. Some part of me was afraid in the midst of my desire, afraid without my knowing it. I stopped.

"I'm sorry," she said.

I kissed her eyes. "No, no, no."

"I don't know about these things."

"Yes. It's strange. Strange territory."

She put her arms around my neck. "Oh why must I go tomorrow? Why must it be tomorrow?"

"Hush. It's all right." I kissed her and put my hand on her breast, covering it with motionless fingers.

"My darling boy," she whispered, hugging me.

We lay quietly until, under the music from the radio, we heard ghostly applause from far away.

"The plays must be over," I said.

"Yes." She didn't move.

"Can you stay?"

She waited so long I raised my head to look at her, thinking she might not have heard. She was staring at the ceiling, tears in the corners of her eyes. "No," she said, and shook her head slowly. "I have to go."

Copenhagen. The room was enormous, a monastery dining room with a smooth stone floor and high walls built of granite blocks the size of small automobiles. There were three of us inside—myself at a table facing the south wall, a Danish boy who wanted to go to Michigan State against the north wall (eighty feet away), and the clerical personage in whom the College Board people had invested such trust at a table midway between us. He was surrounded by various cardboard boxes and manila folders from America, whose seals he had broken moments earlier.

"Now a final check," he said, his voice reverberating through the gloom. "In front of you you should have your special pencils and the first test, test number one, unopened."

"Yes," the boy said. He was so far away I could hardly hear him.

"Right!" I called.

"When I start the stopwatch I will shout BEGIN. You are to break the seals at that moment, and not before. I am instructed to remind you to read all instructions carefully, not to rush, but to pass over any questions you cannot answer rather than waste time in fruitless speculation. Do you both understand?"

"Yes." He sounded even fainter, and I hoped it wasn't fear.

"Right!" I felt marvelous myself. Nothing to lose and everything to gain. I had of course not prepared for the exams, but it seemed to me that my long absence from math was more than made up for by my recent acquisition of French. I was calm, amused by the deadly seriousness with which the proctor undertook his task. Our preposterous placement in the room, for example. He handled folders, pencils, and notebooks as if they were religious objects, and every word he uttered was weighed beforehand. It was a pathetic spectacle, amusing to me, but undoubtedly unnerving to the Danish boy.

"BEGIN!" the man shouted.

I waited a few moments, staring at him as one might stare at an ape in the zoo. Apelike, he began waving his arms at me, afraid to break the holy silence now that the stopwatch was running. I laughed, waved at him, and turned my back. I felt terrific. The world was truly beautiful. Slipping the special pencil into the pages of the booklet, I broke the seal.

In the bedroom (for the first time) of the spoiled, pouty, incredibly sexy sixteen-year-old Danish girl, I forced open her jaw and tasted her tongue. No hesitation here. I knew her game and she knew mine. We had been wrestling for hours. She couldn't speak English (she could write a little, her letters full of thees and thines she had learned at school) and I couldn't speak Danish, but when I tried to feel her breast under rather than through the sweater we understood each other perfectly. She fought me off and I pressed on, both of us drunk with sensation. The maid, a girl her own age and her closest friend, was posted outside the door. Every now and then the girl in my arms would call out to the girl in the hall, they would giggle, and the battle resume. I used force to get under her skirts, but she kept her legs together. At the intrusion of my knee between her thighs a signal was given and the maid rushed into the room. There was more giggling and laughing. In pain, I covered my head with pillows and refused to look at them. After a while they went downstairs to make cocoa.

There were dinners with my relatives, either at my aunt's —where I slept when in Copenhagen, an oppressive bourgeois apartment filled with expensive antique furniture paid for by my uncle's automobile dealership—or at my grandparents'—a lovely house, with a garden, in the suburbs, bought during the fifty years my grandfather had worked as a salesman for the Tuborg Beer company. I called him *Morfar* (mother's father) and despite our inability to communicate a certain tenuous bond arose between us. He would talk louder and louder in Danish, as if I were hard of hearing, smile, pat me on the back, and always try to get me to eat more food. After dinner, in the living room, he would gravely offer me a cigar, which I would gravely decline. But he was a very old man, humbled by a long life with his hypochondriacal, neurotically self-centered wife, and I was a very young man, ignorant of a great deal more than the Danish language, and neither of us knew how to break through. I spent hours watching everyone—the aunts, great-aunts, cousins, uncles—knowing I was related to them but unable to believe it. I felt like an impostor when they fussed over me. I could hear them talking about me, hear my name and see them looking at me the special way people look at you while talking about you in a language they know you can't understand—as if you were dead, or as if you were not sitting in the chair you are in fact sitting in, but had been a few moments earlier. All I could do was smile politely.

I was one of the first students to return to school. Henri and Albert had never left, amusing themselves in their rooms with two girls from the Casino who'd holed up with them the entire vacation. "A mistake," Henri said soberly. "The first few days were fine, but after that, my God. Insatiable! They disregarded me and developed a secret understanding with my tool. As a result I'll never have a hard-on again. I'm going to become a monk."

I spent the afternoon writing my mother. Realizing I couldn't possibly live in Paris on forty dollars a month, I had asked her for the full hundred she received from my trustee. She had declined, explaining that she was maintaining a home for me. I protested that I'd left home, and that although I understood the necessity of that sort of malarky in her dealings with lawyers and judges, she shouldn't try it on me. When I wrote a letter making quite clear the impossibility of staying alive on ten dollars a week in the city of Paris and she still failed to respond, I decided I was dealing with simple peasant avarice and threatened to write the trustee directly. The next mail brought a letter in which she agreed to send the full amount, and denied ever having thought of anything else. It was a spooky moment as I sat at my desk with all three of her letters, the two refusals and the disclaimer, and realized, for the first time, how truly thoughtless she was.

I grew increasingly nervous about Christina's return. Evenings, recuperating from Hysteria in the common room, I'd look up quickly every time the door opened to see if it was she, my body flushing in anticipation. When it wasn't, I was relieved. When, finally, it *was* Christina in the doorway, smiling, her hair loose and the square glasses perched on her nose, walking calmly along the line of seated students, shaking hands, moving closer and closer to me, I wanted to run away. She held out her hand. "Hello."

"Hello. Was it a nice time at home?"

"Yes," she said, giving me a firm shake, "but I'm glad to be back."

She moved past me, shaking hands with the others. I knew she was keeping up a public front, that when she'd said hello to everyone she'd come and sit beside me. I also knew I had to get away. I sneaked out of the room the way I used to sneak out of Stuyvesant for a smoke, and went upstairs, my heart pounding mysteriously.

The next day in class she sent me a note: "Why won't you speak to me? Why won't you look at me? I love you. I would die for you." I held the folded paper in my hands, afraid to read it a second time. I raised my eyes and looked around the room. A lens clicked in my head and reality shifted to a new position slightly farther away from me. Behind the other students Christina sat staring at me, her face dark with blood. Her eyes were the eyes of a madwoman. They *burned,* forcing me to look away.

As the class broke up we remained in our seats. Alone, we sat in silence for several moments. I played with a pencil on the table top.

"Do you understand?" Her voice was loaded with oblique emotions, barely under control.

I nodded, not looking up.

"How can you sit there and do that?" Her accent was suddenly strongly marked with the sing-song rhythms of Swedish.

I dropped the pencil instantly. "Christina, I'm sorry."

She stood in front of me, staring at my chest. Her eyes under the windows. Even her body seemed not to be her own, moving with uncharacteristic awkwardness. Her mouth gleamed as she ran her tongue nervously over her lips. "I love you!" she cried suddenly, "don't you know what that means? If there was a gun and you told me to shoot myself I would do it. I would do it right now!" She reached out as if for a gun. "I would!" she cried ecstatically, looking past me into space.

"Christina . . ."

"You *must* love me. You *must!* You put your hand on me. That means you love me!"

I sat motionless, afraid to move a muscle. Some independent part of my brain, ticking away under its own power, made the irrelevant observation that she was beautiful, more beautiful now than before.

"I'm going back to Sweden," she said, and started for the door.

I got up quickly and intercepted her. "No. Don't do that. Please don't do that."

She stood in front of me, staring at my chest. Her eyes came up and she looked at my mouth. Something happened to her face and I thought she was going to hit me, but she turned away at the last moment.

"Don't go. At least now now. Give yourself time to think about it."

"Why?"

"Please."

She whirled suddenly, ran to the door, and left.

She did not go back to Sweden. After a couple of weeks I began to catch sight of her every now and then, always in the distance, standing on the steps of the girls' dorm, or bringing groceries from the Konditori at the corner. She did not appear at meals, or in the common room after dinner. I would sometimes see her walking along the path below my window with the Frog, but they never looked up.

A cold day in February. The snow was gone, blown away by a week of high winds. All bundled up in sweaters, scarf, and my heavy leather jacket, I walked down the road toward the corner bus stop. Above, the sky was lead, a pale, pearlish glow over the horizon the only sign of the sun. Ahead of me the small wooden shelter stood isolated in the wind, a loose board in its side knocking sporadically. I quickened my step.

She was sitting close against the wall, to stay warm, in such a way that I didn't see her until the last minute. I sat down on the other end of the bench. Motionless, she continued looking straight ahead, hair up tight in the bun at the back of her head, steel glasses gleaming in the pale light.

Her hands were folded in her lap. My face burning, I stared at the ground between my feet.

After a long time she said, "Frank." I looked up. She watched me calmly. When she spoke again her voice was even, almost mechanical. "You don't have to be afraid of me."

She stood up and stepped into the wind without waiting for an answer. The loose board kept knocking beside me as I watched her walking away toward the town.

In the spring I went to Paris.

19

*The Lock
on the
Metro Door*

        I AWOKE at noon in my small room off rue
Mouffetard. Sunlight streamed through the open window at
the foot of the bed. I got dressed and smoothed the
blankets over the straw mattress. Standing at the window, I
lighted a cigarette and looked down into the courtyard.
The Japanese sculptor from the first floor was squatting
carefully on the dark stones, filling a wine bottle from the
building's single water tap. He held the green bottle at a
slight angle under the steady flow. When he crossed the
courtyard and opened the door to his room I could see the
mobiles trembling in the darkness. As he went inside they
brushed against his narrow shoulders. I took a final drag on
the strong cigarette, already conscious of the effect of the
nicotine, and flipped it out the window.

    My room contained a bed, thirty or forty Penguin books
stacked on the floor, my duffel bag and suitcase, and a
single light bulb of clear glass hanging on a black wire at
the exact center of the room. Three strides and I was at the
door.

    Going down the small spiral staircase I kept my head
bent and my shoulders hunched together. A group of cats
scattered at the foot of the stairs as I stepped out into the
courtyard. I yawned and stretched in the open air—eighteen years old, six feet two inches tall, one hundred thirty-
five pounds, wearing blue jeans, a flannel shirt, and
sneakers, and without a haircut for three months.

    I could hear the cries of the Algerian street vendors as
I walked through the short alley toward the square. Passing
the landlord's door I quickened my pace automatically. Out
in the sunlit street hundreds of people moved back and
forth through the market stalls built over the sidewalk.
Everything was for sale—flowers, bolts of cloth, candles,
fruits and vegetables, shoes, coffee beans, toys, cheap jew-

elry, canned goods, religious articles, books, kerosene, candy, nylons, towels—all of it spilling onto the street in colorful profusion. I worked my way through the crowd and crossed Place Monge to the neighborhood café.

The same old waiter brought my breakfast every day. I had only to sit down and a croissant, a cup of chocolate, and a glass of water would appear before me.

"Bonjour," he said. "How is the revolution going?" (His standard line when I wore the bright red shirt.)

"Fine. But we're running out of funds."

"Send Stalin a telegram," the old man said, and went inside.

I checked the other tables to see if anyone had left a newspaper, but I was out of luck. I ate slowly and watched the pigeons cavorting on the roof of the *pissoir* in the center of the square.

The American Students and Artists Center on Boulevard Raspail was my mail drop. I shaved there as well, showered periodically, and invariably shat. I practiced on their piano and borrowed books from the small library. Luckily none of it cost any money. After a short, mysterious interview with the bed-ridden Episcopal bishop in charge I'd been issued a membership card and given free use of the luxurious rooms. I came every couple of days.

The woman at the mail desk took down the C's, went through them quickly, and handed me two letters. One was from Harvard and the other from Haverford. I resisted the urge to tear them open immediately and walked into the lounge. On the far side of the large room a French boy I knew was at the Steinway playing "Laura." I sat down on a couch by the window, put the letters face up on the table, and stared at them.

I hadn't allowed myself to think of the moment now at hand. I felt insufficiently prepared, and sat quite still waiting for something to happen to my mind, for a subtle shift of gears to occur which would indicate I was ready to include the news, whatever it was, in my conceptual universe. Finally I picked up the letter from Harvard. It had gone from Cambridge to Denmark, Denmark to New York, and New York to Paris. I ripped it open and withdrew a single sheet of paper. I had to read it twice before it made any sense. My application had been rejected, but because of my exceptional performance in the college entrance exams they were prepared to reconsider. It was necessary for me to appear in Cambridge for a personal interview and further testing before a certain date. I put the letter back in its envelope. The date mentioned had passed a week ago.

The letter from Haverford was shorter. I was accepted unconditionally. They asked me only to indicate whether or not I was coming. I leaned back on the couch and smiled. It felt a little silly, sitting smiling into the empty air, but I made no attempt to control myself. I held the letter tightly, raising it into the air every few moments to read it again.

That night, in the Select Café with John, a young English painter I hung around with, I wrote a letter to Haverford telling them I was coming. That done, we got drunk on *vin chaud,* and when my friend's wife left work at three in the morning, we walked across Paris to Les Halles for *saucisson* and *pommes frites.*

My sister lived in Reid Hall, a feminine enclave for foreign students off Boulevard Montparnasse. When I was broke I would go there for a meal and some animal warmth. Alison had no more money than myself, but as usual she managed better, and always helped when I was down and out. After dinner we would sit in the garden and talk.

"Frank, you *must* get a haircut."

"Haircuts are a luxury."

"You got that remark from John."

"Well, it's true. Anyway I've got a huge bald spot on the back of my head and this covers it up."

"What? Let me see." She examined my scalp. "Oh, Frank. My *God!*" To my surprise she burst into tears. "What are we going to do? You should see a doctor and we don't have any money. I'll have to borrow from one of the girls."

"Don't worry," I said. "I'll take care of it when I get back to New York."

"But suppose you lose all your hair? We've got to do something!" She paced back and forth on the garden walk, tremendously upset, her face twisted with worry.

There was something odd in her reaction, a certain lack of proportion, and I felt a flash of fear. "Take it easy," I said. "It's nothing to get worked up about. It'll be all right."

"Oh God." She sat down next to me and held her head as she cried. "I can't take any more."

I put my arm across her shoulders. "Alison, it's nothing. Really."

"We're too young to be all alone."

"We're not alone. And you have Jack. He'll be there when you go back."

"I know. I know."

But she kept on crying.

One afternoon at the Select, John handed me a small drawing. "You know what that is?"

I smoothed the paper on the small table and looked closely. It appeared to be a machine of some sort, various cogs, levers, and bars against a flat surface. "You mean something in reality?"

"Yes."

After a while I shook my head. "I don't know."

"It's the lock on the Metro door."

I looked again and recognized it instantly. In a single moment I understood distortion in art. The drawing was highly complex, much more elaborate than the simple bar and catch I had watched interacting countless times on the Metro doors. What he had drawn was the *process,* the way the bar approaches the catch, slides up the angled metal, and drops into the locked position. He had captured movement in a static drawing. For a moment I was speechless. When I looked up he was smiling at me. "You see?"

"Yes, I see," I answered, very serious. "And thank you."

Embarrassed, he folded the drawing and put it in his pocket. "It's nothing. A detail from my Metro painting."

In August I left Paris. I said goodbye to Alison, John and his wife, and a few acquaintances from the cafés, and spent my last night in the little room on rue Mouffetard writing letters. It was hot and I slept in short stretches, waking up each time with my mind abnormally clear, all senses alert, my consciousness reaching out in a last attempt to absorb the city. In the morning I picked up my duffel bag and suitcase and walked out the door.

Alone in the bow of the lighter, I breathed the salt air and looked up at the stars. Going home. Going home. Behind me the other passengers moved in the darkness, their voices muted by the wind. Slowly, the boat swung around a jetty and out into the swell of the open sea. Dead ahead the huge ocean liner spilled light over the black water, its whole long side blazing under the starry sky. My skin tingled as our ship's horn blasted the air. Moments later the liner answered with a deep, bone-shaking note—an immense sea-mother calling her lost child.

The next day I exchanged my money. One of the coins I received was a half-dollar. I turned it over several times, not knowing what it was. The sensation was quite strange.

NOTHING had changed in my neighborhood. The R.K.O., Loew's, and Grande movie theaters were showing pictures I'd never heard of, but the kids still screamed in the children's section and the ushers still flashed their lights across the screen to signal each other. The bars on Eighty-sixth Street were filled with the same heavy men, Wright's and the Automat served the same food, and the Salvation Army band showed up every Saturday night on the sidewalk. My favorite delicatessen smelled the way it always had and the man behind the counter nodded as if I'd never been away. Nothing had changed except myself. I wandered through the neighborhood with a great secret locked in my heart. "I've won. I made it. I'm starting a new life." And it was true. Haverford College would give me the chance to start with a clean slate, and that was all I'd ever wanted. My acceptance into a good college meant I could destroy my past. It seemed to me to amount to an *order* to destroy my past, a past I didn't understand, a past I feared, and a past with which I had expected to be forever encumbered. In the fact of this incredible good fortune life took on an hallucinatory brightness. It was like a religious conversion.

At home I felt like a boarder, a one-night guest impatient to move on to the next town. My room seemed not to be my own. Touching forgotten belongings on the shelves, I felt the echo of another person and an earlier time. Dagmar had thrown out my seven or eight hundred paperbacks, but even that seemed unimportant. Nothing mattered from the past, neither the things I had loved nor those I had hated.

Suddenly a telegram arrived. Alison, who had planned to stay in Europe another year, was being sent home on doctor's orders. She would arrive the next day at Idlewild airport.

I drove out with my mother in a borrowed convertible. (An eccentric millionaire's. He had taken a ride in her cab—she drove occasionally in the afternoons—and was so impressed he took her to the opera every now and then in a chauffeured Cadillac.) It was a warm, sunny day, so I had the top down. My mother was unusually quiet.

"What I don't understand is why they didn't say what's wrong with her," I said.

"Maybe she's pregnant."

"Alison? Are you kidding?" I moved the big car into the fast lane. "No. Maybe it's something they couldn't diagnose. Some rare allergy or something." It made me nervous not to know. I kept running over the possibilities in my head, avoiding certain ones instinctively.

"You're driving too fast."

"Only fifty." I was suddenly annoyed. "Anyway I'm driving. Not you."

"It's simple good manners to slow down if your passenger is uncomfortable."

I kept on at the same speed.

At the airport I dropped my mother in front of International Arrivals, parked the car, and went inside. Alison's plane was down, and a trim woman at the information desk told me the passengers were in customs. On tiptoes, I tried to spot my mother's blond head in the crowd, but without success. I moved to the customs area and stopped at the barrier, leaning forward to look through the open doors into the next room where the inspectors were at work checking baggage. I saw Alison standing with her back to me in one of the aisles. Something was wrong with her hair. I cupped my hands around my mouth and shouted "Alison! Over here! Over here!" She turned around and saw me.

I started to wave, but stopped. She was looking directly at me without the least sign of recognition. Her long dark hair puffed wildly from her head and fell over her shoulders and down her back. Her clothing was wrinkled and food-stained, the buttons on her jacket done in the wrong order, and her lipstick unevenly applied. I stared into her eyes and felt my legs start to go. I held onto the barrier. Neither of us moved. After a moment a faint, quizzical frown appeared on her brow and she leaned forward as if to see me better. Her mouth opened and I realized she was talking to herself. The other people in her aisle hung back, giving her plenty of space.

I went past the guard, ignoring his restraining hand on my shoulder, and moved toward her. From another direction I could see my mother approaching with a stewardess. We converged on Alison at the same moment.

"Here's your mother, dear," the stewardess said gently. "Everything is all right. Just as I told you."

"You stupid bitch," Alison said to the stewardess. "I hope your cunt rots off."

Mother put her arm around Alison's waist and I picked up the bags.

"You're home now," Dagmar said. "It's all over. It's all over now."

We began to walk slowly to the exit. I was aware of people looking at us, passengers from Alison's flight point her out to the people who'd come to meet them. I moved closer to her side.

"The plane almost crashed twice. They wouldn't give me a life preserver."

"All right now. Don't think about it," my mother said. "Let's just go home."

"There were two F.B.I. men sitting behind me. They tape recorded everything."

"Why would they care about you?"

"Because of Jack. Because of his job in the army."

In the parking lot I stood next to Alison as my mother went around the car. "What's wrong?" I asked softly. "What happened?"

She didn't answer and got into the car. I slid behind the wheel. She suddenly became haughty. "Nothing whatever is wrong. You think I've lost touch with reality? Just drive this strange car I've never seen before to eighty-one East Eighty-sixth Street."

I felt tears starting in my eyes and turned away as if I were checking traffic. I pulled into the highway and Alison lowered her head onto her mother's lap.

Alison slept in Mother's bed that night. She lay for hours singing folk songs, her voice trembling when the words were sad. She switched accents for the lighter tunes, overdoing the Irish or Jewish to make Dagmar laugh. I paced back and forth through the hall, checking Jessica's room every now and then to make sure she was covered, unable to stay still for more than a moment. I wondered if we should increase the dosage of Alison's sedatives, and tried not to think of what would happen if they took her to a hospital. It was indescribably weird to hear them laughing and carrying on like two little girls at camp.

Once my mother came out of the room for some water. I was standing in the hall by the bathroom.

"You know," she said, pursuing her lips and giving a series of quick nods (her everything's-under-control look), "I think Alison is faking just a little bit." She smiled, relieved and tolerant, as if it were a game she was willing to allow.

Early in the morning, just before dawn, something woke me. I got up from the couch and went to the head of the hall. Halfway down the corridor, under the single light by the bathroom, Alison stood in a white nightgown with her fists clenched and her teeth bare, making a continuous hissing sound something like the noise of a steam radiator. I remained in the doorway until she caught sight of me and then began to advance. She raised her fists slightly as I came close, her lips drawn back like an animals, her whole head trembling, the tendons in her neck standing out like ropes. "Take it easy," I said softly. "Just take it easy." Her eyes watched me from another world. Expecting anything, I reached out for her. Her arm was hard as steel. "Better try and sleep," I said.

She went along stiffly, still hissing. At the door to Mother's room I stopped and urged her inside. Dagmar lay motionless under the blankets, fast asleep.

"There's the bed," I said. "Just lie down and try to sleep."

She got under the covers and turned toward her mother. I stood watching them for a moment and then went back to the living room. In the darkness, I stared at the ceiling. After five or ten minutes I went into the kitchen and collected all the knives. I put them under a cushion on the sofa and slept on them.

After a day or two it became clear that Alison would not have to be hospitalized. But she re-entered reality a different person from the one who had left. The responsible, self-sufficient Alison was gone. The new Alison was an infant—love-starved, grasping every available scrap of attention, physically passive as if her very bones and muscle had gone back to childhood softness, and utterly blind to everything but her own needs. More than once I saw her curled up on the sofa or a chair, sucking her thumb abstractedly. She hung on my mother's skirts, constantly reaching out to hug and be hugged, to kiss and be kissed, simply to touch—joking all the while to cover the desperate importance of her desire.

Jack obtained special leave from the Army and came directly to the house. He never faltered for a moment. Alison stayed more or less permanently in his lap and they began talking about marriage. The old Alison had hesitated, but the new Alison was eager, to say the least.

And so the day came when I packed my bag and took the train to college. Jean had started a used-car lot in Florida, Alison was to marry Jack, and my mother and Jessica would continue at eighty-one. My trustee had paid my tuition and agreed to an allowance of a hundred dollars a month. I was rich and I was free.

Stepping onto the station platform in Haverford, Pennsylvania, I took a deep breath and looked at what I could see of the town. A quiet suburban village. Tree-lined streets and clapboard houses. Some kids shouted as they rode their bikes down the hill into a tunnel under the tracks. A taxicab waited in the sunshine and I approached the driver, who stood leaning against the front fender.

"Do you know where Haverford College is?"

"Why sure."

"Is it far?"

"No, but with that bag you better let me run you over."

"Okay." I got in the back, my suitcase beside me, and lighted a cigarette. The driver adjusted his baseball cap and pulled away from the curb.

"You a new freshman?" he asked.

"Yes."

"I figured. I took a few boys over already, today."

"Will it take long?"

"Just a couple of minutes."

"I hear it's very pretty," I said.

"You mean you ain't never seen it?"

"No. I've been away."

"Well, it's pretty, all right. They got a big duck pond you can skate on in the winter."

I sat back in the seat and finished my cigarette.

"This is the main entrance."

We drove between two stone pillars and a vast expanse opened before us. Across a long, open green I could see a small lake shining in the sun. Three swans moved slowly across the surface.

"The whole place was planned by a gardener they brought over from England in eighteen something or other. Mr. White told me that."

"Who's Mr. White?"

"He's the president. Nice fella."

We drove through a stand of elms and turned up a slight rise toward the main group of buildings. The smell of freshly cut grass filled the car. We pulled up under a huge oak tree. Two card tables were set up in the shade, and a group of young men sat on folding chairs, some with their feet up on the tables. I got out of the cab and paid the driver. As I reached for my bag one of the young men came trotting across the lawn. "Let me take that," he called out. Smiling, he approached, picked up the bag, and held out his hand. "Hi. It's nice to see you." We shook hands and he laughed. "I know how you feel. It's a little strange."

"Yes, it is."

"My name's Bob. Welcome to Haverford."

Epilogue

ABOUT ten years later. England. 4:30 A.M.
Approaching the village on a long straightaway, I braked
down to ninety, shifted into third, touched the brakes
again, and took the turn into the town square at about
fifty. There was a sudden rumbling under the car as the
road surface changed from asphalt to cobblestone. My
headlights lit the concrete fountain directly ahead, a fountain I sometimes passed on the left, sometimes on the right,
depending on how well I'd taken the previous corner. I
waited an instant too long, and as I eased the wheel over,
the rear tires broke loose and the car began to skid.

"Hooray!" I shouted, spinning the wheel to the left, into
the skid. "Whee!"

The car stabilized in a sideways position. I looked out
the open window toward the fountain. It was coming directly at me, coming very fast as the car skidded broadside
across the square. It would strike the center of the door and
the car would bend like a beer can, with me inside. I was
going to die. As the fountain grew larger I felt myself relax. I leaned toward the door. Let it come. Let it come as
hard and as fast as it can. Touch the wheel, make an adjustment so it will strike right beside me. Here it comes!
Here it comes!

But the front wheel caught a low curb and the car spun
around the fountain like a baton around a cheerleader's
wrist. I became disoriented, knowing only that something
freakish was happening. The side of the car bumped very
gently against the fountain, inches away from my face.
Then, with a slight lurch, everything stopped. The fountain
was a few yards behind and the car was pointed in more or
less the right direction.

After a moment I got out and walked over to the fountain. I put my hands on the damp concrete and vomited.
From the corner of my eye I saw a light go on in the
upper story of one of the buildings fronting the square. A
window was raised, and after a moment a man's voice
called out.

"Here. What's all this?"

My throat burning with bile, I started to laugh.

FOR THE BEST IN PAPERBACKS, LOOK FOR THE

In every corner of the world, on every subject under the sun, Penguin represents quality and variety—the very best in publishing today.

For complete information about books available from Penguin—including Penguin Classics, Penguin Compass, and Puffins—and how to order them, write to us at the appropriate address below. Please note that for copyright reasons the selection of books varies from country to country.

In the United States: Please write to *Penguin Group (USA), P.O. Box 12289 Dept. B, Newark, New Jersey 07101-5289* or call 1-800-788-6262.

In the United Kingdom: Please write to *Dept. EP, Penguin Books Ltd, Bath Road, Harmondsworth, West Drayton, Middlesex UB7 0DA.*

In Canada: Please write to *Penguin Books Canada Ltd, 10 Alcorn Avenue, Suite 300, Toronto, Ontario M4V 3B2.*

In Australia: Please write to *Penguin Books Australia Ltd, P.O. Box 257, Ringwood, Victoria 3134.*

In New Zealand: Please write to *Penguin Books (NZ) Ltd, Private Bag 102902, North Shore Mail Centre, Auckland 10.*

In India: Please write to *Penguin Books India Pvt Ltd, 11 Panchsheel Shopping Centre, Panchsheel Park, New Delhi 110 017.*

In the Netherlands: Please write to *Penguin Books Netherlands bv, Postbus 3507, NL-1001 AH Amsterdam.*

In Germany: Please write to *Penguin Books Deutschland GmbH, Metzlerstrasse 26, 60594 Frankfurt am Main.*

In Spain: Please write to *Penguin Books S. A., Bravo Murillo 19, 1° B, 28015 Madrid.*

In Italy: Please write to *Penguin Italia s.r.l., Via Benedetto Croce 2, 20094 Corsico, Milano.*

In France: Please write to *Penguin France, Le Carré Wilson, 62 rue Benjamin Baillaud, 31500 Toulouse.*

In Japan: Please write to *Penguin Books Japan Ltd, Kaneko Building, 2-3-25 Koraku, Bunkyo-Ku, Tokyo 112.*

In South Africa: Please write to *Penguin Books South Africa (Pty) Ltd, Private Bag X14, Parkview, 2122 Johannesburg.*